COLLABORATE,
Communicate,
& *Differentiate!*

We would like to dedicate this book to the many students who have taught us everything we know about effective teaching.

A special shout-out to the teachers who have collaborated with us and inspired us over the years: Randi, for always being willing to take the "tough" kids; Mr. C., for standing on the table and singing when the occasion called for it; Linda, who moved from co-teacher to family member; Rebecca, who is both creative and hysterically funny; Lynne, for mentoring both of us in the art of collaboration; June, who taught us what it means to advocate for kids; Rachel, our first reader and our constant cheerleader; and all the other teachers who've been generous enough to share their classrooms, their strategies, and their hearts with us. You, the teachers and students whom we've known and loved, are why we wrote this book.

A final dedication to our own families, who have helped us keep energized, motivated, and sane. We love you, Layne, Christien, and Kiernan.

COLLABORATE,
Communicate,
& *Differentiate!*

How to Increase
Student Learning in
Today's Diverse Schools

Wendy W. Murawski
Sally Spencer

CORWIN

A SAGE Company

CORWIN
A SAGE Company

FOR INFORMATION:

Corwin
A SAGE Company
2455 Teller Road
Thousand Oaks, California 91320
(800) 233-9936
Fax: (800) 417-2466
www.corwin.com

SAGE Ltd.
1 Oliver's Yard
55 City Road
London EC1Y 1SP
United Kingdom

SAGE India Pvt. Ltd.
B 1/I 1 Mohan Cooperative
    Industrial Area
Mathura Road, New Delhi 110 044
India

SAGE Asia-Pacific Pte. Ltd.
33 Pekin Street #02-01
Far East Square
Singapore 048763

Acquisitions Editor: Jessica Allan
Associate Editor: Allison Scott
Editorial Assistant: Lisa Whitney
Production Editor: Cassandra Margaret Seibel
Copy Editor: Tina Hardy
Typesetter: C&M Digitals (P) Ltd.
Proofreader: Sarah J. Duffy
Cover Designer: Scott Van Atta
Permissions Editor: Karen Ehrmann

Copyright © 2011 by Corwin

Printed in the United States of America.

Library of Congress Cataloging-in-Publication Data

Murawski, Wendy W.

Collaborate, communicate, and differentiate! : how to increase student learning in today's diverse schools / Wendy W. Murawski and Sally Spencer.

p. cm.

Includes bibliographical references and index.

ISBN 978-1-4129-8184-2 (pbk.)

1. Language arts—Social aspects—United States.
2. Literacy—Social aspects—United States.
3. Multicultural education—United States. 4. School improvement programs—United States. I. Spencer, Sally (Sally A.), 1955– II. Title.

LB1576.M86 2011 371.102—dc22 2010051778

This book is printed on acid-free paper.

11 12 13 14 15 10 9 8 7 6 5 4 3 2 1

Contents

Additional materials and resources related to *Collaborate,
Communicate, and Differentiate!* can be found at
http://www.corwin.com/diverseschools.

Acknowledgments

Corwin gratefully acknowledges the contributions of the following reviewers:

Marsha Basanda
Fifth-Grade Teacher
Bell's Crossing Elementary School
Simpsonville, SC

Mark Bower
Director of Elementary Education and Staff
    Development
Hilton Central Schools
Hilton, NY

Dolores Burton
Chairperson, Teacher Education Program
School of Education
New York Institute of Technology
Old Westbury, NY

Sally Coghlan
Teacher, SPED
Rio Linda Junior High
Rio Linda, CA

Laurie Emery
Principal
Old Vail Middle School
Vail, AZ

William Richard Hall, Jr.
Principal
R. C. Longan Elementary School
Henrico, VA

Cindy Harrison
Consultant
Broomfield, CO

Katie Morrow
Technology Integration Specialist/Adjunct
    Faculty
O'Neill Public Schools/Doane College
O'Neill, NE

Lisa Parisi
Co-teacher
South Paris Collaborative
Denton Avenue Elementary School
New Hyde Park, NY

Kathleen Prisbell
Eighth-Grade Integrated Language Arts
    Teacher
Russell O. Brackman Middle School
Barnegat, NJ

Christine Southard
Co-teacher
South Paris Collaborative
Denton Avenue Elementary School
New Hyde Park, NY

Bambi Thompson
Principal
T.C. Walker Elementary School
Gloucester, VA

About the Authors

Wendy W. Murawski, PhD, is the Michael D. Eisner Endowed Chair for the Center for Teaching and Learning at California State University, Northridge. She is a tenured Full Professor in the Department of Special Education, as well as the Director of Research for the CHIME Institute, an institute devoted to the inclusion of individuals with disabilities. She was the recipient of the Distinguished Teacher Educator Award for the state of California in 2004. Wendy has published numerous articles, book chapters, and teachers' guides in the area of co-teaching, collaboration, and teacher training. Her most recent books are published through Corwin and are titled *Collaborative Teaching in [Elementary/Secondary] Schools: Making the Co-Teaching Marriage Work!* Wendy is the CEO and President of 2 Teach, LLC, an educational consulting company (http://www.2TeachLLC.com). As a high school teacher in both Virginia and California, Wendy taught German and special education, spending most of her time co-teaching, which led to her passion on the topic. She is a national presenter and is often requested to speak at schools, districts, conferences, and training seminars about her classroom experiences and her research in the area of co-teaching. She lives in Winnetka, California, with her handsome husband, stupendous son, cute cat, and ferocious fish.

Sally Spencer, EdD, is an assistant professor in the Department of Special Education at California State University, Northridge, where she teaches courses in assessment, special education teaching methods, reading instruction, and collaborative processes. Prior to that, she was a special education teacher for the Los Angeles Unified School District, where she experienced the joys and challenges of collaboration as a teacher of self-contained special education classes, as a resource specialist, and as a co-teacher in a fully inclusive elementary school. In 2001, she was awarded Outstanding Special Educator of the Year by the Southern California branch of the Council for Exceptional Children, and her heart is still in the classroom with the hundreds of students who touched her life and taught her everything she knows about special education. Sally is a national presenter on the subject of teaching reading to students with mild to moderate disabilities, and she is published in the areas of reading instruction, collaboration, and inclusion. She lives in Northridge, California, with her husband (who's every bit as handsome as Wendy's), three dogs, and six birds.

Introduction

AN OVERVIEW OF THE BOOK

Collaboration. That means playing nicely with others, right? Essentially, yes. To be more technical, we're going to say that collaboration is when a few folks work together to accomplish a particular goal, but ultimately this book *is* about adults playing nicely together—specifically those involved in the education of children. Why do we need a whole book devoted to collaboration? Don't adults—especially those in education—already know how to do this? And if they don't, aren't they able to just shut themselves in their own classrooms and do whatever they want? The answer now is *no*, to both questions. As you might surmise from this first paragraph, this is a different kind of book. It's a book that talks to you directly and that addresses issues head-on. Our language is straightforward and our strategies for improving collaboration in schools are practical. That's not to say that we don't care about research or that we are writing off the cuff; both of your authors have their doctorates in education and both of us conduct research, publish in peer-reviewed journals, and are national consultants. However, we are also former teachers and currently teach teachers, so we know that the last thing a working educator wants to read is a boring, dry textbook full of citations and research and very little practical application. That's not our goal.

Our goal for this book is to focus on collaboration as a means toward improving student success in schools. When we say students, we mean *all* students—kids with and without disabilities, students who are on 504 plans, or children who are gifted or homeless or at risk or cheerleaders or English language learners or all of the above. You get the picture. In addition, when we are talking about success, we recognize that there are multiple ways to be successful in schools. First and foremost we want to help students in K–12 classes improve their academics; we believe that the collaboration among educators can help accomplish that task. We also write about how collaboration can improve social skills, self-esteem, and behavioral success. All of this is currently abstract, however. As you read the different chapters, you'll see how we link concepts with practical, concrete strategies that demonstrate how you can use collaboration as a tool to increase success in these various areas. Again, notice that we keep the focus on student learning and student outcomes—that's the reason we are in schools. It may be more fun to work with a colleague on a common goal; it may decrease our workload; it may even decrease teacher attrition. While these are fantastic outcomes for educators, we don't want to lose sight of the fact that we are all in education to help *students*. That must remain the focus of everything we do. If collaboration is not necessary to improve the education for students, we wouldn't suggest it. We do, however, believe it is often the lynchpin for whether or not a child, especially one with a disability, is able to achieve success in the inclusive classroom. We believe that so strongly, in fact, that we wrote a book about it.

Our belief system is not the only impetus for encouraging increased collaboration in schools. A little law known as the No Child Left Behind Act of 2001 (NCLB), with its mandate of more accountability for all children, including those with disabilities, and its emphasis on the need for "highly qualified" teachers, has greatly impacted the makeup of today's typical classroom. In addition, the reauthorization of the Individuals with Disabilities Education Improvement Act of 2004 (IDEA) continues the emphasis on least restrictive environment for students with disabilities while supporting the need for access to the general education curriculum for all students. These laws have led to a complete paradigm shift in the way students with disabilities are educated and, subsequently, how teachers in schools are utilized to meet those needs in an inclusive environment. What this means is that we have laws telling us to work together or else. We go into these laws and more in Chapter 1.

How should we work together to ensure we are addressing the requirements of NCLB and IDEA? One of the main ways that schools are addressing these needs is through collaboration. Teachers in both general and special education classrooms are being asked to step outside their comfort zones and work together to give all kids access to the general education curriculum. This is easier said than done. Think about it. This is a major paradigm shift for many teachers, who have spent years behind closed doors reigning as the kings and queens of their individual classrooms. Now we are asking those same teachers to not only work with others, but in many cases we are even asking them to allow other educators into their own classrooms to teach together. No wonder there is resistance! We address how to overcome some of that resistance, even if it is your own.

Despite the growing demand for collaborative situations and inclusive settings, teachers receive very little training in the skills critical to successful collaboration. Very little has been done in many districts to genuinely prepare teachers to collaborate with their colleagues. Educators are merely told to collaborate, consult, co-teach, or otherwise "include" kids with special needs. While there are textbooks that teach collaboration and communication skills, it is often in a lifeless, abstract, or theoretical context, with very little connection to the practicalities of everyday school life. The goal of this book is to take collaboration out of the abstract and apply it to the tasks that teachers perform every day. How do you collaborate with other professionals to teach math or English more effectively? How do you collaborate with office personnel to get your Individualized Education Programs (IEPs) done on time? What are the tips and tricks that can make collaboration reasonable, feasible, less onerous, and more effective given teachers' resistance, time constraints, and control issues? This book answers those questions and more.

As we said in the first paragraph, since the subject is collaborating *in schools*, this book is centered around student learning. If the goal of all classrooms is to increase positive student outcomes, then the goal of collaboration in schools *must be to increase student learning*. This book takes the skills involved in collaboration and applies them to practical tasks such as planning instruction, working with families, and conducting student assessment, all with the goal of increasing the desired outcomes for all learners. While we hope you will read the book from cover to cover, devouring each page and frequently admiring the brilliance of the authors, we also recognize that you may have a need in a particular area or you may be consulting with someone who does. In those cases, you may want to select a particular chapter from the Table of Contents or section from the index and use those specific strategies to help you get through a sticky situation.

In order to be as practical and teacher-friendly as possible, there are a variety of special materials in this text. In fact, we purposefully avoided having a book that is so heavy on narration and theory that it screams university course textbook. As you may have noticed, we decided to adopt a conversational, informal tone that is easy to read and more fun to write. We want you to read this book as if we are actually in the same room having a conversation—a one-sided conversation, granted, but a conversation nonetheless.

What other "special" items can you look forward to in this book? We are big believers in humor; it's always easier to contemplate difficult content if it's put in a humorous context. Each chapter starts with what we call *Voices From the Field* so that you can connect with the focus of the chapter right away. We move immediately into *The Big Picture* so you know what to expect in that chapter. Throughout the chapter, we have pulled aside key words and concepts and put them in boxes to draw your attention; we have also created *In A Nutshell* pages to eliminate the need for lots of narrative when you may want to have a boiled-down version of the information to reference. As we mentioned earlier, we are big believers in making sure information is practical and realistic. Thus, we have vignettes and real-life scenarios called *In Practice* that demonstrate various aspects of collaboration and the impact on students. These will help you "see" what the strategies look like.

This book is created for the variety of individuals impacted by inclusive education. We anticipate that our readers will be administrators, general and special education teachers, paraprofessionals, counselors, staff developers, special service providers, and parents, among others. Thus, we recognize that there will be different frames of reference in terms of your reading of the content, as well as your issues related to collaboration. To make these different perspectives explicit, we have call-out *Frames* indicating when someone's frame of reference may color his interpretation of the information. Strategies for an administrative point of view are called *Principal Points*. Different readers also require different levels of research-related support to our suggestions; some of you will skip right over any citations, while others will want to know where we got our ideas and what research was involved. Thus, while we keep our citations minimal in order to enhance readability, we also provide *Eye on the Research* pages and *Diving Deeper* references in our website supplement (http://www.corwin.com/diverseschools) so that those interested in studying further can go to primary sources.

To keep the focus on practical strategies and student learning, each chapter ends with a section devoted to taking the focus of that chapter out of the abstract. These sections provide bulleted suggestions for educators to grab and go. We know that the last thing educators have is time and we want to be respectful of that. Chapters are short, to the point, and focused on tips and tricks. That is just up your alley, isn't it? How did we know? Because in our hearts we are teachers, and our goal with this book is to reach out to other educators to make it all work better. It's as simple as that.

Well, now that you know what to expect, let's stop wasting time on an introductory chapter and get to the meat of the matter—finding ways to work together better so that we can help our students succeed!

1

Understanding the Historical Context

Voices From the Field

"I went into teaching because I wanted my own class—why should I have to collaborate with *my* kids included in someone else's class? I have a special education credential—give me a special ed class, please, and quit treating me like a glorified assistant!"

Katia G., special education teacher

"I have to say, I don't really get the whole inclusion thing. The extra workload that is created by having students with disabilities in my class makes it harder for me to give the other kids the time they need. It just seems unfair to me and the other kids in the class."

Rebecca S., general education teacher

THE BIG PICTURE

No doubt in the course of your career you have heard many comments like these. What are the benefits of collaborative programs? If a teacher has a teaching credential of her own, why should she be forced to teach with someone else, or to share students across placements? What is the point of this whole move toward more collaborative and inclusive schools, anyway?

We understand the uncertainty, so in this first chapter we think it's imperative to tell you a little bit about the history of special education in America and how we came to the place in which we find ourselves today. We are going to take you on a brief trip back in time to examine how individuals with disabilities have been treated and, most specifically, educated. This is important, because without a historical perspective, you—like Katia and Rebecca in our *Voices From the Field*—may not realize why it is that collaboration, inclusion, and differentiation are so truly critical in today's schools.

We are lighthearted authors, and this is a pretty lighthearted book, but unfortunately the story of special education isn't particularly pretty. We ask you to bear with us in Chapter 1 as we take you on a journey that isn't always pleasant, but which is, we believe, very, very important. (We promise that after this we'll kick back, crack open some snacks, and have some laughs as we explore how to make your collaborative schools more effective!) In the meantime, put on your comfy traveling clothes and brace yourself for one heck of a ride.

In this chapter we do the following:

- Look at the history of special education and examine some of the important laws and issues that have shaped the educational programs we have today.
- Discuss how those laws and issues impact our classrooms and what we need to do to address them.
- Consider the other ways that our classrooms have changed and how collaboration can help us meet the needs of a wide variety of learners, including students from diverse cultural and linguistic backgrounds, kids with identified and unidentified special learning needs, and students who are gifted.

Let's Get STARTED!

A LOOK AT THE HISTORY OF SPECIAL EDUCATION: WHAT'S CHANGED OVER THE YEARS?

People with disabilities have always been treated differently. For the most part, we think it's fair to say that they have been treated poorly. For years, individuals with identifiable disabilities such as physical impairments, cerebral palsy, intellectual disabilities (previously referred to as mental retardation), blindness, and so on were either kept at home with no access to education or institutionalized with very limited education. The education that *was* provided at those institutions was generally limited to a particular skill or task (for example, putting wicks in candles, creating crafts).

As compulsory education laws began to be enforced in the early 1900s, however, students with disabilities began to show up in public schools, and administrators and teachers wondered how to handle this influx of students who had challenging special needs. Anderson (1917) pondered in a book titled *Education of Defectives in the Public Schools* whether "defective" children should be allowed in public schools at all or whether they should be trained in other settings.

Also around this time, methods of identifying disabilities were becoming more specific, so more students with special needs were being documented in the public school system. The emphasis on rigid control in the general education classroom led to segregated classes for many of these students, who were considered unmanageable, "incorrigible, backward and otherwise defective." (Osgood, 2008, p. 43). Classes identified as being for "feebleminded," "backward," or "subnormal" children began to spring up in major cities such as New York and Chicago. Separate classrooms and schools were also created for students who were blind, deaf or deaf-mute (called "deaf and dumb"), students with physical disabilities (labeled "crippled"), or those with cognitive impairments (known as "mentally retarded"). Some children, particularly those with severe physical and/or cognitive disabilities, ended up in mental institutions, hospitals, or asylums—out of sight and out of mind. The outlook for children with disabilities who couldn't conform to the rigid expectations of public schools was dim; they were hustled off to isolated locations where they were often denied the opportunity to learn even basic academic and social skills and where their troublesome cognitive or physical differences could be ignored by the general public.

> **Want more info?**
>
> Check out *The History of Special Education: A Struggle for Equality in American Public Schools*, by Robert Osgood (2008).

What about those children with what we today call "invisible disabilities"? Labels like *learning disability, autism, Asperger syndrome, Tourette syndrome, obsessive compulsive disorder, oppositional defiant disorder,* and *emotional disturbance* didn't exist at the time. These students often dropped out, were kicked out, were ignored, or were simply known as the "weird" kids in school. Ask your parents or grandparents what happened to students in their classes who simply did not fit in. Were their specific educational or behavioral needs addressed? That really depended on the individual teacher. There were certainly no laws in place to ensure that they received additional support.

Thankfully, in the late 1950s and 1960s, many things in American society began to evolve. The landmark case of *Brown vs. Board of Education* in 1954 began to change the face of the American educational system. *Brown vs. Board of Education* demanded for the first time that schools become integrated racially—it established that *separate* education was not the same as *equal* education for students of color. Gradually, that concept also began to be applied to education for children with disabilities.

President John F. Kennedy, whose sister Rosemary was born with a cognitive disability, was a major champion of education for kids with disabilities. When Rosemary was young, the family ignored the advice of doctors and kept her at home rather than sending her away to live in an institution, as was the common practice at that time. As she aged into her 20s, she began to experience violent outbursts, resulting in her family deciding to try an experimental medical procedure recommended by her doctors. In 1941, Rosemary Kennedy underwent a lobotomy; sadly, it left her uncommunicative and unable to care for herself. She spent the rest of her life institutionalized and separated from her family.

Likely as a result of this experience, President Kennedy took a personal interest in what happened to children with disabilities in our nation's schools. In the early years of his presidency, he pushed through legislation that formed a Division of Handicapped Children and Youth in the Office of Education. This legislation began to focus the federal government's attention on the problem of educating students with disabling conditions. In a presidential statement in October 1961, Kennedy expressed his concern about the issues:

The manner in which our Nation cares for its citizens and conserves its manpower resources is more than an index to its concern for the less fortunate. It is a key to its future. Both wisdom and humanity dictate a deep interest in the physically handicapped, the mentally ill, and the mentally retarded. Yet, although we have made considerable progress in the treatment of physical handicaps, although we have attacked on a broad front the problems of mental illness, although we have made great strides in the battle against disease, we as a nation have for too long postponed an intensive search for solutions to the problems of the mentally retarded. That failure should be corrected. (Kennedy, 1961, p. 1)

Although President Kennedy's personal crusade was cut short by his untimely death, over the next decade Presidents Johnson and Nixon both continued his focus on this important cause.

In 1966, two photojournalists, Burton Blatt and Fred Kaplan, shone a brilliant light on the plight of individuals with disabilities, and this time it was too vivid to be ignored. Blatt and Kaplan (1966) published a photographic exposé titled *Christmas in Purgatory: A Photographic Essay on Mental Retardation,* that for the first time made the appalling conditions in residential facilities apparent. The journalists snuck hidden cameras into five institutions for the cognitively disabled, documenting conditions of filth and squalor. Children were warehoused in rows of desolate cribs, with little or no human interaction. Adults were kept naked and soiled in empty rooms with no stimulation of any kind. People with disabilities were housed in conditions that today would be considered unfit for an animal. As they described it in the introduction to their book, "There is a hell on earth, and in America there is a special inferno. . . . Although our pictures could not begin to capture the total and overwhelming horror we saw, smelled, and felt, they represent a side of America that has rarely been shown to the general public, and is little understood by most of us" (Blatt & Kaplan, 1974, p. iv). America as a whole, and education professionals in specific, could no longer afford to ignore the crisis of individuals with disabilities in our country.

At the same time, other organizations and individuals were beginning to raise their voices in support of more thoughtful and humane treatment of people with disabilities. The Council for Exceptional Children (CEC) and the National Association for Retarded Children (later renamed the National Association for Retarded Citizens and more recently renamed simply The Arc) began to advocate for change in the educational system, while the Disability Rights Movement pushed for comprehensive change in educational, work, and public settings. The efforts of all these organizations helped bring the plight of kids with disabilities into the public consciousness, and gradually they began to step out of the shadows.

A NEW ERA: HOW CAN WE EDUCATE ALL OUR STUDENTS?

In 1975, about 75 years after students with disabilities first began to attend public school, President Ford signed the Education for All Handicapped Children Act (EAHCA or PL 94-142), finally guaranteeing educational rights for students with special needs. This landmark legislation recognized the injustice that existed when children with disabilities were excluded from typical school experiences. It mandated equitable education as a civil right and required that the educational rights of children with disabilities be protected by law. Although it was just the beginning, PL 94-142 required school districts to take a good, hard look at how they were providing services to students with disabilities, and it forced them to drag their most shameful practices out into the open.

One of the most important elements of PL 94-142 was that it identified 11 types of handicapping conditions that were to be protected by law. Those eligibilities (plus *Autism* and *Traumatic Brain Injury,* which were added when PL 94-142 became the Individuals with Disabilities Act in 1990) can be seen *In a Nutshell* on page 6. (Please note, current language recommends the use of the word *disability* in lieu of *handicap.*) PL 94-142 also identified six key cornerstones on which the education of students with disabilities still rests today. We've summarized five of these here. (Don't worry; the sixth is coming!)

1. *Nondiscriminatory evaluation.* As methods of detecting disabilities became more standardized, more and more students of color began to be identified as having cognitive disabilities. Investigation revealed that standardized measures of IQ were often biased against students from diverse cultural backgrounds, resulting in the overidentification of these minority students. This section of the law states that testing for special education must be free from bias, and it must avoid the overidentification or underidentification of children due to culture, race, or language.

2. *Free and appropriate public education.* This segment of the law moves beyond the idea that students have a right to an education, and it ensures that the education they receive is also appropriate to their individual needs. The principle of free and appropriate public education (FAPE) guarantees that public schools provide every child with disabilities a meaningful education, designed to meet each child's unique needs and to prepare that child for future employment and independent living. This free education must include appropriate preschool, elementary, and secondary options.

3. *Procedural due process.* In order to assure that families of children with disabilities were not pushed around by their local schools, and to provide them with legal protection if they didn't agree with decisions that the school personnel made, two provisions were included. The first was that individuals involved in special education proceedings have the right to appeal school district decisions in a court of law.

4. *Parent participation.* The second provision in support of parental protection was that special education decisions cannot be made without the participation or consent of a child's parents or legal guardians.

5. *Individualized Education Program (IEP).* The fifth key element of PL 94-142 guaranteed that each child with a disability would have an educational program specifically tailored to his needs. An IEP must be developed for each student identified with a disability. The plan must be developed by a collaborative team, and it must outline specific academic goals and objectives for the child, as well as how and when that child will meet those objectives. IEP team members should include an administrator or administrative designee, a special education teacher, parents, a school psychologist, the student (when appropriate), and other designated instructional service providers when appropriate. (General education teachers were always encouraged to attend, but they were not added as mandatory participants to the IEP team until IDEA was reauthorized for the second time in 1997.) Social, behavioral, and transition goals should also be recommended, according to the needs of the child. The IEP must include a statement of the student's current levels of functioning, the educational services that will be provided, and the duration of those services. It must also specify the percentage of time a student will spend in general education, and it must be reevaluated and rewritten annually. (See *In a Nutshell* on pages 7–8 for specifics about how the provisions changed when the law was reauthorized.) We go into detail about the IEP team in subsequent chapters.

In a Nutshell

The 13 Eligibility Categories for Disability Under IDEA

Category	Description
Autism (not originally identified in PL 94-142 but added in 1990 by IDEA)	A developmental disability that significantly affects children's verbal and nonverbal communication skills, social interactions, and educational performance. It is generally evident before age three. Consider a "spectrum disorder," which includes Asperger syndrome.
Deaf-Blindness	Simultaneous hearing and visual impairments that cause significant communication and learning deficits. These needs cannot be accommodated in programs designed specifically for children who are solely deaf or blind.
Deafness	A hearing impairment of such significant severity that it affects a child's ability to process linguistic information through auditory means and negatively affects the child's educational performance.
Emotional Disturbance	A child who exhibits an inability to learn that cannot be explained by intellectual, sensory, or health factors; has the inability to sustain interpersonal relationships; exhibits inappropriate behaviors and feelings; or has a pervasive mood of unhappiness. These behaviors must be exhibited over time in a variety of settings. Includes schizophrenia.
Hearing Impairment	An impairment in hearing (stable or fluctuating) that adversely affects a child's educational performance and isn't covered under the definition of deafness.
Mental Retardation	A developmental disorder that includes subaverage general intellectual functioning along with deficits in adaptive behavior that adversely affect a child's educational attainment. (This is more often referred to currently as a *cognitive* or *intellectual impairment*.)
Multiple Disabilities	Concomitant impairments, the combination of which causes such severe educational impairment that it cannot be accommodated in programs designed for a single disability. Does not include deaf-blindness.
Orthopedic Impairment	Any severe orthopedic impairment that impedes a child's educational attainment.
Other Health Impairment	Includes children with limited strength, vitality, or alertness that is due to chronic or acute health problems such as asthma, attention deficit disorder, etc., which adversely affects a child's educational performance.
Specific Learning Disability	A disorder in one of the basic psychological processes involved in understanding or using spoken or written language. Results in impaired ability to listen, think, speak, read, write, spell, and/or do math. Includes terms such as *perceptual disabilities, brain injury, minimal brain dysfunction, dyslexia,* and *developmental aphasia.*
Speech or Language Impairment	A communication disorder such as stuttering, impaired articulation, and/or a language or voice impairment that adversely affects a child's educational performance.
Traumatic Brain Injury (not originally identified in PL 94-142 but added in 1990 by IDEA)	An acquired injury to the brain resulting in total or partial dysfunction that adversely affects a child's educational performance.
Visual Impairment	Total or partial blindness that, even with correction, adversely affects a child's education performance.

In a Nutshell

Key Elements of EAHCA and IDEA

Six Key Elements of the Education for All Handicapped Children Act (EAHCA) Public Law 94-142 (1975)	
Nondiscriminatory evaluation	Students must be evaluated using assessments that do not discriminate based on culture, race, language, etc.
Due process	Parents have the right to examine all records, to receive written notification of proposed changes to a child's program, and to have an impartial hearing to mediate disagreements.
Free and appropriate public education (FAPE)	All children, regardless of the severity of their disability, must be provided with a no-cost education that meets their individual needs.
Parental participation	Parents must be full participants in all decisions regarding their child's education.
Individualized Education Program (IEP)	Every child with a disability must have an individualized plan that documents his or her educational program, including the following: • Present levels of performance • Individualized goals and objectives • Outline of educational services • Degree to which child will participate in general education • Plans for services and duration of services • An annual reevaluation
Least restrictive environment (LRE)	Children with disabilities will be educated to the maximum extent possible with their typical peers. States must provide a continuum of placement options.
Other Important Features of PL 94-142	
Child find	School districts have an obligation to go out and try to locate students with disabilities and make sure that they are provided an education.
Early childhood	Schools must provide an education to preschoolers with disabilities.
Zero reject	All children, no matter their disability, have the right to an education, and public schools have an obligation to provide that education, without exception.

(Continued)

(Continued)

Major Changes in 1990; Reauthorized to Become IDEA	
Change in name	The name of the law was changed to the Individuals with Disabilities Education Act (IDEA); became PL 101-476.
Individual Transition Plan (ITP)	All students with disabilities, beginning no later than age 16, must have an individualized transition plan in place to provide for the transition from school to life.
Added identifications	Autism and Traumatic Brain Injury (TBI) were added to the list of eligibility categories for IDEA.
Major Changes in IDEA; Reauthorized in 1997	
Behavior	Students with disabilities who experience minor infractions of school rules can be disciplined in ways similar to typical peers.
General education	IEPs must now specifically state how a child will be involved and progress in general education.
Transition planning	The age for transition planning was changed from 16 to 14.
IEP team	General educators were added to the IEP team.
Assistive technology	The IEP team must consider and address a child's needs for assistive technology.
Assessments	Students with disabilities must participate in statewide standardized assessments or be given an alternate assessment.
Major Changes in IDEA; Reauthorized in 2004	
Change in name	The name of the law was changed to the Individuals with Disabilities Education Improvement Act (IDEIA); most still refer to it as IDEA.
Highly qualified teachers	Language from NCLB was added, requiring highly qualified teachers in special education classrooms.
IEP	A pilot study to examine the option of three-year IEPs was created.
Response to Intervention (RTI)	States were granted permission to use Response to Intervention as a method to identify students with learning disabilities, instead of the discrepancy model previously used.

Why, you might be asking yourself, did we only summarize five of the six cornerstones of IDEA? Because the last one is the whopper, the Big Kahuna, particularly for those of us collaborating to teach students with disabilities. The sixth principle of PL 94-142 is the principle of least restrictive environment (LRE), and it was LRE that brought about the beginning of the inclusion movement.

Key Term

Least Restrictive Environment (LRE)—A special education placement that meets a child's needs and is as close to general education as possible.

LRE specifies the following crucial concept: *Children with disabilities must be educated in a setting as close to the typical classroom as possible.* In other words, the target destination for kids with disabilities is no longer a segregated classroom or site or a filthy institution with minimal care and even less curriculum; it is the typical classroom in your neighborhood school. LRE requires us to give access to general education to *all* children, no matter how severe their disabilities, and to provide the accommodations and modifications a student needs to be successful in a typical general education class. (See Chapter 2 to learn more about how LRE impacts deaf students.) The principle of LRE assumes that with the right supports, the vast majority of students can succeed and flourish in general education. LRE was the beginning of a new world for kids with disabilities and the beginning of a new paradigm for education in our nation's schools.

As you can see, the supporters of PL 94-142 were determined to bring kids with disabilities out of the dismal conditions that were documented in the 1950s and 1960s and make them a part of the community of school children in our public schools. Happily, the foundational concepts of PL 94-142 have survived for more than 30 years, and they have been strengthened as it has been reauthorized, first as the Individuals with Disabilities Education Act (IDEA; PL 101-476, 1990 & 1997), and later as the Individuals with Disabilities Education Improvement Act (IDEIA; PL 108-446, 2004). Thanks to the tenets laid down for us in IDEA, we no longer make assumptions about a child's ability just by his looks, his IQ, or even his ability to communicate orally. As a society, we have begun to acknowledge the amazing potential of kids who were previously isolated and ignored. We are discovering how to reexamine our prejudices, raise our expectations, and provide more opportunities for all. (See *In a Nutshell* on page 10.)

That's the good news.

The bad news is that there are still major obstacles to overcome. There are still biases that remain, and many individuals with disabilities still do not have full access to the same education as their peers. We have some teachers who do not want to work with "those kids," and there are parents who treat their own children as though they are incapable of real learning. We still have many children who are relegated to decrepit bungalows at the back of the campus and classes taught in former closets. We have kids with disabilities failing out or dropping out of school at a much higher rate than their nondisabled peers and ending up on welfare or state support. We have kids (in real life and in the media) calling each other "retards" and children who feel isolated and stigmatized by the special services they're receiving. We have students of color and second language learners being overidentified for special education services due to testing bias and lack of cultural understanding. Although we've come a long way, it's clear we still have a lot of work to do. Our society is resistant to change.

Key Term

IDEA—Individuals with Disabilities Education Act—Was later renamed but is still commonly called IDEA. Guarantees the rights of students with disabilities in public schools.

But we're optimists, so let's go back to the good news. In addition to the changes that have already occurred educationally for students, we also have many teachers who are embracing

In a Nutshell

Major Laws/Court Cases Impacting Special Education

Law/Court Case	Year	Impact
Brown vs. Board of Education	1954	Stated that "separate is not equal." Abolished educational discrimination by race. Acted as the foundation for the argument against segregation by disability.
Section 504 of the Rehabilitation Act	1973	Established rights for individuals who have a disability or are treated or seen as having a disability. Still used in schools today for students who don't qualify for special education but need individualized services.
Public Law 94-142: Education for All Handicapped Children Act (EAHCA or EHA)	1975	First major law establishing special education. Legalized concepts of free and appropriate public education (FAPE), individualized education programs (IEPs), child find, and least restrictive environment (LRE).
Public Law 99-457: Handicapped Infants and Toddlers Program	1986	Created a new provision that covered children with disabilities from birth through age two. Created statewide, comprehensive, coordinated services for infants and toddlers with disabilities.
Americans with Disabilities Act (ADA)	1990	Prohibits discrimination against people with disabilities in employment, transportation, hotels, governmental agencies, and communications. Also established the guidelines for telephone relay services for deaf individuals.
Public Law 101-476: Individuals with Disabilities Education Act (IDEA); now PL 108-446: Individuals with Disabilities Education Improvement Act (IDEIA)	1990, 1997, 2004	Emphasizes rights in special education. Added Autism and TBI as disability categories. More focus on LRE. If a child with a disability is not in a general education setting, the IEP team is required to explain why.
Jacob Javits Act	1993	Defines gifted/talented. No federal funding support to schools through this Act.
No Child Left Behind Act (NCLB)	2001	General education law establishing, among other things, that children have the right to highly qualified content teachers and to equal accountability and standards. This law led to higher expectations for special education and inclusion in standardized assessment for most kids with special needs.

change and who recognize the need for collaboration. These teachers are asking for more training to work with this diverse population and for help in working with each other. Parents are supporting the move to inclusive education and are working with schools to ensure that their children have more access to typical educational and social opportunities. School professionals in districts across the nation are taking a hard look at which students are sent to nonpublic schools, which are educated in self-contained settings, and which students can be successful with support in a general education class. The numbers of students with disabilities in general education classes is rising each year. However, placement alone is not an indicator of success; the real success comes when students are actually having their needs met in their classes and are given the opportunity to develop all their skills and talents to their maximum potential so that they can take their rightful place in society alongside their peers. PL 94-142 and IDEA created the foundation that made this possible.

MAKING SENSE OF THE LAW: HOW DOES IT IMPACT OUR CLASSROOMS?

Thank you for joining us on our quick trip through the history of special education. We hope that now you have an understanding of the powerful momentum that led to the creation of more collaborative and inclusive schools. This isn't just another crazy educational trend, any more than the equal rights of individuals of different races is a trend. It came about as the result of pervasive and long-standing inequity and discrimination in our society. But many questions still remain: How does this movement for more collaborative programs impact our classrooms? We know that IDEA mandates that kids with disabilities be given the opportunity to get their education in a conventional classroom alongside their typically developing peers, but we also know that it isn't always easy! Students who have severe cognitive or physical needs often require special accommodations such as assistive technology devices and adaptive equipment that may be beyond the expertise of most general education teachers. Kids with more common special needs, such as learning disabilities and attention deficit disorder (ADD), may need supports or adaptations to the curriculum in order to be successful. Others need instruction that is planned in such a way that it engages them using a variety of modalities and gives them choices in how to express their knowledge. Seriously, what's a teacher to do?!

Believe it or not, there's a miraculous answer that we've decided to unveil for you here, that can make all these unmanageable demands seem manageable again. This incredible discovery is convenient, inexpensive, and it can be implemented by even first-year teachers. Are you ready? Wait for it . . .

Collaboration!

"Oh please!!" We can hear you saying it even as we write it. "Collaboration can solve all those issues? Give me a break!"

We believe it can and it will. Sure, you may not have the expertise to adapt that seventh-grade novel for the student with the third-grade reading level, but there's someone in your school who does. You might not know how to operate an Eco language device, but there are people across the campus or around the corner who have the skills you need. You may not know how to engage that kindergartener who is already reading at the sixth-grade level, but there are experts out there who have the answers. It's all about learning to reach out and work together.

So seriously, how do these laws impact our classrooms? They require us to break out of the stereotypical paradigm of the teacher as the king/queen of the classroom, laboring away behind closed doors with nary another adult in sight. They compel us to reach across the hallway to our colleagues and ask for help. They demand that we let go of the vision of ourselves as the all-knowing experts and work as a *team* to educate our learners. All of our learners. Simply put, they *require* us to collaborate.

Throughout this book we will be teaching you how to plan and adapt instruction for students with special needs, whether you are a special educator, general educator, administrator, or other professional. Our goal is to give you more of the expertise you need to provide for the wide range of learners you can find in any classroom today. Even more important, we will be teaching you how to collaborate to fill in the gaps. There is no book in the world that can teach you everything required to service all kids—teachers spend their whole careers trying to acquire that expertise—but what we can teach you is how to work with others to get the information you need when you need it. Rick Lavoie, a special education guru and the author of the classic video *F.A.T. City* (Lavoie, 2004), said it best: "We have been doing closed-book teaching in an open-book world." In other words, it's no longer about knowing everything or being the ultimate expert; it's about knowing where to *access* the information you need to get the job accomplished.

So consider this your open-book introduction to the world of collaborative education, where we work together to share what we know and where the *real* expertise involves knowing how to get the information you need to be successful with the diversity of learners in our schools today. Welcome to the world of collaborative schools!

RESPECTING DIVERSITY: HOW HAVE OUR SCHOOLS EVOLVED?

Speaking of diversity . . . all you have to do is look at the kids in any public school and it is clear that schools have become diverse. Even if you look beyond the crazy hairdos and wild clothes, the diversity is obvious. We have students of many different races, cultures, abilities, genders, and preferences included in our classrooms. But how are we doing addressing their *learning* differences?

Why do we mention this? Because collaboration goes well beyond students with disabilities! Think about it. Have you ever worked with a child who had no special education eligibility at all but you thought, "Hmmmm . . . something is going on here"? We have a lot of learning differences in our classrooms that need to be addressed, and only a small percentage of them have anything to do with special education. Collaborating only to work with kids with identified disabilities will do a disservice to all the kids—and the teachers too. What if others would benefit from the information? We need to teach based on our students' needs, not on their labels.

In Practice

Ms. Jenkins is a general ed math teacher in an urban high school. When she first started teaching, the policy for dealing with kids who didn't learn, behave, or fit in was to refer them for special ed. Her new principal is actively against this action and wants teachers to collaborate with other school specialists.

Skeptical of this new regime change, Ms. Jenkins decided to investigate how many people would need to get involved to make this work. She contacted a special ed teacher for strategies in dealing with Eric, a student with major behavioral issues; she asked the ELL teacher for help with Ramon, a student who recently immigrated from Mexico; she called on the GATE teacher to provide enrichment activities for Emma, Zoe, and Quinn, who were working at advanced levels; she talked to the school psychologist about Ben, who was too shy to participate, Barb, who seemed depressed and anxious, and Darren, who was teased for being gay. Each time Ms. Jenkins spoke with one of these colleagues, they provided her with strategies and ideas that helped not only the target student but also other students in her classes. Although it took a fair amount of time, in the end Ms. Jenkins was convinced— the collaboration worked. With the help of her colleagues, she was meeting the needs of her diverse classroom better than ever before.

There are many ways to look at educational diversity. We are fans of anything that gets teachers thinking about individual students' learning and then collaborating with other professionals to address that diversity in the classroom.

Consider the *In Practice* box. Obviously, it is not easy to address the wide variety of needs that occur in the typical general education classroom. To be able to effectively teach all these students is a daunting task. However, when Ms. Jenkins turned to her colleagues and asked for help, the collaboration she experienced enabled her to meet her students' learning needs without going crazy. To be sure, it can take time to collaborate with this many people, but we address that issue later. Consider, however, how helpful it is to know you are not alone in this. Consider, too, how the students in this scenario were "typical" learners. Not one of them had an identified disability or special education label, yet all had issues that were impacting their learning. Without the specialized assistance and collaboration of Ms. Jenkins's colleagues, all of these students might not have reached their potential in math because she was too overwhelmed by their unique learning needs. And whether you're an elementary, middle, or high school teacher, there are specialists in your school or district who are available to help. Of course, it's up to you to reach out to them and to solicit their collaboration.

Before we move into some hints and tips regarding ways to address the various needs in the inclusive classroom, we have one more bit of critical information for you. Just as our philosophy toward individuals with disabilities has evolved over the years, so too has our language involving those individuals. We hope that society has moved far away from considering it socially acceptable to call anyone a "retard," but other than that one, how can you know what terms are considered acceptable these days? Here is the key. Use what is known as *People-first language* (Snow, 2010) and you'll be fine. People-first language considers that each of us is a person first, though some of us may also have disabilities. Instead of talking about the "autistic kid" or the "LD child," you would mention the "kid who has autism" or "the child with a learning disability." Better yet—talk about the kid in the red sweatshirt or the child who cracks you up during PE. Whenever possible, look at these students as who they are—people. People who happen to have disabilities. As you continue to read this book, we hope you will also pick up on the fact that we staunchly avoid stereotyping kids by their labels whenever possible. You won't get a chapter on working with children with learning disabilities (LD) and one on working with students with emotional/behavioral disabilities (EBD). Instead, you will get strategy after strategy on working collaboratively with other adults to help all students. We like to focus on strengths, rather than deficits. In fact, the remainder of this chapter focuses on starting you off with practical strategies for working with your diverse learners—whoever they may be.

TAKING DIVERSITY OUT OF THE ABSTRACT

This chapter is focused on starting you on a journey, a journey to a more collaborative and inclusive classroom and school. To start that journey, we took you on a brief trip through time. We had to go back in order to go forward. Now, however, we hope you are ready to recognize the very real situation in which you find yourself. Kids with identified and unidentified special needs will—*without a doubt*—be in your classroom. Rather than bemoaning this fact, now that you know the evolution of inclusive education, we hope you will embrace your diverse classroom and look for ways to address any curricular, behavioral, instructional, or social issues that may occur. As we mentioned, there are lots of strategies that can help you meet the needs of the diverse learners in your classroom. Second language learners, students with special needs, gifted students, students who don't like school—all benefit from specialized teaching strategies that can help them make the best of your classroom. So the rest of this chapter is devoted to some of the hundreds of strategies that can help you provide for the wide variety of learners we know you have in your classroom. However, in order to continue our journey of collaboration to benefit *all* kids, and to avoid falling into the "label trap" of disabilities, we divide these strategies according to learning styles. Although we aren't big believers in matching learning styles to teaching styles—research doesn't support the effectiveness of that approach—we *are* big believers in teaching to all learning styles, so that all types of learners can be accommodated and supported.

Here are some ideas that may help you make your curriculum more accessible to *any* learner.

Strategies for visual learners

Most learners benefit from visual supports as they learn. These can be as simple as pictures to illustrate the topic at hand or as engaging as videos. Here are some of our favorites:

• Keep it simple! Reduce visual clutter on the page by using a single clean font and minimizing the unnecessary use of colors, bolding, italics, all capital letters, and so forth.

• Enrich your instruction with meaningful videos. Watch them twice—once to get the overview and then once with pauses and discussion of important points. Provide a graphic organizer for students to take notes from the videos.

Strategies for auditory learners

Auditory learners have the learning style that is best adapted for most classrooms, since most teachers love to talk. Nevertheless, here are some strategies that can help them be even more successful:

- Give them lots of opportunities to share verbally with peers.

- Encourage and teach self-talk.

- Allow students to audiotape or create podcasts or videoblogs of their responses to content questions.

Strategies for kinesthetic learners

Kinesthetic learners are often the ones who are challenged the most by the traditional classroom. They usually have trouble sitting still, and they don't learn well unless allowed to interact with the materials. This is *not* a disability, and a kinesthetic learner does *not* necessarily have attention deficit disorder (ADD). Here are some strategies that can help students who are kinesthetic:

- Allow them to move around as they learn. Sometimes moving them to the back of the room where they can stand without disrupting other students is helpful.

- Give them a rubber ball to manipulate or a Koosh ball to squeeze while they sit and listen.

- Be okay with students who doodle while listening to a lecture or quietly tap their pen on their leg when you are talking.

On the web

For more strategies for teaching visual, auditory, and kinesthetic learners go to http://www.corwin.com/diverseschools.

In Practice

"The first year I was teaching I had a young man named Jeffrey in my room. He was a really great kid, but ACTIVE!! He was a kinesthetic learner, times 10! It was difficult for him to sit down for more than about five minutes, and after a little while his behavior would start to deteriorate as he struggled to keep himself still in his seat. Before long his wiggliness would affect the whole class.

After a couple of months I came up with a strategy that really worked. Every so often I would write a note to the office that said, "Jeffrey needs a break. Please keep him there for about five minutes, then send him back." I would staple the note closed, then ask Jeffrey to race to the office as fast as he could to deliver this very important note. He loved the break and loved feeling important, and the physical exercise would make it possible for him to come back to class and work without problems—a true win–win strategy!"

Sue S., fifth-grade teacher

THUMBNAILS OF RESOURCES ON THE INTERNET

The following elements can be found on the companion website for *Collaborate, Communicate, and Differentiate!* at http://www.corwin.com/diverseschools.

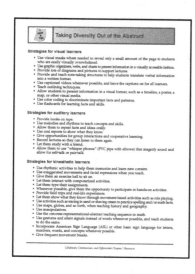

2

Unscrambling the Range of Settings and Services

THE BIG PICTURE

As we mentioned in Chapter 1, IDEA mandates the least restrictive environment for kids with disabilities, but that environment may look very different depending on the specific needs of the child. Although we believe that well-implemented inclusion is the most appropriate setting for the vast majority of students, it's still important (not to mention legally required) to have a variety of settings and services available to meet the needs of our diverse student population. *No one setting or service delivery model can work for all kids!*

No matter what setting a student is in, however, you'll need some form of collaboration in order to create the most effective learning and social environment possible. The types of collaboration needed, and the levels of interaction, may be quite different depending on the setting in which a teacher is working. For example, Yolanda (in *Voices From the Field*) may need to begin her collaborative efforts by setting up monthly meetings with the grade-level teachers at her school in order to create relationships with them and to discuss how to get her students more involved in the school programs. On the other hand, a general ed teacher who has students in a resource program might need to collaborate with the special ed teacher once or twice every week in order to give his students the level of support they need to be successful. Teachers in other situations will engage in different levels and types of collaboration to support their students effectively.

In this chapter we do the following:

- Explain some frequently used terms just to make sure we're all on the same page. (You say inclusion, I say mainstreaming . . . let's call the whole thing off!)
- Review placement options, figure out what they are, and discuss which students they might serve.
- Introduce you to our concept of "the Collaborative Continuum." Just how much collaboration might you need in order to make one program work for Emma, a child who has ADD and a learning disability, and another work for Javier, who is gifted and an English language learner? What strategies can you use to make this collaboration more convenient in your busy school day?

Keep Reading!

DEFINING TERMS: WHAT THE HECK DO ALL THESE WORDS MEAN?

Well, that's the point, isn't it? Much of our educational jargon means different things to different people. The purpose of this section isn't to tell you the *"right"* meaning for these terms; it's to develop a *common* meaning so that we can discuss these topics throughout the rest of the book and know that we're talking about the same things. Remember, these are *our* definitions—you may use some of these terms differently at your school site, but we want you to know how we use them throughout this book. We've put these terms in our *In a Nutshell* easy reference guide (see page 19) so that you can copy them and get to them easily whenever you need the information.

As you may see by looking at the chart, even among close friends and colleagues at your school, these terms may be interpreted in various ways. For good communication to occur, it is critical that all stakeholders use terms in the same way when collaborating. Take the time to talk about what they mean to you and to clarify what they mean to others. While you are thinking of mainstreaming as a model you want to avoid, someone else might be thinking of

In a Nutshell

Commonly Used Terms About Placements and Services

Term	Quick Definition
Inclusion	Inclusion is when a student with a disability receives instruction in a general education classroom or setting with all the supports and services in place to allow him equitable access to the curriculum and the social constructs of the classroom. When truly included, students with disabilities are full members of the classroom just like their typically developing peers. A student may be "included" in a general education classroom for one specific subject or activity or for the full day with no services outside the general education environment (called *full inclusion*). No matter the amount of inclusion, *the services are in place to help that student be successful*, both socially and academically.
Mainstreaming	Although the terms *mainstreaming* and *inclusion* are often used interchangeably, we believe they are critically different. Mainstreaming typically involves placing a student with a disability in a general education environment *without* effective supports or services. This was considered a "readiness model"; kids were put in general education classes when adults thought they were ready for the experience. Over time, this became known as the "sink or swim" model based on the fact that many students were unable to make it without additional support.
Collaboration	Collaboration is a style of interaction: two or more people working cooperatively together toward a shared goal (Friend & Cook, 2009). Collaboration can be done with *any* activity where you work together toward a goal: you can collaborate to bake cookies, plan a school dance, or create an IEP. It's the way you do it that's important—cooperatively and with a shared outcome in mind.
Consultation	Consultation is a way of giving indirect services to a child with a disability, usually one who needs less intensive support. In a consultation model, a general teacher and a special ed teacher might meet regularly to collaborate on strategies to support students in a general education class, but the special education teacher will rarely work directly with the students; she serves only as a consultant. In some instances, special educators may provide "monitoring" services to students by observing and/or consulting with their general education teachers.
Co-Teaching	Co-teaching is when two or more adults co-plan, co-instruct, and co-assess a group of students (Murawski, 2003). Teaching requires planning, instructing and assessing; *co*-teaching means we do all of these together. This is often done with general and special ed teachers, but others can co-teach as well. It's important to note that in co-teaching, *both* teachers are participating in all three elements in a *meaningful* way.
In-Class Support	This is another way for a special service provider to assist a student with a disability in a general ed classroom. Whereas in co-teaching the teachers are working together to provide instruction, in some cases that may not be possible or desirable. Sometimes a special education teacher may come into a general education classroom once or twice a week and provide discrete support services for a student or group of students who need a little extra help. In this case, the teacher is serving more as a coach or a tutor rather than a full-blown classroom teacher. Other support providers, such as speech-language pathologists, occupational therapists, and physical therapists, may also provide support services in the classroom.

it as synonymous with inclusion. The result? Conflicts. Tantrums. Gnashing of teeth. And that's just between the teachers. Without common language, misunderstandings are bound to occur.

THE RANGE OF PLACEMENTS: WHERE DO KIDS WITH SPECIAL NEEDS END UP?

As we mentioned earlier, IDEA mandates that students with special needs be educated in the least restrictive environment (LRE). But what the heck does that mean? Is the LRE always the general education classroom, or is it the classroom with the best fit for that particular child? Will LRE look the same for all kids, or will it even be the same for one child throughout her school career?

What IDEA gives us is a range of placement options. In other words, the law recognizes that not all kids will be successful in general education classrooms, and it lays out a series of options for IEP teams to consider. Typically, the range of placements includes such options as these:

- *General education classes (which may include a variety of supports, ranging from consultation to pull-out services).* General education classrooms can serve students with the full range of special needs, from severe physical and cognitive disabilities to students who are gifted, but the correct supports and instructional techniques must be in place to help the students achieve success. Providing the necessary supports is what differentiates inclusion from mainstreaming.

Want more info?

Author June Downing has published several books with practical information on including students with significant disabilities in general education classrooms. Check out the *Diving Deeper* section on the web for a list of her great resources.

- *Special classes on a general education campus (usually resource or self-contained).* Special classes are generally reserved for students with more challenging learning, behavioral, or physical needs. However, it's important to point out that inclusion in general education is considered best practice for students with severe physical and cognitive disabilities. Placement in special classes must be carefully considered for both the drawbacks and the benefits. In secondary schools, special classes may be available for students who are English language learners or for students who are gifted; these are typically considered pull-out classes and replace other classes the students might have taken (e.g., Honors Science in lieu of Basic Biology; ESL English in lieu of English 7).

- *Special schools (such as nonpublic schools).* From time to time, a student's needs cannot be effectively met in the public school setting, especially if the student is considered a danger to himself or others. For this very small percentage of students, a special school may provide the supports they need to be successful. Special schools are sometimes considered effective for students with very severe behavioral challenges, or very significant learning disabilities, where small class sizes and increased services are helpful. In addition, some magnet schools are available for students who are highly gifted and may not have their instructional or social needs met in the typical classroom setting.

- *Home instruction.* Home instruction can be useful for students with specific challenges that make it difficult for them to sit all day in a classroom. For example, a student with a health condition that requires ongoing medication may receive home schooling through a school district. It is also occasionally used as a transitional placement for students who are struggling behaviorally. Home instruction is often a short-term placement.

• *Instruction in hospitals.* For students with very severe mental health or physical challenges, hospital schooling is available. Students are housed and educated in a hospital with ongoing access to counseling and medication. Like home instruction, hospital schooling is often a short-term solution.

• *Live-in institutions.* A very small percentage of students, most of whom have very significant behavioral and emotional challenges, will receive schooling in a live-in setting. These institutions help support schools and families who don't have the resources to give their children the emotional and behavioral support they need at home. There are other instances in which children may be taught in a "live-in institution" (see the *Learn More* box).

> **Learn More**
>
> IDEA addresses the LRE for students who are deaf or hard of hearing (DHH), specifically recognizing the unique communication needs of this population of learners. For these students, the IEP team must "consider opportunities for direct communication with peers and professionals in the children's language" (IDEA, 1997). This may mean that, for students who are DHH, a live-in setting like a School for the Deaf may be a very appropriate placement and the LRE for those children.

Our friend June Downing, who has done much of the seminal work on the inclusion of students with severe disabilities, asks us to remind you of a few things here. The law specifying continuum of placements was created LOOOOONNNGGG before students with significant disabilities were ever considered for inclusion in general education classes. As a result, this law is sometimes used to exclude students with significant cognitive and physical disabilities under the excuse that "the placement won't work for them." Often the teacher is afraid that he won't have the skills needed to teach a particular student, and so the placement is made based on the needs of the *teacher* and not the student. This is never okay. As June says, "You often have to do it before you feel comfortable doing it. Then you'll realize what you don't know and need to learn" (personal communication, August 9, 2010). In other words, you just gotta jump in (with the appropriate collaborative support, of course)! Don't use the continuum of placements as an excuse to exclude children with significant disabilities from their rightful place alongside their general education peers.

We must make one other note on this population: placement in general education classes for children with significant disabilities gives them access to high expectations, accountability for learning, and entrée into the social learning environment of 20 to 30 typical children with strong skills and appropriate behaviors. For a child with a significant disability, that kind of role modeling can make the difference between a life lived as part of society or a life relegated to exclusion and segregation. Inclusion for these students is about learning skills for life, not just about academics.

THE RANGE OF PLACEMENT OPTIONS: WHO MAKES THE DECISION?

Individualized Education Program (IEP) teams

The critical concept here is that the IEP team (discussed in detail in Chapter 3) decides what the LRE is for any particular student with an identified disability—it shouldn't be determined according to the convenience of a teacher, a school, or a school district. And the LRE can change as a student's needs change; for example, a child could be home schooled for a year or so while dealing with a medical issue, then transition into a special class or a general ed setting as appropriate. Or a variety of concurrent settings may be appropriate as well. Consider this: a student might start in a general education class, receive instruction for part of the day in a special ed resource class, and end the day in a general ed class that is co-taught. Determining the LRE for a particular child at a particular time can be tricky, though. For an example, let's look at the following *In Practice* box.

In Practice

Larry is a young man with an emotional disability (ED). In elementary school, general education was the LRE for Larry; he was quite successful in a general ed classroom, with pull-out resource services available when he was overwhelmed by the classroom demands. However, as he got older, his emotional needs grew more significant and his frustration in the general education classroom became more profound. By high school, Larry was no longer able to control his emotional outbursts in general education classrooms. At that point, his IEP team, with Larry included, determined that a smaller, more supportive environment would be helpful to him. They looked around for a place that not only could give him more security and less frustration, but also where more mental health services would be available to him and his family. The team settled on a nonpublic high school that provided very small classes, many activities designed to build self-esteem and self-control, and a full range of mental health and counseling services for both Larry and his parents. In high school, then, general education was no longer the LRE for Larry—the high academic demands and lack of individual support in a typical high school classroom no longer met Larry's needs. He was much more successful once his team found a placement with more intensive, individualized supports for him, and we're proud to say that Larry earned a diploma and graduated from his high school in June!

Principal Points

One of the pitfalls of being a principal in an IEP meeting is that you can have *too much* power! The IEP was designed as a collaborative team process, in which all participants have a valued voice. As a collaborative principal, you need to work hard at providing an informed perspective without being the final word. If the team feels strongly that a student should have a service and you don't agree, avoid bringing down the hammer. Provide information and data that support your point of view, and if the team still doesn't agree, consider giving everyone a chance to think it over by reconvening at another time. See Chapter 3 for more information on teams and how they should function.

As you might imagine, for most students, a nonpublic school would be a very, very restrictive environment—these schools typically have fewer choices, fewer opportunities, more rules and regulations, and students are not with their nondisabled peers. However, for Larry (see *In Practice* above), this setting was appropriate, and he was able to complete high school in this setting. *Nevertheless, we need to reiterate the point we made at the beginning of this chapter: We believe that for the vast majority of students, a well-implemented inclusive setting is the most appropriate and least restrictive environment.* It is a tragic reality of special education that placement options such as special classes and special schools have long been the dumping ground for kids that schools didn't know how to or didn't care to serve (Kavale & Forness, 2000). This is not the intention of IDEA, and it shouldn't be the impetus behind any placement decisions.

So how does an IEP team decide what placements *are* appropriate and "least restrictive"? It all comes back to collaboration! The team has to work together to identify Larry's strengths and areas of challenge and proceed from there. All perspectives are critical to this dialogue—a parent may know a lot about a student's interests and affinities that school personnel don't know. The general education teacher probably has information that the special education teacher doesn't and vice versa. The administrator is often the expert in district services, budget issues, and placement options. Other educational professionals may also have input on specific areas (e.g., speech/language, school psychologist, nurse). And Larry, as a member of the IEP team, certainly might have something to add about himself! However, IDEA mandates that consideration of the general education classroom as the least restrictive placement needs to be the starting point for all discussions, and if team members decide that general education is not appropriate, they need to specify why in the IEP.

Section 504 teams

Section 504 of the Rehabilitation Act of 1973 also provides guidance on the education of students with disabilities, or for students perceived as having a disability, identified or not. Section 504 states that any public agency that receives federal funds (like schools, of course) must make every effort to educate students with disabilities in the general education environment (Smith, 2001). As with IDEA, Section 504 assumes that it is most appropriate to educate kids with disabilities in the general education classroom with supports and accommodations.

Section 504 defines a disability as "any impairment that substantially limits one or more life activities" (Rehabilitation Act of 1973, Section 504, 29 U.S.C. § 79). School is considered a life activity and is subject to Section 504 regulations. Obviously, students who qualify for special education would qualify for services under this definition, but if they are already receiving services as a student with special needs, then they would not need 504 protection. However, this one gets tricky, because students whose disabilities do *not* qualify them for services under IDEA *may* be eligible for protection under Section 504. These protections usually take the form of basic classroom accommodations such as extended time or preferential seating, and though protected by law, there is no funding to ensure their effective implementation. Much like the IEP teams, all of these decisions are made by a group of individuals who work together on what is typically known as a 504 team. This team also should have a broad representation of various stakeholders.

As IDEA has been reauthorized and rewritten over the years, many of the students who would previously have been covered under Section 504 are now protected under IDEA. As a result, Section 504 is used less frequently. You still need to know about it, though, because when a student does not require much more than basic accommodations in order to be successful in the general education classroom (for example, additional time or copies of notes), parents may advocate for 504 accommodations in order to avoid the stigma attached to having a special education label for their child. Having a 504 Plan ensures that their child will have access to those accommodations each year. There's a catch, though. Services provided under a 504 designation are not funded, so schools are more likely to push for a special education designation so that they get funding for the services. As you can see, there's potential for conflict between these two opposing interests. (See why collaboration is so critical?)

SERVICE DELIVERY OPTIONS: WHAT IS THE COLLABORATIVE CONTINUUM?

So your IEP team has met, and you've collaboratively agreed on a placement that meets the needs of the student. What now? Does your obligation—as a general education teacher, a special education teacher, an administrator—end once the student begins her new placement? If a child is moved into a self-contained special education classroom, you're done, right? Only *that* teacher is responsible for the student now, right?

Wrong! We believe that any program that serves a student with a disability requires collaboration among a wide variety of parties in order to be successful (McLeskey & Waldron, 2002b). If the goal is to make a student's education as close to typical as possible (and that's really the idea behind LRE), then it's important that the stakeholders keep in touch with what "typical" is. One of the biggest traps of noninclusive placements is that the teachers and parents can lose track of what kids are doing in general education, so they begin to set the bar lower and lower for the kids in special education. It's an insidious process that can be overcome with . . . say it with us . . . COLLABORATION!

In order to describe this process better, we have created what we call the Collaborative Continuum (Friedman Narr, Murawski, & Spencer, 2007). The goal is to illustrate in graphic terms how the need for collaboration changes as a student's placement changes. Note, we didn't say it goes away—it changes and will continue to change as a student's strengths and needs and therefore services evolve over time. Check out Figure 2.1.

As you can see from Figure 2.1, the amount of collaboration needed to support a child in a self-contained special education class may be less than is needed for a child in a pull-out or co-taught setting, but nevertheless, collaboration is still needed! Whenever possible, teachers of self-contained special ed classes should find opportunities to collaborate with general ed grade-level or subject-matter teachers in order to align instructional goals and keep expectations high (Huber, 2005). Remember, IDEA mandates that students with disabilities be educated in the general education curriculum, guided by state standards (Thurlow, 2002). Sharing strategies and teaching techniques to help all students access those standards is critical to the success of diverse learners. Additionally, teachers should work together to decide which parts of the standards are most critical for each student to master, and collaboration is essential to this process.

In Practice

Carol is a general education teacher in a large city on the East Coast. At her school, the special education services were completely separate from general ed, and she freely admits that she didn't have a clue what was going on in the special ed classes at her school for most of her career. It wasn't until a new special ed teacher joined the faculty that the general education teachers had the opportunity to see beyond the labels and start to get to know the kids. This new teacher was a good musician, and he volunteered to direct the music for the school's graduation ceremonies. All the students loved him, and suddenly the students in his special ed class had new status. They were proud to be "Mr. M's kids." As Carol puts it, "I have to admit, it was pretty heartwarming to see the way they opened up when their teacher stepped up to the podium. Suddenly, for the first time in my memory, these kids were legitimately part of the school culture. And many of us veteran teachers had a chance to realize that 'those' kids were really not very different from the kids we saw every day in our own classes."

Figure 2.1   Understanding the Differences in Support Along the Collaborative Continuum

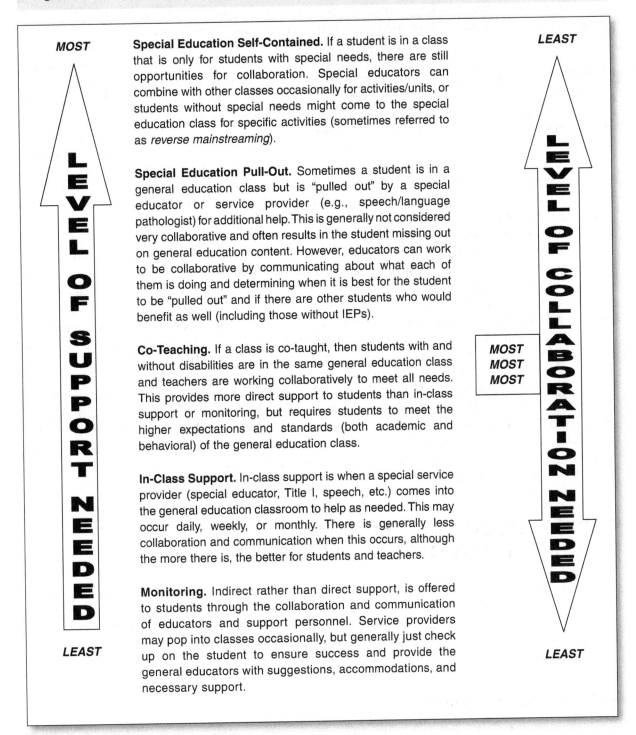

Source: Murawski, W. W. (2008a). *Co-teaching for success: Effective strategies for working together in today's inclusive classrooms.* Bellevue, WA: Bureau of Education and Research. Reprinted with permission.

Working outside the curriculum is also important for developing a collaborative environment. Teachers should grab chances to work on special events such as planning a dance or coaching cheerleading in order to be seen as a vital member of the school community. If the TEACHERS aren't part of the community, the kids won't be either!

Want more info?

Building a collaborative school environment is discussed in more detail in Chapter 10.

We know how easy it is to stop collaborating when you're working in separate settings. (I'm in general ed; you're in the self-contained special ed classroom across campus . . . we're oil and water—we just don't mix!) Yet for both special and general educators alike, the need for collaboration is critical to the education of kids with special needs. Let's say you're a general ed teacher, and you have a student with a significant learning disability in your classroom. You have been collaborating with a special ed teacher who has been giving you strategies for making your instruction more kinesthetic to meet the needs of that student. And guess what? Turns out those strategies work really well for your English language learners, too. And even some of your gifted students. Who knew?

After a while, however, the student with LD is moved out of your classroom. So you are no longer working with that special ed teacher, and you no longer have access to those engaging methods she was suggesting to you. What do you do? You keep collaborating! Reach out to the coordinators and coaches at your school. Talk to the ELL teachers. Ask them for tips and strategies that will work with your kids. Talk to the special educators, even if you no longer have a child on their caseload. Build that culture of collaboration with *everyone* at your school. Your students (and your teaching) will be all the better for it. Granted, we may be asking you to do even more than you already are doing. We realize that some of you might be ready to put this book down when you read that. However, we do it because we passionately believe that by building a culture of collaboration that goes beyond what is mandated by your caseload, you are ultimately creating a school community in which everyone helps one another and shares the workload. Yes, we truly believe that collaboration will eventually *reduce* your work, not create more. But it's a process, and you have to lay some foundational blocks to get there.

TAKING THE COLLABORATIVE CONTINUUM OUT OF THE ABSTRACT

We know that ongoing collaboration isn't always easy. Teachers are busy, and reaching out to communicate takes time and effort. So we wanted to include some concrete tips to keep you communicating, collaborating, and connected to the world outside your ~~kingdom~~ classroom (oops!). The rest of this chapter is devoted to hints, tips, and strategies for collaborating across the continuum.

Collaborating across campus

Hints & Tips

- Pair up for specific units in a subject area such as history or science. Hands-on units are particularly good for this!

- Schedule informal "lunch meetings" or "strategy swaps" with colleagues once or twice a month to touch base and keep up with the latest news.

• Create opportunities for group assignments and projects that can be completed by kids working across classroom barriers. (Examples include murals, gardens, and sports activities.) Be sure to work with colleagues to select group assignments that won't humiliate any one child by highlighting his areas of weakness to his peers. If you have students at multiple grade levels in one class, consider carefully how you implement these projects, however. Students need to work with peers at their own age levels.

Collaborating across school sites

• Use technology to teach intercampus classes. Perhaps a Spanish or computer class could be offered at multiple campuses via webcam or distance learning, allowing the kids with special needs the opportunity to continue taking courses in their areas of interest.

> **Principal Points**
>
> When setting up your school's classes, try not to isolate special education classrooms in the back of the school or cluster them all together. Any convenience you might gain by putting them together will be far outweighed by the negative stigma attached to the kids when they have to walk the "special ed corridor" to get to class. Organize your classrooms by grade level, and make sure that the students in special classes are side by side with their typical peers of the same age.

• If one of your students moves from your classroom to another school site, make the effort to reach out to the new teacher and provide as much information and insight as you can about the student who is leaving you. Don't assume that the IEP has everything she needs to know—it rarely does—and more important, the teacher often won't receive the IEP in a timely manner or know what to do with the information it contains. Your phone call or e-mail will be much more personal and informative. Think about it: isn't that what you would prefer if a student was just dropped into your class?

On the web

For more strategies for collaborating across campus and across school sites go to http://www.corwin.com/diverseschools.

In Practice

Ross M., a middle-school teacher, got a new student named Stefan. Stefan had behavior problems from the moment he came into the class. He was always ranting about his old teacher and how much better she was than Ross. Finally, Ross figured out a strategy. He made arrangements to have Stefan's mother come after school, and together the three of them sat down to talk on the phone with Stefan's previous teacher. All four (Stefan, his mom, Ross, and Mrs. Munoz, the former teacher) collaboratively brainstormed how to make the new classroom more palatable to Stefan, as well as identified strategies that Ross could use to curb the behavior problems. Stefan participated in all the discussions. From that day on, Stefan's behavior improved. As Ross puts it, "I can't say it was perfect, but it was definitely much better. I kept in touch with Stefan's former teacher, and she would e-mail suggestions and strategies when I needed them. It was excellent! I think it would have taken me much, much longer to come up with ways to work with Stefan that I got in minutes just by collaborating with Mrs. Munoz."

THUMBNAILS OF RESOURCES ON THE INTERNET

The following elements can be found on the companion website for *Collaborate, Communicate, and Differentiate!* at http://www.corwin.com/diverseschools.

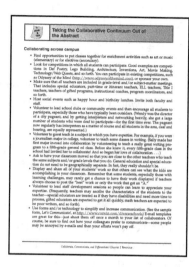

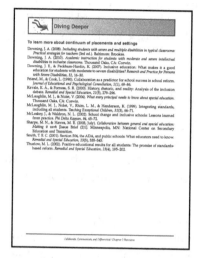

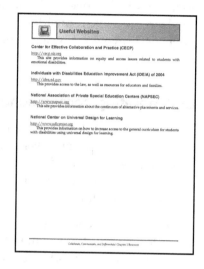

3

Improving Student Outcomes by Working in Teams

Voices From the Field

"I was absolutely terrified before my first IEP meeting. All I had heard from other parents was how contentious they were, and how I would have to fight to get my daughter the services she needed. I was afraid I wasn't going to be strong enough or knowledgeable enough to be Katelyn's advocate. What a surprise, then, when I got into the room and found a team of people who were willing to listen to what I had to say! I went into the meeting determined that my daughter needed hours of pull-out speech services, but after talking to the speech pathologist and general ed teacher, and having them listen to my opinions about my daughter's speech needs, we came up with a solution that seemed to work better for everyone. I really feel like I have a partnership with my daughter's teacher and the other professionals at the school."

Tori R., parent

THE BIG PICTURE

Most educators already know that IDEA mandates that special education decisions be determined by teams. If you haven't been to an IEP meeting, you've certainly heard the stories! As in Tori's experience in the opening vignette, many people think of IEP teams as contentious and frightening.

However, the IEP team was originally conceptualized as a planning medium, not as a bare-knuckle boxing event, with the goal of having parents, teachers, administrators, students, and other professionals come together and work collaboratively for the good of students. It has one simple purpose: to be a vehicle for creating partnerships. Other school teams exist for this purpose as well. Despite the fact that the word *team* may send shudders down your spine, these teams can meet a real need and even do some real good when used effectively and efficiently. In this chapter, we explore the various school-related teams that require collaboration in order to benefit student learning. We demystify some acronyms and clarify some roles—maybe even your own!

In this chapter we do the following:

- Discuss how different frames of reference can bring richness and improve outcomes on our team meetings and collaborative interactions.
- Identify the different major school teams (i.e., IEP, SST, RTI), make sense of their function in a child's schooling, and discuss your possible roles on those teams.
- Review the range of partners you might work with as part of your collaborative school team experience.
- Share strategies on how to collaborate with other educators and develop worthwhile relationships with various school personnel.

Let's Jump In!

BUILDING PARTNERSHIPS: WHY CAN'T I JUST DO ALL THIS ALONE?

As we've mentioned previously, IDEA mandates that people involved in special education work in teams. There's a reason for this, and it isn't because the framers of IDEA thought educators had too much free time on their hands. No, they had a much more thoughtful and important purpose when they created the notorious IEP team: *collaboration!* Believe it or not, the creators of IDEA actually believed in that old chestnut, two heads are better than one. In fact, they thought that many heads were better than two, particularly if they all had different perspectives and points of view. Check out the words of our friend, Fred Weintraub, in the *In Practice* sidebar. Fred was one of the instrumental folks who actually crafted the first special education law (PL 94-142), now known as IDEA, and helped come up with the whole concept of the IEP team.

In Practice

"When we got together to discuss how we thought special education should look, we talked about getting all the major players in a student's life together: kid, parent, general and special education teachers, administrator, school psych, and any other key people. Then we'd talk about where the student currently was, where we wanted him to be in a year, and how we would get him there. That made sense. That was how the concept of an IEP started. At no time did I or my colleagues think it would develop into a 20-page document indicating that the kid would have to show how he could hang his red hat on the third peg from the left with 72.5% accuracy on Wednesdays."

Fred Weintraub (personal communication, July, 2, 2010)

What Fred and the framers of PL 94-142 understood was that *none of us alone knows as much as all of us together.* We know it's a cliché, but in a very real way, it takes a village to create a good IEP. Let's look at the example from the *Voices From the Field* box at the beginning of the chapter describing Tori's IEP meeting for her daughter Katelyn. Before going into the meeting, Tori believed that Katelyn needed multiple pull-out sessions of speech therapy per week. However, once she talked to the general education teacher, she discovered that many young people experience problems when they are pulled out of class to receive services—inevitably they miss academic content, and some start to struggle where they never had difficulty before. The speech and language teacher, an itinerant teacher for the school district, told Tori and the other team members about a collaborative speech program she was implementing in a school across town. Twice a week she ran a reading group in the first-grade class that allowed her to integrate speech remediation into the regular classroom instruction. This was a new idea for the general ed teacher, but both she and Tori felt it could be a win–win solution for everyone involved, including the other kids in the class. In fact, the first-grade teacher was excited about the prospect of reducing pull-out services and having additional reading and speech expertise in the classroom.

Furthermore, the administrator in the meeting reassured Tori that the decision they made today didn't have to be permanent. She explained the process through which Tori could call for a new IEP meeting if she felt Katelyn's speech needs weren't being met, and she even encouraged Tori to come sit in the classroom to observe once the program got under way. By the end of the meeting, Tori felt that her opinions about Katelyn's speech and language program had been respected and honored, and she felt that a higher-quality intervention had been created than the one she had originally imagined. By bringing together a variety of experts—parents, teachers, specialists, and administrators—with a variety of frames of reference, the IEP team collaborated to create a program that was better than any the participants could have created on their own.

Authors' Note: Be sure to read the "Frame of Reference" box on the side. This is a key term we will be referring to over and over again throughout this book. In many cases, understanding others' frames of reference can make or break your collaborative and communicative endeavors!

As we can see, bringing together people with a variety of perspectives and skills can be a powerful paradigm. But it can

Key Term

Frame of Reference—The point of view people bring with them to all situations. Shaped by past experiences, opinions, and beliefs. Influences the exchange of ideas and helps shape the unique perspective that every individual brings to a collaborative interaction. Because this is also a *key term*, you will see us use a *picture frame* motif from now on to alert you that we are pointing out the impact frame of reference may have on a particular topic.

also be intimidating! Facing a table full of professionals, all with sheaths of paperwork and test results, is overwhelming for any mere human. And then when you add the acronyms—LRE, OT, PT, APE—it might start to feel like you've fallen in a bowl of alphabet soup. Help! I've fallen and I can't get up! Before we go into the individual team members—and introduce their accompanying acronyms—let's first take a moment to talk about some of the key school teams that relate to inclusive education. Understanding the purpose of these teams will provide a context for understanding the folks who are working on those teams . . . we hope.

THE RANGE OF SCHOOL TEAMS: WHAT ARE ALL THESE GROUPS AND WHAT DO THEY DO?

Teams and meetings are ubiquitous in education. And by "ubiquitous," we mean there are way too freakin' many of them! Let's get one thing straight. We are not against teams—we are *for* them—if . . . and *only* if . . . they are effective. Meeting for meeting's sake drives us insane! (Hmmm. We suspect we aren't the only ones who feel that way.)

Nevertheless, how do we know if a team is going to be effective? Research is available that clarifies the key characteristics of effective teams—check them out in the *Key Concept* box. Our suggestion is to look at these, and if your team is *not* displaying these characteristics, you have three choices:

1. Communicate with your teammates so that you can work together to improve the team.

2. Get off the team and let someone else deal with the pain.

3. Dissolve the team altogether.

While choices 2 and 3 are options, they are probably not the most collaborative of your choices. And since this is a book on collaboration, we strongly recommend choice 1. *Talk* with your team members about why the team does not appear to be as effective as you might like. If you are feeling frustrated, chances are other team members are, too! Have your team members complete a quick evaluation using the Team Evaluation Checklist on page 33 or ask the following questions:

- Are you all clear on what the team is trying to accomplish?
- Do you feel that your role is respected and that you are allowed to clearly communicate your point of view?
- Do you understand how the team functions and what the rules are to maintain its effectiveness?
- Are you encouraged to take a leadership role, or do you feel constrained to following someone else's lead?

Once team members have answered these questions, share the results and discuss changes that might make the team more effective. It takes time and commitment, but the outcomes are worth the effort. Remember, *none of us alone knows as much as all of us together!*

Key Concept

Characteristics of an Effective Team

- There is a shared goal that is mutually agreed upon.
- All members feel equal and valued.
- The participation and decision making are truly shared.
- All participants share in the responsibility for the team outcomes.
- Resources are shared among team members.
- Participation on the team is voluntary.

Source: Snell & Janney, 2000.

Team Evaluation Checklist

Check whether you agree or disagree with these statements. Be prepared to support your response.

	Agree	Disagree
The goals of our team are clear.		
The members feel respected and valued.		
The members all have clear roles.		
The norms and expectations of the team are clear.		
Team members can exercise leadership skills.		

Source: Adapted from Friend & Cook, 2006.

Although there are many different types of school teams, we'd like to pay special attention to three teams that relate directly to the instruction of students with special needs: the Response to Intervention (RTI) team, the Student Study Team (SST), and the Individualized Education Program (IEP) team. Let's take a closer look at these.

RTI: How can we collaborate to provide high-quality intervention?

Response to Intervention (also referred to as Response to Instruction or Responsiveness to Instruction) is a relatively new concept that has lots of schools creating another team: the RTI team. A major premise behind RTI is that when all students are provided with high-quality instruction in the general education classroom, students who are struggling academically can be identified early and provided with more intensive support (Brown-Chidsey & Steege, 2005). The emphasis in RTI is on individualized, proactive instruction; ongoing assessment; data-based decision making; and systematic, explicit remediation. While these seem like things we've been doing for a while in schools, in RTI there is a mandate to provide additional support services to students *before* they get so far behind that they have to be identified as having a disability. In fact, RTI was actually approved by IDEIA in 2004 as a new method by which students with learning disabilities can be identified. Everyone remember the discrepancy model? In order for a child to be identified with a learning disability, the IEP team had to show a significant discrepancy between his ability (as typically measured by IQ tests) and his achievement in school. Many people call it the "wait until they fail model" because the majority of students didn't show a large enough discrepancy to get services until they were in third grade or later. So that's four years of schooling in which a child really needed extra help, yet frequently got very little.

RTI is designed to eliminate those wasted years. In RTI, children who need extra help are identified early—as early as kindergarten in many cases—and then given the type of individualized intervention that used to only exist in special education and solely through pull-out services. At the same time, they continue to receive general education instruction like

> **Want more info?**
>
> Check out the website of the National Center on Response to Intervention: http://www.rti4success.org

all the other children. If the child does well, in other words, if she *responds to the intervention* (hence the name), the intervention ceases. If the child is still struggling, the RTI team will designate more intensive, smaller-group remediation for her and continue to assess her progress. Eventually, if the child is a genuine nonresponder who is not making significant improvement even with this intensive, small-group remediation, the child may be identified as having a disability and receive special education services (Fuchs & Fuchs, 2006).

We urge you to remember that just because a child needs Tier III intervention does not necessarily mean that he should be taken to a separate classroom. Students with more significant disabilities will almost always need the third level of intervention, and it can often be given in the general education classroom by a special education service provider. Remember, service does NOT equal setting! In a true collaborative school, we need to move beyond the idea of "change of services, change of placement" and begin to explore what can be done within the general education classroom, without the stigma of pull-out or separate classrooms.

The role of the RTI team is to help make decisions regarding which children need intervention, what level or tier of support is appropriate, and what assessments should be done schoolwide or for an individual student, and to follow up with teachers. If you are a member of an RTI team, you might be involved in assessment, problem solving, data collection, and even modeling instruction. "For RTI to be successful, a wide array of stakeholders need to collaborate. These will include administrators, parents, students, staff, community and educators of all types" (Murawski & Hughes, 2009, p. 69). Again, a diversity of perspectives and expertise makes for the most effective RTI team at any grade level.

It's important to mention that RTI isn't just an elementary school phenomenon. It is beginning to be implemented in both middle and high school as well. It can go across subject areas, and it isn't restricted to reading and writing skills—in fact, RTI for positive behavior support is quickly gaining in popularity. Our *Eye on the Research* on page 35 identifies some of the benefits. Although there is not yet much research on the effectiveness of RTI in secondary schools, many schools are moving ahead in response to national and state mandates. In some secondary schools, educators begin by documenting their existing resources, then organizing them into tiers to fit the needs of a variety of students (Samuels, 2009). Other schools are using block scheduling and other creative scheduling to build students' deficit skills (Elliott, 2008). In any case, if you haven't yet been invited onto an RTI team, it's likely that you will be before too long.

The SST conundrum: Why do we have this extra hoop?

Another important and often misunderstood team is the SST: the Student Success or Student Study Team. Many states or districts use a variety of different terms for this team and we can't go over them all, but this is the team that is generally thought of as the "prereferral team" or "the-hoop-you-have-to-go-through-in-order-to-get-a-child-into-special-education" team. However, this team is actually *not* designed to be part of special education. In fact, the SST is designed to be a general education team. The function of the SST is to give struggling students the supports they need to be successful in their general education classrooms by clearly identifying their problems, generating high-quality solutions, and organizing resources to implement those solutions (Male, 1991). Unfortunately, in many schools, the SST has become the pipeline to special education instead of the general education support service that it was designed to be.

Like other teams, a well-functioning SST should include members with a variety of perspectives and areas of expertise. Typical membership might include several general education teachers with expertise in different subject areas and/or grade levels, a special

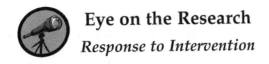

Eye on the Research
Response to Intervention

RTI Benefits	What has the research found?
Academic	• Fletcher, Coulter, Reschley, and Vaughn (2004), D. Fuchs (2003), and Kovaleski (2007) show that RTI methods are accurate for identifying which students need and will benefit from special education. • O'Connor (2003) and Torgesen (2003) provide data to show that RTI methods reduce the number of students receiving special education services while increasing the quality of educational outcomes for all students. • Tiered intervention in elementary math can reduce instances of student failure (L. S. Fuchs, Fuchs, & Hollenbeck, 2007).
Behavioral	• RTI can be used as a method to identify students with emotional and behavioral disorders (Gresham, 2007). • Combining positive behavior support with RTI can decrease student misbehaviors and referrals in secondary school (Sprick, 2009).
Other	• Both sides of the issues related to using RTI as a method for identifying students with learning disabilities are covered in the April 2009 issue of *Child Development Perspectives*. Articles by renowned experts Lynn Fuchs and Douglas Fuchs, Sharon Vaughn, Jack Fletcher, Sally Shaywitz, and others discuss the pros and cons of this method of identification.

For more research in this area go to http://www.corwin.com/diverseschools.

education teacher, an administrator, and other interested school personnel. (For example, if there is a paraeducator or a staff member who knows the student well, this would be an important addition to the team.) Additionally, it should always include the parents of the student who is being discussed and the student herself when appropriate. Remember, all these different frames of reference make for a well-balanced team with the potential for diverse and high-quality ideas.

Most effective SST meetings begin with a listing of the student's strengths and affinities. By starting this way, the problems that are addressed later can often be remediated by leveraging these areas of strength. For example, if a student is having trouble with reading comprehension, using books on a subject of choice such as basketball or soccer might be an effective strategy. If a student is skilled on the computer, online practice activities might be a motivating learning tool. By starting with the positive, you also give the parents the impression that the team is understanding and supporting of their child's needs, rather than feeling like everyone is out to get them.

Well-run SSTs can be a fantastic resource to a school and a shining example of an efficient team. Because the team membership tends to remain stable over the course of one or more school years (with the addition of parents at each meeting), members often have the opportunity to work through the stages of team development to become high performing, interdependent, and trusting of each others' expertise (Bonebright, 2010). Volunteering to be a member of an SST can be a wonderful opportunity for true collaboration and professional growth—as you work with your team members, you can learn from each other and develop a new set of skills and perspectives that can improve your own practice. We urge you to give it a try!

But again, we want to caution you: please don't let your SST become the one-way express highway to special education. If you do, you are undermining the valuable resource available to you when you have a diverse team collaborating to improve student performance. We will say it again: the goal of the SST is to come up with strategies that will help make a student successful in the *general education* classroom. Make sure every team member has that shared goal. If you can focus your team meetings on that goal, together you can achieve astonishing results.

Making sense of IEP teams: How do we get everyone in the loop?

Okay, we are finally to it—the giant meatball on our plate of collaborative spaghetti—the dreaded and feared IEP meeting. Even though it has a horrible reputation, and we know that sometimes it's an exercise in hostility and conflict, we truly believe that the IEP meeting, if handled with good collaborative skills, can be an experience in which everyone leaves the room with a smile and a handshake. And, oh yeah—a big old wad of paperwork.

Let's be honest: IEP teams can be one of the hardest places to institute true collaboration. Most IEP teams get together once a year, and even then the membership changes. In some cases, the only stable members of the IEP "team" are the parents and the administrator. The special education teacher, the instructional specialists, and the general education teachers may all change every year. (We'll discuss in more detail the various members of the IEP team in a later part of this chapter). Sometimes even the administrator is new, and it's left to the parents to be the stable members of the team. With a rotating crew such as this, how can we even really call it a team?

Let's take a second and look back at those characteristics of an effective team that we discussed earlier. We think you will see that given good collaboration and the ability to appreciate diverse frames of reference, an IEP meeting can be a true team experience.

1. *Shared goals.* This is a critical component of any effective IEP meeting (or any other meeting, for that matter). If one member's goal is to get Anthony the heck out of her classroom, and the other member's goal is to help Anthony be more successful in that classroom, conflict *will* arise. So it's really important in any IEP meeting to set a clear goal on which everyone can agree right up front. In this case, a good goal might be to find systems and strategies that will make Anthony more successful in school. As simple as that. With a clear, simple goal that everyone agrees on, you're now free to discuss, brainstorm, and find a group consensus. Whew. Conflict avoided. Or at least minimized.

2. *Members feel equal and valued.* This one is trickier than it sounds. Although the framers of PL 94-142 had the vision of an equal team in which all stakeholders have a voice, in reality the school members often have a huge advantage. Have you ever walked into a room where people in professional clothes were all sitting around a table with stacks of important looking papers, and you come in and sit down with nothing but your overcoat? If you have, then you've experienced what it's like to be a parent at an IEP meeting. Many parents feel overwhelmed, uninformed, and overlooked in their children's IEP meetings, and many teams fail to give the parent an authentic voice.

Is it any wonder, then, that during the 2005–2006 school year, more than 19,000 due process hearings were initiated in the United States (Mueller, 2009)? Many IEP teams consist of a school administrator or school psychologist who wields most of the power, some teachers (who may or may not feel comfortable expressing their opinions), and parents, who are rarely allowed the opportunity to weigh in on important decisions. The concept of valued, equal membership goes right out the window.

What are some steps we can take to facilitate IEP meetings that give everyone equal voice? Well, first of all we can give everyone the opportunity to talk. One way of doing that is that every time a new topic is raised, members go around the table and have a chance to speak to the topic *before* there is a group discussion (Mueller, 2009). However it's done, each team member needs to be able to express an opinion on each relevant topic as it comes up; it may be up to the meeting facilitator to offer that opportunity by directly soliciting input. "Mr. Corzo, what do you think about your son's reading program?"

Another important team member who can be overlooked is the general education teacher. IDEA mandates that a general education teacher needs to be present at every IEP meeting. The idea behind this mandate is to make sure there is someone there who can always relate the discussion back to grade-level standards and expectations. However, in many schools (particularly secondary), the administration will schedule a teacher to attend the meeting who barely knows the student in question, just to fulfill that legal mandate. In other cases, the teacher knows the student and the student's work well, but his opinion is never solicited other than to ask him to share the student's grades in his class. Remember, general education teachers may not have a lot of experience with IEP meetings, and they may feel overwhelmed by the specialized language and paperwork. It is incumbent on the facilitator to give the general education teacher many opportunities to weigh in, just like the parents. If a general educator feels superfluous, he's going to want to share his limited information and then leave, and the team will lose the possibility for true collaboration and his valuable perspective.

We have to admit, however, that in some cases there may be a facilitator who is hesitant to give up the floor to other team members. Whether it is an administrator, a special education teacher, a district-level person, or the president of the world, the leader of your IEP meetings needs to be a facilitator, not a dictator, and she needs to provide team members with plenty of opportunities to have meaningful input into the topics discussed. If that is not happening, help the process by being an advocate for collaboration. Speak up and say, "Excuse me, Dr. Frump. I'm not sure everyone has had a chance to share their experiences with Omar. Could we possibly go around the room and make sure each of us can share? I'm really interested in hearing what the others have to say too, especially Omar's dad."

> **Principal Points**
>
> While the role of the administrator in an IEP meeting is critical, the role of the administrator in *scheduling* the IEP meeting may be equally or even more important! An effective administrator will schedule the IEP meeting at a time when a general education teacher who knows the student and his work can attend. The effective administrator will also provide a substitute, if needed, to allow the general educator to attend the whole meeting, even if it goes beyond her planning period. The general educator's point of view is critical to the success of any IEP meeting, and providing a sub sends the message that this person is an essential component of a student's educational team.

3. *Shared participation, decision making, and responsibility.* One of the ways to make an IEP team a true team is to ensure that all participants feel valued, know that their participation is important, and know that there are meaningful jobs for every member. If the team decides that Keisha needs more instruction in decoding skills, and an IEP goal is written to address that need, each member of the team can participate in determining for which part of that IEP goal he should be accountable. For example, Keisha's mom might commit to working with her three times a week on some interactive materials that the teacher sends home. The general ed teacher can give Keisha time in class for peer tutoring. The special ed teacher might come to the classroom twice a week for small-group instruction to a group of students with similar needs, and the administrator can allocate planning time for the general ed and special ed teachers to collaborate on Keisha's program. By sharing the participation, decision making, and responsibility, we all become accountable for Keisha's success—that's true collaboration at work. And most important, it's true collaboration that clearly leads to improved student outcomes.

> ### In Practice
>
> Randi was a particularly creative teacher who needed some help to complete one-on-one reading assessments with her class. She looked around the school to see what resources were available to assist her.
>
> Out of sheer coincidence, Randi found out that the school custodian was a skilled ceramic artist. With the principal's permission, she recruited him to come to her class for half an hour every day for a week, to teach her students how to make ceramic flowers. While the class did ceramics, Randi pulled some students to the back of the room to complete her assessments. At the end of the week, she had completed all her assessments, and her students had all created beautiful Mother's Day presents. A true win–win collaborative solution!

4. *Shared resources.* Often when we think of resources we think of such things as textbooks, instructional materials, computers, and so forth. But shared resources can actually go way beyond the typical supplies we see in school. If the speech and language teacher has expertise in pragmatic communication, and Blanca needs to build those skills, the speech teacher could "share his resources" by showing the general education teacher some quick, easy, pragmatic language activities she can do in her classroom. Expertise is a wonderful and inexpensive resource to share.

Another excellent way to share resources is to share time. For example, the special ed teacher might send a special education paraprofessional to the general education classroom for three hours a week, supervising students in independent work while the teacher works with students who are struggling. Or a parent might volunteer to create a website for a teacher to post homework and regular class updates that will benefit the teacher himself, the special service providers the teacher works with, and any parents or students who want to access that site. When you think about sharing resources, we encourage you to think outside the box. There are lots of sources of information and support that we can overlook because we haven't been creative enough with our thinking.

5. *Voluntary participation.* Okay, we admit it—this one is kind of a scam. Because who would voluntarily attend an IEP meeting? If we had our druthers, we'd all spend our time doing things directly with our students rather than going to meetings and filling out paperwork. However, a truly collaborative IEP meeting can be a pleasant and fulfilling experience. Look back at the *Voices From the Field* box at the beginning of this chapter. Katelyn's mom left that meeting feeling like she had created friends and partners at her child's school. Even though IEP meetings might not be truly voluntary, good ones can create a sense of "voluntariness" that dispels the feelings of doom we so commonly associate with meetings of all kinds. You may not volunteer to attend the IEP meeting, but when you are there, you can volunteer to be an active, thoughtful, and collaborative participant or choose to be a resentful and inactive one. We hope this chapter has helped you see the benefits of volunteering for the former!

THE RANGE OF COLLABORATIVE PARTNERS: WHO ARE ALL THESE PEOPLE AND WHAT DO THEY WANT FROM ME?

Speaking of team participants, as you can tell there are a wide range of professionals and stakeholders in every typical school, any of whom could show up in your team meeting; we want to introduce you to a few of them. Hopefully, next time you are asked to collaborate to plan graduation ceremonies, select curriculum, participate in an SST, RTI, or IEP meeting, or even just meet to talk about a particular student, you'll have a better idea of who is across the table from you.

School administrators

There are a variety of administrators that you could run into in any school parking lot. (Not literally, we hope. . . .) Two of the key roles of an administrator in a collaborative school are to provide leadership in evidence-based instruction that meets the needs of all students (Boscardin, 2005) and to facilitate a culture of collaboration and collegiality (J. Murphy, 2001). Functioning as a team member in collaborative meetings can play a significant part in developing that culture of solidarity.

Many schools also have assistant or vice principals, school counselors, or other personnel who serve as the administrative designee on teams. These designees are empowered to make decisions and assign resources, just as the principal can. However, whether it is the principal or a designee, the chief function of an administrator as a team member is to keep in mind the resources, needs, and requirements placed on the school through the function of that particular team. The administrator needs to be aware of how the outcomes of this particular team meeting may impact the sometimes delicate balance of overall school resources and be mindful of the school as a whole during the decision-making process. Important note: the administrator should not have the final say in your collaborative meetings, particularly not IEP meetings! Decisions about special education services need to be made by the team as a whole, with the administrator serving as one critical cog in the wheel.

> **Principal Points**
>
> If you are assigning an administrative designee to attend your IEP meetings, make sure that person understands the collaborative role the administrator should uphold. In the scenario of Katelyn's IEP meeting (at the start of the chapter), the principal fulfills the perfect role—informing the parent of her legal rights, working as a member of the team, providing perspective on school resources and possible services. All too often designees end up "running" IEP meetings without any clear idea of how to do that in a collaborative manner. It's up to you, Ms. Principal, to make sure he knows what to do!

District-level personnel

Program specialists, coordinators, inclusion facilitators, and directors are all district-level specialists whose job might include attending team meetings. Their role on most teams is to provide expertise on services and programs available at the district level. If you are part of an IEP meeting that is particularly disputed or is requesting unusual services for a child, a district-level special education administrator may well be involved. Remember, the job of the district administrator is not to be the boss or the "decider"—it's to be part of the team like anyone else. However, because that person is at the district level, he may have specialized knowledge to suggest options and opportunities that others at the table might not know about. The same holds true for curriculum team meetings that a district curriculum specialist attends or an RTI meeting that the RTI coordinator attends. For a team to function in the way it was intended, there needs to be a sense of parity and communication. If one person holds all the cards, the others may feel like they didn't even need to show up.

Teachers

Teachers are a major part of any team meeting in a school. A grade-level team meeting requires all teachers of a particular grade level to collaborate. A department meeting facilitates communication between the teachers of a certain subject. A school site council meeting may involve a variety of teachers, as well as administrative, parent, and student representatives.

IEP teams are required by law to have teacher representatives from both general and special education, yet all too often, as we previously said, an authentic general education point of view is missing. Either the teacher isn't invited, she shows up but doesn't really know much about the student, or she doesn't feel comfortable expressing herself during the meeting. Yet research shows that the participation of a general education teacher who knows the student is critical to the success of an IEP team. IEP teams that include a general education teacher are better able to make informed decisions and have more conversations about the strengths and challenges of the students (Martin, Marshall, & Sale, 2004). The combination of a variety of points of view, from teachers and other stakeholders, can be critical to the success of any team meeting.

FRAME OF REFERENCE

As you can see, with all these different people on an IEP team, there are liable to be many different frames of reference at play. In order to keep the meetings productive, it's critical for members to have the opportunity to discuss things from their own point of view. Don't think of this as an imposition—think of it as an amazing resource! The more frames of reference you have, the richer the bank of ideas and strategies from which to draw. Just be careful that you don't assume that everyone sees things the same way you do. Keep an open mind and listen to what they have to say.

Designated instructional personnel

Aside from general and special education teachers, there are a wide variety of other instructional personnel who may participate in a team meeting. Many different types of instructional specialists may be asked to address topics ranging from speech and language services to physical education. Some of the most common of these instructional specialists and their roles are presented *In a Nutshell* on page 41.

Instructional support personnel

Another important player in our parade of collaborators is the paraeducator. These invaluable partners can be found in classrooms for a variety of purposes: functioning as general classroom assistants, floating assistants, or one-on-one aides for students with special needs. Paraeducators, also known as paraprofessionals, aides, or assistants, can often provide a unique perspective in team meetings, as sometimes their relationship with students is more personal than a teacher's. Additionally, a one-on-one paraeducator may be the only adult who gets to see a student with a disability across multiple settings. Their frame of reference is unique and important but sadly all too often overlooked. Don't forget to invite your paraprofessionals to the team meeting or you'll miss out on some valuable insights!

Families and parents

Without a doubt, one of the key collaborators in many team meetings is the parent or family member. Parents provide an important frame of reference on school leadership teams, fundraising teams, restructuring teams, IEP teams, school site council teams, SSTs, and in many more critical school functions. The parents are our customers—it is their children we are educating, and their lives are the ones impacted by the services we provide. No wonder their point of view is so critical to a team's success! On student-centered teams (such as IEPs and SSTs), parents can often inform us about a side of their child that educators may not get to see. Without the parent's point of view, we may be making decisions based on a limited understanding that doesn't represent the true picture of the student.

In a Nutshell

Collaborative Team Members

Collaborative Partners	Acronyms	Typical Frame of Reference
Administrators	Admin	Concerned about the whole school, logistics, and the dispersal of resources
General Education Teachers	GET	Trained to think of the "forest"—how to get the whole classroom to succeed and move to the next grade level; subject matter specialists
Special Education Teachers	SET	Trained to think of the individual "trees"—how to modify or adapt to meet students' individualized needs; disability specialists
Paraprofessionals/Paraeducators/ Aides	Para	Focused on supporting teachers and students, despite often receiving little to no training
School Psychologists	Psych	Often focused on formal assessment results, paperwork, and procedural requirements
Speech/Language Pathologists	SLP	Concerned with the student's articulation and language skills
Physical Therapists	PT	Usually focused on the student's ability to use gross motor skills for purposes such as balance, positioning, etc.
Occupational Therapists	OT	Concerned with the student's ability to apply fine motor skills to functional use (e.g., job skills, turning pages in books, writing)
Adaptive Physical Education Teachers	APE	Trained to work with students in physical education who have gross motor needs
Nurses	Nurse	Concerned with the child's physical health
Behavior Intervention Case Managers	BICM	Trained in providing positive behavior support strategies for the student
Parents/Family Members/ Guardians	Family	Concerned with the home context of the student, as well as familial goals and norms
Advocates	Advocate	Focused on ensuring that the family and student's rights are maintained

There are many different issues (e.g., cultural differences, communication challenges, varied frames of reference) that can arise when trying to collaborate with families, so we'll spend more time on these communication challenges in the next chapter. Suffice it to say for now that while collaborating with parents can be daunting at times, it can also end up being exceedingly rewarding when done well.

Students

The purpose of this book is to improve positive student outcomes. To do so, however, we are focusing on collaboration among adults. That is not to say, however, that students themselves should not be part of a team. In fact, if the team meeting is about a particular student, we definitely believe the child should learn to self-advocate and be an active member of the team. That said, keep in mind that teams need to be comprised of members who have parity and feel equal in the process. This can be difficult with a child and can be compounded by the child's age or disability. If the student is a true member of the team, then she needs to feel like a valued participant and not like someone who has to sit and listen while others make decisions about her future. Keep in mind that research shows that students usually feel uncomfortable expressing themselves in meetings and often can't follow what's going on (Martin et al., 2004). Make sure you give them enough genuine opportunities to participate and the time to process what is said.

We started this section by asking, "Who are these people and what do they want from me?" As a team member it is not unusual to feel overwhelmed and intimidated by the strangers sitting across the table from you. Remember, effective teams take time to develop. In fact, research tells us that teams move through stages in which they gradually learn to trust each other, to fulfill their individual roles, and to productively deal with conflict (Bonebright, 2010). If you are a new member of a team, or your team does not meet often, you may not feel empowered to participate in a significant way.

So the question remains: What *do* these people want from you? As a team member, they want you to value your role on the team, feel equity with the other members, and share your own unique perspective so that it can contribute to the overall success of the process. You are important, and your voice is imperative. That's what being a team member is all about.

So now you have a renewed sense of optimism about your work on school teams, right? We are choosing to assume you agree. From time to time we all have to attend meetings that we would really rather skip, but there are ways to make the time productive (other than trying to surreptitiously check your e-mail) and give team members a sense of accomplishment and a job well done. For some concrete strategies for making your team meetings more productive and satisfying, take a look at the tips and strategies that follow.

TAKING TEAMS OUT OF THE ABSTRACT

Strategies for working on teams

- Start meetings with a review of the roles of each member and what areas of expertise members are bringing to the meeting. Emphasize that *each* member is valued and has an equal role on the team.

- Have extra paper, sticky pads, and writing utensils available on the table for those team members who always forget their materials. This way they aren't embarrassed, and they also don't get to "forget" their assignments because they didn't have paper to write the information down.

- Have one team member type up the notes and discussions on the computer while it is being projected on the wall by an LCD projector so all participants can follow along and agree or disagree.

Within one day of the meeting, be sure to e-mail the notes to all team members so everyone has a copy. If your room has Wi-Fi, you might be able to do it right as the meeting ends.

- Identify an "acronym catcher." That person's job is to stop the meeting if an acronym is used in order to make sure everyone knows what it means.

- Vary the team makeup. While having individuals serve on a team for multiple years certainly does help with "institutional memory" (they are the ones who remember how things are typically done), it also can result in a lack of necessary change (they may also be the same ones who say, "We don't do it that way. This is the way we've always done it."). Mixing up team members allows for different frames of reference, more insight into the school community's opinions, and a willingness to change as needed. It also allows a break for those who are "teamed-out."

On the web

For more strategies for working on teams go to http://www.corwin.com/diverseschools.

THUMBNAILS OF RESOURCES ON THE INTERNET

The following elements can be found on the companion website for *Collaborate, Communicate, and Differentiate!* at http://www.corwin.com/diverseschools.

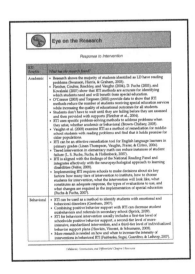

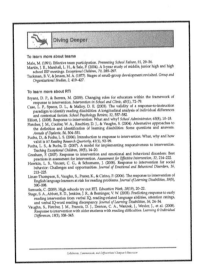

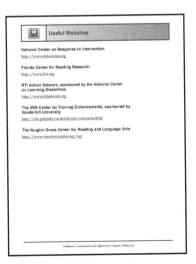

4

Improving Collaboration Through Powerful Communication

Voices From the Field

"I am amazed how often I hear general educators complain that the special educators with whom they are supposed to be collaborating 'don't do anything' or just 'sit around.' At the same time, those same special educators complain to me that 'the general ed teacher won't *let me* do anything, so I end up just sitting, walking around, or leaving to go work in another class where I am needed.' The need for good communication is so evident in these examples!"

Lisa D., Teacher Educator

THE BIG PICTURE

We can all agree that one of the keys to any successful collaborative school relationship is communication (Spencer, 2005). Good collaboration involves two or more adults trying to achieve a common goal, and without effective communication, this is often impossible. The importance of high-quality communication is well known. So why is miscommunication so rampant in our schools? In this chapter, we identify some of the reasons for the frequent miscommunication that occurs between adults. We also identify specific skills for improved communication, as well as strategies for improving those skills. Who knows? Maybe after reading this chapter you will not only be able to communicate better with your school colleagues and students' parents, you'll also be able to improve your communication with your significant other, your children, or your pets—there can be all kinds of benefits to improving your communication skills!

In this chapter we do the following:

- Discuss various purposes and styles of communication.
- Identify the role of culture as it impacts the communication between individuals.
- Describe active listening techniques that educators can employ with students and other adults.
- Explain strategies for both seeking and providing information that result in strong communication between individuals.

Let's Do It!

THE PURPOSE OF COMMUNICATION: WHAT'S THE POINT?

Simply put, teachers need to communicate. In the context of education, it is simply not possible anymore to get away with closing your door and pretending the rest of the school doesn't exist. Adler, Rosenfeld, and Towne (1995) described the basic needs that cause people to communicate with others: physical needs (e.g., "I need food!"), identity needs (e.g., "Am I a good teacher? Are you?"), social needs (e.g., "Do you mind if I vent a bit?"), and practical needs (e.g., "Where's the nearest restroom?"). In education, our purposes may be even more specific, including sharing information, identifying and achieving educational goals, making requests, and solving problems (*Family-Teacher Partnerships*, n.d.). We need to communicate effectively to accomplish any of these things. Additionally, because children with disabilities often have special issues that impact home, school, and the community, there is usually a considerable need for frequent and in-depth communication between educators, families, specialists, and others who are serving students with disabilities. We owe it to our students to find ways to communicate effectively—even with people we find difficult to talk to.

> **Key Term**
>
> *Communication*—Exchanging information in a form that is mutually understandable. May include listening, speaking, signing, use of a communication board, writing, or any other format in which two or more people can interact to share information.

STYLES OF COMMUNICATION: WHAT'S THE BEST APPROACH?

Consider this: when you want to get in touch with a friend, what do you do? Do you drop by, make a phone call, e-mail, text, or poke them on Facebook? Your choice is probably based on your own personal preference for communication as well as what you know about your friend. Moreover, these preferences can vary based on what you need to say, the time of day, and the person. For a casual conversation with a friend, the choice you make may not be critical. However, when you're working with a family or communicating with your principal, the method you choose can make all the difference in the world. Recognizing the different types of communication available—as well as their relative strengths and drawbacks—can help you as a potential collaborator select the most appropriate way of communicating for the situation at hand.

FRAME OF REFERENCE

Sometimes you may need to collaborate with more than one person on a regular basis, and if they have different styles of communication it can make it difficult. One teacher may be "old school" and like to talk in person, which may result in what seems to you like lots of unnecessary meetings. On the other hand, another teacher may never have the time or interest to meet in person. That teacher's standard response to requests to talk about kids' progress may be, "Oh, just e-mail or text me. We'll work it out." With some teachers, you may be left feeling that important issues haven't been addressed because they can't be adequately discussed in writing; with others you may feel the need to hide when you see them in the hallway. Whatever their style of communication, however, discussing what works for *you* in different situations can only make the process smoother and the outcomes more productive.

Frankly, the style in which you choose to communicate can greatly impact the success of a collaborative effort. People feel differently about information they receive in an e-mail than they do about a phone call. For example, would you text a friend to tell him another close friend was gravely ill? Probably not. Would you drive across town to remind your husband to pick up a gallon of milk on the way home? Again, unlikely . . . we hope. The style of communication we choose and the way we interpret information is greatly affected by the content and the method of the communication.

So what are these styles, exactly? Different authors have used different terms for the three major communication styles; some identify them as *directive, instructional,* or *inclusive,* while others have called them *linear, interactive,* or *transactional.* Collaboration gurus Friend and Cook (2009) prefer the categorization system first identified by Schmuck and Runkel (1994) in which they identified communication as *unilateral, directive,* and *transactional.* These are the terms we are going to use here. Remember, once you familiarize yourself with the various styles of communication, you can then identify which style is most appropriate for the specific communication and collaboration desired at that moment. Knowledge is power.

Unilateral communication is basically a one-way exchange. An example of a unilateral communication would be an announcement, phone message, text, e-mail, or letter home. While e-mails and texts may be efficient and at times critical, they are definitely limited in their ability to establish a collaborative relationship. Additionally, one-way communication is easily misunderstood. Have you ever sent an e-mail that you thought was funny, only to find that the recipient thought it was slightly insulting? That kind of misunderstanding is common with unilateral communication. Obviously, a unilateral approach can be useful, especially if you just need to deliver a quick piece of information (e.g., "Johnny's IEP meeting today at 1:00 pm was cancelled. I'll let you know when we're able to reschedule it."). This approach can save time, but you also want to be careful that you are not trying to convey important information that really deserves input from the other person. In collaborative interactions, it's best to use unilateral communication sparingly and with caution.

A second style of communication is known as the *directive approach*. In this case, communication is usually being used to instruct or guide. This approach tends to be in person, but it is still more of a one-way interaction. Directive communication may be used inappropriately when school personnel act as the "experts" or "consultants" during a team meeting, while treating family members as subordinates. A more appropriate example of directive communication might be when one teacher is training another on a particular instructional activity. While this communication style may be *somewhat* interactive in nature (Adler et al., 1995), it does not tend to encourage the parity that is necessary for two equal parties to work together collaboratively. It is most appropriate when one person is considered the "expert" on a topic (e.g., a speech therapist relating her instructional methods, a teacher describing a unit students are doing in class, a mother explaining her son's interests and chores at home). Again, consider the context and situation before you choose a directive communication style. However, if you need to give instructions or make sure that something is done in a particular way, a directive style of communication might be your best bet. Being aware of the styles and using them thoughtfully is a critical step toward effective communication.

The third communication approach is the *transactional,* or *inclusive, approach*. In this approach, all parties have input and all input is valued. Communication flows back and forth in both directions. The open environment enables participants to feel comfortable, respected, and empowered to share, and it facilitates effective listening. When individuals demonstrate through their communication that they are open to one another and willing to give and take during an interaction, collaboration can occur. Obviously, face-to-face transactional contact is the most effective approach for facilitating this kind of open collaboration, and webcams can be a powerful tool for transactional interactions as well. However, it's important to note that not every interaction needs to be transactional; certainly there are times when the other approaches are more appropriate and time efficient. (Can you imagine someone using this approach 24/7? "Gee, there seems to be a fire. Which exit do you think we should take? Let's chat about it and come to an agreement." Eek.)

> **Want more info?**
>
> Check out *Interplay: The Process of Interpersonal Communication* (6th ed.), by Adler, Rosenfeld, and Towne (1995).

Nevertheless, schools interested in establishing a more collaborative environment need to consider the styles of communication most often in evidence; how inclusive are most interactions? Are you and your colleagues picking the right communication style for the right job? Are the people you regularly communicate with doing the same? If not, consider discussing your communication options with them. *How* you discuss it is up to you!

THE ROLE OF CULTURE: HOW CAN WE COLLABORATE WHEN WE'RE SPEAKING A DIFFERENT LANGUAGE?

Cultural factors can have a major influence on collaboration and communication. In fact, "attitudes and beliefs about cultural differences often present more of a barrier to cross-cultural communication than language" (*Family-Teacher Partnerships*, n.d., p. 3). Because our cultural beliefs and expectations can influence our priorities and concerns, we really need to be aware of and sensitive to these varying priorities and concerns when we are working with other people. As we said in the previous chapter, there are numerous issues that can make collaborating with families difficult, and culture is one of the most significant of these issues.

While culture can influence collaboration in a variety of ways, a major one relates to the cultural interpretation and value of educational interactions. For example, some cultures may value frequent communication with teachers and school personnel, resulting in a parent who seems to never go away. In another scenario, a family may opt to attend meetings but members rarely speak: they don't make requests, ask questions, or voice concerns. This may be because they believe that it is disrespectful to question authority figures such as teachers (Park & Turnbull, 2001; Song & Murawski, 2005). The parity that is needed for two people to truly collaborate can be lost when one person or group of people, the education professionals, seem to hold all the power (Friend & Cook, 2009). Understanding families' cultural values about school and communication can help educators understand how to work with culturally diverse families in a manner that is respectful, and this can aid in the establishment of a relationship that gives the families equal voice in the interactions.

> **Key Term**
>
> *Culture*—The beliefs, practices, attitudes, and behaviors of a particular group of people. May be influenced by country of origin, religion, sexual orientation, age, gender, and many other factors.

Many students come from families who have a variety of other mitigating factors that can impact the communication and collaboration between parents and teachers. "Culture" can encompass far more than a country of origin, and it is imperative that educators are aware of these other "cultural" factors. For example, a child who comes from a family with same-sex partners or from a single-parent home may have had unique cultural experiences. Similarly, the Deaf culture can be very different from that of the hearing culture with which the majority of educators are familiar. For example, in Deaf culture, it is considered polite to tap the shoulder of a person with whom you are communicating but rude to leave the room without saying where you are going (Moore, 2010). A family with a strong religious background may bring the family's religious philosophies into meetings and those beliefs need to be respected by educators, even if the beliefs are not shared (Poston & Turnbull, 2004). In some societies, individuals with disabilities are viewed as shameful to the family, and families from those cultures may be embarrassed, defensive, or unwilling to acknowledge a disability in their child (Song & Murawski, 2005). In each of these instances, it is incumbent upon the school to learn about the cultural impact on communication and collaboration so that a respectful and productive relationship can be achieved. You don't need to know or share everyone's culture; you just need to be open to the differences and willing to truly honor them.

In Practice

"About 20 years ago, before I began teaching, I was working at a youth center in a depressed urban area. I was tutoring three students who were all in the same fifth-grade class, and one day they asked me to help them with a big science project that was due at the end of the week. They were required to make an operating circuit board that showed their understanding of the electrical process.

I took them out to buy supplies, using my own money, as their families had none to spare. We spent several days making intricate circuit boards on sheets of Styrofoam, which was the only material I could afford, but we were all quite proud of them when they were done.

The following week I asked one of the students, Henry, what grade he had gotten on the circuit board. He told me he got a B. When I asked him why he hadn't received an A, he told me that many of the students came from rich families, and their parents had helped them make fancy circuit boards out of wood and copper. Those were the students who received As on the project.

From that day forward I was aware of the profound effect poverty could have on a child's education and on a family's ability to support their children in school."

Nazik R., teacher

Another factor that can impact collaboration is poverty. Many educators are not aware of the socioeconomic factors that impact their students and their students' families, but these can definitely create a barrier toward true collaboration. Park, Turnbull, and Turnbull (2002) found that poverty impacts children in five ways. It impacts their *health* (e.g., hunger, lack of care, limited access to health care), *productivity* (e.g., no child care or money for educational toys or leisure activities), *physical environment* (e.g., no heat, no room, unsafe neighborhoods), *emotional well-being* (e.g., higher stress, anxiety, lower self-esteem), and *family interactions* (e.g., inconsistent parenting, fewer positive interactions). Each and every one of these factors can negatively affect children and make it difficult for family members to find the time, interest, or motivation to work with school officials. A financial struggle is usually not one that individuals are eager to share, and families may be less likely to divulge these issues with teachers at their child's school. How often have we heard or maybe even said ourselves, "Those parents just don't care!" Unfortunately, we often have no way of knowing if the passivity and disinterest we think we are seeing is really a sign that the parents are struggling to hold down a job or even to maintain their home.

Despite the cultural, social, or economic barriers that may prevent families from approaching a school, there are strategies that can be used by educators to promote effective communication and collaboration between home and school. The first and most important is to be sensitive to, and respectful of, differences (Rothstein-Fisch & Trumbull, 2008). Consider the following questions when interacting with families of diverse cultural backgrounds:

- In what manner are you providing information to the families? Is there a need for a sign language interpreter or foreign language translator? Does information need to be provided in writing, Braille, or another format? Is the family literate enough to read and understand written communication sent home in any language (Purcell-Gates, 1995)? All too often we send home notes and announcements that end up in the circular file because the people on the other end can't read the language of the announcement, or they can't read at all.

- Are phone calls an effective tool? Certainly, using phone calls in English to communicate with parents with limited English skills may demonstrate a lack of respect and understanding for their needs. In a case such as this, a home visit or personal conference may be the most appropriate and sensitive way to communicate.

- Is the setting a "safe place" for the parents to speak with you? Some parents may feel that they need a private space in order to communicate concerns or questions, while others are quite comfortable in a public setting. In some cases, a male member of a household may not feel comfortable talking with a female teacher. Even if you find this objectionable, a female teacher may need to make an effort to have a male staff member present in order to communicate effectively with some parents.

- Do the parents have enough information in advance? When people are communicating in a second language, it usually takes more time for them to process and digest new information. Providing information in advance, and in the native language whenever possible, can allow parents the opportunity to come to a meeting prepared with questions and concerns, and it models respect for their culture and language.

- Do you know enough about the cultures of your community to effectively communicate with the families in your school? If not, you probably aren't the only one. Consider asking a staff member from the community to present information on the cultural norms and practices. Ask your district or administrator for training and professional development in multicultural awareness and cultural perspectives on disability and education for your faculty and staff (Park & Turnbull, 2001).

- Is your perspective one of an individualistic nature, one that values independence and personal achievement? Do the families of your students share your individualistic perspective or do they come from a collectivistic culture, one that values interdependence and group achievement? If so, you need to learn how to bridge these different cultural perspectives (Rothstein-Fisch & Trumbull, 2008).

We just focused on the impact of culture as educators work with families, but before we move on to the next section, we also want to point out that culture may play a large role in our interactions with other educators as well. Go back and reread those tips we just gave you, and in lieu of the word *parent* or *family,* put in the word *colleague* or *principal.* Just as it is helpful to find out about the implications of working with families of different cultures, so too will you find it helpful (and often critical) to learn about the cultures of the people with whom you work. For example, you may burn a few bridges—or at the least hurt a feeling or two—if you organize a faculty Christmas party or "Married Couples mixer" in order to increase faculty collaboration and interaction, only to find out there are a number of Jewish, or homosexual, or single teachers on your faculty who now feel left out. You certainly can't learn everything about everyone, but you can make an effort to respect and value differences of the individuals with whom you interact on a regular basis.

GATHERING INFORMATION: LISTENING—WHY BOTHER?

It really goes without saying that one of the most important skills in good communication is listening. There is very little that can put the damper on a conversation more than one member of an interaction feeling that the others are not really paying attention. What do you do when that happens to you? Chances are, you either become annoyed, demand attention, or totally disengage. Any of these options can negatively impact the communication and ultimately the collaboration. Let's face it; if folks are not listening, we stop talking . . . at least to them.

Research has identified numerous barriers to listening and we're sure that you're familiar with many of them. So instead of just reviewing them, we'd like you to do a little activity here. Please indulge us.

Before you read on, think about one recent situation in which you felt you weren't doing an effective job of listening to someone. It doesn't have to be a situation with a student's parent or with a colleague at a school—it may have been with your spouse or your teenager. Chances are it could have happened 10 minutes ago. Do you have the situation in mind? Take your time. We can wait.

Ready? Okay, now that you are thinking about that situation, let's consider the most common barriers to listening and see which ones were taking place in your situation. Were you daydreaming or only partly listening to what the other person was saying? Did you stop listening when the speaker stumbled on a "hot topic" that caused an emotional reaction in you? (Talking about diets does it for many of us!) Maybe you were so busy constructing your response to the person that you stopped listening completely. Or perhaps it was as simple as you being distracted by some extraneous detail—the smudge of mascara under your principal's left eye or your friend's new tattoo. Any one of these things can put a halt on your normally *stellar* listening skills and cause you to become the dreaded "head nodder"—a person who is pretending to listen while actually being completely engrossed in a private inner monologue. By the way, we saw it when your eyes glazed over. You are not fooling us.

So, back to your situation. Which was it for you? What was it that negatively impacted your listening situation? Be honest—if it wasn't one of the aforementioned barriers, what do you think *was* the barrier? It's helpful if you can identify and admit it now; if it happened before, it's likely to occur again. Remember, the first step to recovery is admitting there's a problem. We all have our "go-to" reasons for not listening, and identifying them is the first step in becoming a better listener.

How can you improve your listening skills? We have provided numerous practical tips at the end of this chapter, but first we want to emphasize that it's really all about your attitude. Do you truly want to hear what the other person has to say? Do you view the other person as someone who is worth listening to? Can you genuinely accept the other person's feelings and opinions, no matter how different they are from your own? What if that person has a very different way of seeing the world—can you accept that and be flexible? Finally, do you trust that person's capacity to work through his or her own problems without feeling that you have to be the Almighty Problem Solver? If so, then you may be on your way to being a good listener. J. T. Murphy (1988) stated the following:

> Good listening involves an active effort to understand the world from another's perspective. It requires both an instant analysis of what has been said (and of the accompanying tone and body posture) and a sense of what has been left unsaid. Good listening involves testing aloud what one has heard, to make certain that the speaker's meaning has been captured. Good listening requires the ability to act as if the speaker's topic is central—even when the listener is preoccupied with other matters. To listen well takes practice, patience, energy, and hard work. (p. 658)

We couldn't have said it better ourselves.

It may not be easy to engage in active listening, but the results are worth it. Use active listening skills such as silence, minimal encouragers, and positive nonverbal signals to indicate your interest in what someone is saying to you. (See *In A Nutshell* on page 53 for more information on each of these.) Put yourself in someone else's shoes. How do *you* feel when you aren't being listened to? Yeah. We thought so.

In a Nutshell

Listening

Communication skill	Example	When to use it
Active Listening	Selecting a quiet room free of distractions, occasionally asking questions that demonstrate understanding, using body language and minimal encouragers (see below) to show interest and engagement	When it is critical that your partner knows you take her information seriously; when the message is important
Silence		When your partner needs to vent; when your partner needs to explain something; when your partner tends to get distracted or forgets his message when you interrupt; when you need to provide space in a conversation to allow the other person room to participate; when you just need to stop talking for a while
Minimal Encouragers	"um," "yeah," "I see," "okay," "great"	On the phone so the speaker knows you are there; during long monologues to provide ongoing feedback that you are still listening and to help you focus; when you sense your partner needs encouragement to go on
Nonverbal Signals	Head nod, wink, yawn, looking at your watch	To communicate your interest (or noninterest) without interrupting the speaker

PROVIDING INFORMATION:
HOW IMPORTANT IS HOW WE SAY THINGS?

So, you've learned to listen, to *really* listen. That's great! What now, though? Now do you get to go ahead and say whatever's on your mind? Sorry, good communication doesn't work like that. Just as there are better ways to listen, there are also better ways to go about sharing your opinion. Have you ever gotten a daring new haircut only to have an "honest" friend say, "Oh no! Why'd you do that?" Right. Sometimes blunt opinions are just not all that welcome. That said, we do value honesty—we just think there are good ways to share and not-so-good ways to share. Paul Simon says it best in his song *Tenderness*. He sings, "You don't have to lie to me. Just give me some tenderness beneath your honesty."

Let's break it down. Talking involves questions and statements—seeking and giving information. So far, so good. There are different types of questions and different types of statements, and believe it or not, it actually does matter which ones you use, when, and with whom. For effective communication, you need to select the right tool for the job.

In Practice

Ms. Trimble, a 10th-grade science teacher, is having a conference with Mrs. Santiago, Lupe's mother. Ms. Trimble has asked question after question of Mrs. Santiago in order to learn more about Lupe and to determine how better to help her. However, her answers have been short and uninformative; it feels like pulling teeth to get a response. Ms. Trimble suddenly realizes she's been asking closed questions ("Does Lupe have a place to do her homework?" "Yes." "Does she seem to like science?" "Yes." "Do you have any idea why she's not really doing her homework every night?" "No."). Upon reflection, she tries to change it up by asking open questions ("What does Lupe's typical evening look like?" "Can you tell me more about how Lupe prefers to spend her time on weekends?"). While Mrs. Santiago doesn't all of a sudden become exactly loquacious, she does start to answer some of the questions with more detail, providing Ms. Trimble more information and providing more of an opportunity for the two of them to collaborate on ways to help Lupe in science.

Using questions. Spend a little time looking over the *In a Nutshell* chart on verbal communication (see page 55). We have identified two basic types of questions—closed and open. Depending on how you use these two types of questions, you may elicit different types of information from an interaction. For example, using closed questions often elicits short, direct answers. This can be useful in certain situations, but in others it may limit the amount and type of information you receive.

Open questions can provide a listener with the opportunity to elaborate or provide richer detail in a conversation. On the other hand, they may also allow a person to run amok and get off track—if you need to get right to the point, you might sometimes need to stick with closed questions. Get it? Open questions = more opportunity for expansive information. Closed questions = more direct and to the point. Consider the example of Ms. Trimble and Mrs. Santiago in the *In Practice* box. Ms. Trimble doesn't get any useful information from Mrs. Santiago until she starts using open questions that allow Mrs. Santiago the opportunity to elaborate on her answers. The type of question you choose often shapes the response you get.

Using statements. Similarly, the type of statements you use can also shape the response you get, but in a very different way. Our *In A Nutshell* chart on verbal communication on page 55

In a Nutshell

Verbal Communication

Communication skill	Example	When to use it
Closed Questions	Questions with yes/no or finite responses ("Are you cold?" "How many pieces of chocolate are left?" "Does he ever have meltdowns in class?")	When you want specific information quickly; when you need to steer a "talker" to a quick response; when you have a reluctant speaker
Open Questions	Questions with an infinite number of responses ("How do you feel today?" "What do you want to be in life?" "What happens when he has a meltdown in class?")	When you want more general information; when you want to encourage a reluctant speaker to provide more detailed information
Descriptive Statements	"I heard you say you are at your wit's end with Sam." "When I entered your class, 10 kids had their head down, and five were sitting on the floor playing cards."	When you want to have a conversation that may be emotional; when you want to open a conversation without being judgmental; when you want the other person to make the evaluations
Evaluative Statements	"Boy, you really don't know what to do with Sam, do you?" "It seems like you are really overwhelmed with this class." "That activity really worked with this class. I'm amazed."	Typically to be avoided (whether positive or negative) in collaborative interactions; can lead to agreement but may also lead to frustration if the other person feels judged or belittled (However, they might be used by those in evaluative positions such as observers or administrators.)
Advising Statements	"Have you considered using a point system with Sam? I think that would help." "You really should call the parent in situations like this."	Also typically to be avoided, unless advice has been requested (Friend & Cook, 2009); if not, even advice couched in the form of a question can be taken poorly and seen as judgmental (When advice is requested, however, these statements may be welcomed.)

provides information on three of the main statement types: descriptive, evaluative, and advising. Depending on how you use these in your collaborative activities, you can build relationships and alliances or alienate your colleagues for a long, long time. It's all in how you communicate. What is our recipe for good communication? A heavy dollop of descriptive statements with only a light sprinkling of evaluative and advising statements. In fact, we believe in most cases the evaluative and advising statements should be like vermouth in a perfect martini—more of a hint than an actual ingredient.

Think about it. How do you feel when you begin to discuss a problem with a colleague, only to have the colleague start giving you unsolicited advice or making judgments about your actions? For most of us, that is an immediate turnoff and we want to shut the conversation down. We aren't saying that you can't ever make judgments or provide advice when you are collaborating or communicating with others. What we *are* saying is that you have to be careful—evaluative or advising statements can have a very negative impact on communication if interpreted in the wrong way. This is particularly true when you don't know the person very well. (So yes, feel free to continue advising and evaluating your spouse. That's what you got married for.) We're also saying that evaluative and advising statements are the ones that most humans naturally gravitate to. Sadly, it's the nature of humans—we are all too willing to criticize and give advice.

On the other hand, it's hard to misinterpret a descriptive statement. Descriptive statements are also known as "fly on the wall" statements or "just the facts, ma'am" statements—they tell it like it is. If we said, "You moved Jana to another class in the middle of the semester" (descriptive), that is merely a fact, with no value implied. The recipient of the statement can determine if it's a good or bad thing. On the other hand, if we said, "You seem really upset that Jana was in your class this semester" (evaluative), the listener may not agree, and it could cause him to become uncomfortable or feel judged. If we said, "You should talk to the principal about getting Jana out of your class" (advising), the listener can roll his eyes, thinking, "You think I haven't already pursued that route? How dumb do you think I am?" Evaluative and advising statements can be fraught with opportunities for miscommunication and hurt feelings—a surefire way to end a collaboration.

Principal Points

While administrators need to exercise good communication skills with even more urgency than the typical person, given their job, they also need to be wary of being put in the role of "marriage counselor" or "mediator." Helping *others* to communicate effectively can be difficult. Consider getting additional skills through a course or professional development on working with poor communicators. It's likely you will need to use these skills daily!

Consider the examples in the Situation Chart that follows. Notice how the same information can be communicated in an honest but thoughtful and sensitive manner by using positive comments, descriptive statements, and questions designed to encourage collaboration. As Paul Simon said, just use a little tenderness. We know that it sometimes may feel disingenuous to manipulate or rephrase the way you give information rather than just coming out and saying what you think or feel, but we again caution you that *how* you say things will greatly impact the result of your interaction. After reading the first two examples in the chart, don't look at the responses to the next two and see what you come up with. What statements could you use that would not be effective (but might be true)? What would be more effective? Ask a friend or colleague to read over your examples. Do they agree? Based on their frame of reference, would they interpret your examples in a different way? Now read our responses for ineffective and effective examples (see Table 4.1). Do you agree? Did we make our case? (If we didn't, don't let us know. It would hurt our feelings.)

Table 4.1   Strategies for Improving Your Communication

Situation	Ineffective Communication	Effective Communication
A special education teacher (SET) observed a general education teacher's classroom and has identified some instructional techniques that are not effective with kids in the classroom.	SET: When I was in your class today, I noticed that the kids weren't interested. They were bored. For some, it was totally over their heads. I think you need to slow down, check understanding, and use more concrete examples. (evaluative; advising)	SET: When I was in your class today, I noticed that six kids had their heads down during the explanation on slope of a line. Four kids said they didn't understand. When you used the concrete examples, all of the students had their heads up and were paying attention. Is that what you remember? (descriptive; checking question to encourage communication and agreement)
A teacher is talking to a parent about her son during a parent–teacher conference.	Teacher: Luis doesn't pay attention during class. It seems like he's lazy and really doesn't care. I know he's good in sports, but he's just not cutting it in the academic classes. (no sensitivity; negative; evaluative)	Teacher: I'm concerned about Luis. I know he's good at sports and enjoys them, but I also want him to be successful in his academic classes. Right now, he doesn't do any of his class work or homework. Do you have suggestions for how we might engage him more at school? (positive; descriptive; open-ended question seeking input)
A teacher is talking to an administrator about the lack of planning time due to numerous meetings.	Teacher: You keep giving us more and more to do and also scheduling more and more meetings, and there isn't enough time to plan our teaching! You are being totally unreasonable. (evaluative; negative)	Teacher: I'm having some issues with time management and I'd like to discuss them with you. It feels like there is more to do and less time to do it, and I'm feeling overwhelmed. Do you think you could give me some support with this? (descriptive; nonevaluative)
A Title I teacher is talking to a classroom teacher about the possibility of providing services to students in the class as opposed to doing a "pull-out."	Title I Teacher: The pull-out model we're doing now isn't working. Pull-out is old-school anyway, and we need to move into the 21st century. We should do an in-class model instead. (evaluative; advising; no sensitivity)	Title I Teacher: I wonder if we should consider using another model. Maybe Giovanni would have more success if he wasn't missing class for his pull-out sessions. Are you interested in getting together to brainstorm some options? (indirect question to reduce threat; nonevaluative; seeking input)

There are numerous benefits to good communication. Being able to be open and honest, but also sensitive, in your conversation with others will increase trust and respect. Using active listening skills and knowing what questions to ask will help you gain information that can improve your collaborations. Finally, using more positive and descriptive statements and avoiding those that can sound overly judgmental or advising will also aid in your communication. Improving your communication skills is not just a good idea; research supports the positive benefits that can come of increased communication between educators and families. Increased communication can lead to better services for students, more collaboration between teachers and parents, reduced stress in the work environment, and an opportunity for teachers to share, vent, and celebrate their successes with one another. We can't think of better reasons to work on our communication skills, can you?

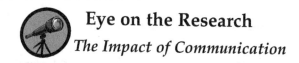

Eye on the Research
The Impact of Communication

Issues	*What has the research found?*
Gender Differences	• Differences in interaction styles commonly attributed to gender may be due to differences in status or social role, situational context, or stereotype effects (Aries, 2006).
Cultural Differences and Educational Differences	• Cultural differences in communication styles may be more profound in work settings than in nonwork settings (Sanchez-Burks et al., 2003). • Individuals from different cultures are socialized to use language in different ways, which may cause conflict between families and schools (Lovelace & Wheeler, 2006).
Positive Outcomes of Improved Communication	• Institutional communication such as invitations to Open House or weekly newsletters are less likely to solicit parent participation than personal communication. Personal letters and phone calls can increase communication and build a stronger parent-school relationship (Halsey, 2005). • Regularly communicating with families helps us understand each other's frames of reference and build partnerships (Arndt, 2008).

For more research in this area go to http://www.corwin.com/diverseschools.

TAKING COMMUNICATION OUT OF THE ABSTRACT

Strategies for improving communication

• If you frequently work with individuals who have a habit of interrupting or there is a meeting wherein everyone needs to participate and it is likely to get heated, consider the use of a "talking stick." The idea is that no one gets to talk unless they are personally holding onto the "talking stick." A cute variation on this is to use a piece of floor tile and to say that you can only speak when you have "the floor."

• Be careful of e-mail and text messages. What may seem clever and funny on your end may not read that way on theirs. Much miscommunication has occurred as a result of written communication that was misinterpreted.

• Be VERY careful about what you put on Facebook, MySpace, or other networking sites. Stating that "Today I had the IEP from Hades! Some parents are just clueless!" may actually get back to that parent. In addition, you also need to be careful not to accidentally share confidential information.

• Remember that difficult interactions can be minimized by humor and a positive outlook. If you know you are about to engage in a difficult discussion with a colleague, parent, administrator, or team, walk in with a smile and the determination to work positively. Make a light joke if possible to break the ice or, if you are humor-challenged that day, bring a bag of candy to share.

- When possible, create and agree upon agendas for lengthier, more problematic, or more complex interactions. This will help you all stay on the same page and will help you avoid diverging off the topic.

On the web

For more strategies for improving communication go to http://www.corwin.com/diverseschools.

THUMBNAILS OF RESOURCES ON THE INTERNET

The following elements can be found on the companion website for *Collaborate, Communicate, and Differentiate!* at http://www.corwin.com/diverseschools.

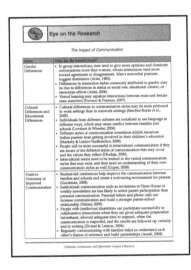

5

Proactively Planning and Differentiating Instruction

Voices From the Field

"When I first started teaching I was spending a lot of time creating behavior systems to bribe my students into good behavior. I became a master at giving out tickets and food, randomly rewarding on-task behavior . . . sure, my kids were behaving, but were they really interested in what they were learning? Didn't seem like it. Then, as I became more experienced, I found that making my lessons more interesting, more hands-on, and more accessible to all my learners made a HUGE difference in my kids' behavior. I didn't have to implement so many behavior supports because my students were actually involved in the curriculum. Suddenly the behavior problems in my class decreased significantly. It was a moment of awakening for me as a new teacher. Sure, not every lesson I teach is fun and interactive, but you can bet I make an effort. It makes not only my students' lives better, but mine, too!"

Dean W., middle-school teacher

THE BIG PICTURE

 One of the biggest concerns we often hear from new teachers is, "How can I reach all the students in my class? I have such a wide range of learners!" Although most teachers get some training in differentiating lessons in their credential programs, many feel it isn't enough, and meeting the hugely diverse needs of the students in a typical class can be overwhelming. You've got students with disabilities, students who are gifted, students who are English language learners, students with attention problems, students with emotional problems, students at risk, students who are homeless, students whose parents are divorcing. . . . And that's not to mention the typical learners who all need your concern and attention as well. Geez! What's a teacher to do?!?

In this chapter, we look at strategies for planning instruction that will increase the learning of all the students in your classes and make life easier for you, too. We know that differentiating for all those kids can be time consuming and overwhelming, but we also know that there are ways to make your daily planning easier. And remember, it all can be done most effectively *with collaboration.*

In this chapter we do the following:

- Look at techniques to make your curriculum more manageable for the diverse learners in your class.
- Explore the Triangle of Learning and its implications for teaching grade-level curriculum to students with a variety of learning needs.
- Introduce the principle of Universal Design for Learning (UDL), a proactive differentiation strategy for instructional planning.
- Learn how UDL can make your teaching more accessible to a variety of learners.
- Explore strategies and materials for proactively differentiating instruction, including approaches that support students who are gifted, students with disabilities, students with language needs, and everyone in between.

Here We Go!

TEACHING TO THE STANDARDS: HOW DO WE MAKE IT WORK FOR STUDENTS WHO AREN'T WORKING AT GRADE LEVEL?

Not too many years ago, students who were not learning according to grade-level expectations had one of two things happen: they were held back, or they were tracked into classes that worked on skills below grade level. Sadly, for most of these students, tracking into a "slow" class, or worse, a special education class, meant that they were consigned to a future of low expectations and below-average performance.

Then came the movement toward standards-based instruction, and teachers had a much more specific notion of what they were supposed to teach, when they should teach it, and how it related to what was being done in all the other grade levels. Gone were the days of teaching dinosaurs in every elementary class just because kids like them! Gone were the days of special education and tracked classes using textbooks that were two, three, or more grade levels below the age of the students. Gone were the days of teachers developing a favorite unit on their favorite topic and teaching it every year come hell or high water, no matter what grade they were assigned. Schools were expected to present students with a logically sequenced and connected curriculum from year to year that built on the skills taught the year before. For many teachers, that was a huge relief. For others, not so much.

However, the standards-based movement brought with it other challenges. For example, standards don't tell *how* a concept should be taught or in what ways students should be engaged in the content, they just give us an outline of the essential facts and concepts that our state thinks our kids should learn (Solomon, 2009). How we teach them is still pretty much up to us . . . and to the textbooks we select for our schools. Which brings us to the second part of this conundrum: textbooks.

Did you know that the textbooks you adopt may have the standards from lots of different states embedded in the curriculum? It makes sense when you think about it—textbook companies have to design books that can be used by teachers in a variety of states, not just one. Though the standards for ninth-grade math in Tennessee may be quite different from the standards for ninth-grade math in Utah, the textbook companies have to create a book that works for both groups of teachers. This brings us to the *huge* planning challenge that we all face: there is just too much content in our textbooks for us to cover it all in a meaningful way! In fact, research tells us that teachers would need between 22–26 *years* to teach all of the standards and objectives in their state's curriculum (Marzano & Kendall, 2007). Are you feeling better about not getting through all your content? To make it worse, in many states and districts, this content is also covered by a pacing plan, which expects teachers to move through the content at a quick, steady pace. There is little to no consideration for needing extra time due to snow days, fire drills, school assemblies, or repetition for kids who simply "don't get it" the first or second time. In these instances, with too much content and not enough time, all but the most proficient learners will fall behind or end up confused. Is the answer simply "covering the content" and moving forward, even if your students aren't with you? No. We believe teaching is about "uncovering the content" rather than covering it; teaching is about having kids learn, not just talking at them. How, then, do we address this conundrum?

We would advocate that your job as a discriminating teacher is to *be choosy!* Yep, you need to *choose* which of the concepts in your textbook are critical to the learning of your students, and teach those important concepts thoroughly and explicitly. You need to *prioritize* which of the standards are essential, which are important, and which would be nice to know. Work with colleagues in the same grade and subject to make these decisions, as well as with those in the grades before and after the one you teach. Some states have already done some of this work for you by introducing "key" or "power" standards. In some schools, teachers are taught to sit down with their textbooks, with the state standards at hand, and to use these two sources to create their curriculum. This process, called Curriculum Mapping, can help teachers identify what material is closely aligned to their standards and what is not (Solomon, 2009). Sure, you may end up exposing your students to most of the other concepts, or you may choose not to cover them all, but at the very least, teachers have the responsibility to identify *what is really important for their students to know* from the morass of information found in most textbooks. Then their job becomes a bit simpler: to focus the instruction on what's important instead of covering every detail in every textbook chapter and every standard in minutiae.

Let's look at an example. How many of you can tell us anything about the Sugar Act? Anybody? Sure, we know that in fifth-grade social studies you are supposed to teach about the Stamp Act, the Sugar Act, and several other acts the names of which have escaped us, but what's the Big Idea of that social studies unit? Taxation without representation (we know you would have gotten that eventually). Unfortunately, all too often that critically important Big Idea gets lost in the muddle of less significant details involving the Sugar and Stamp Acts. As a teacher, if you don't identify that important Big Idea and focus on it during your lessons, your students, particularly those with learning difficulties, will end up lost, uninspired, and with no real sense of the importance of the subject you are teaching. And that would be a crying shame. We all need to know and understand the concept of taxation without representation, but many of us don't remember the particulars of the Stamp Act . . . and we probably don't need to, either! (No offense to any Sugar or Stamp Act enthusiasts.) What's more, research has identified that students who understand the Big Ideas in curriculum gain a longer-lasting and more thorough understanding of the concepts (Greenes, 2009).

So, how do we choose these important Big Ideas? It's up to you as the teacher to make those choices because you are the expert on curriculum and content, as well as the expert on your students. You didn't take all those years of classes and fieldwork for nothing—you know your stuff! One of the first things to do would be to establish an "Essential Question" (EQ; Wiggins & McTighe, 2005). Essential Questions are broad, real-world questions that students should be able to answer after walking away from your lesson. For example, if the Big Idea is "taxation without representation," the EQ for that lesson might be "How would you feel if someone took your money without asking you?" That would be a question that could be posed at the kindergarten level as well as to seniors in high school, to individuals with cognitive impairments and to those who are identified as gifted. The complexity of response should certainly differ, but this demonstrates a real-world question that students should be able to answer after leaving that lesson. So, now all you have to do is figure out your Big Idea and Essential Question. Simple, right? Um . . . okay, maybe not. Don't fret; we aren't going to leave you hanging without strategies to help you—you know us better than that. Let's begin by taking a look at the chart titled Identifying Essential Concepts for Learning: The Triangle of Knowledge (see Figure 5.1 on page 65).

The Big Ideas, or "Content for all students" at the bottom of the triangle, should be the main focus of the majority of your lessons, and all of your students should be assessed on their acquisition of these critical concepts. Go through your textbooks and identify these Big Ideas first.

As previously stated, some states may already have identified these concepts as key, power, or essential standards; in others, you will have to make those choices yourself. In all cases, however, these are the profound, important concepts that students need to know in order to be successful at the next grade level. In our previous example, "taxation without representation" would be an example of an important Big Idea. It should directly relate to the state standards, which might look like this: *Understand how political, religious, and economic ideas and interests brought about the Revolution (e.g., resistance to imperial policy, the Stamp Act, the Townshend Acts, taxes on tea, Coercive Acts).* We recommend you identify one to three Big Ideas in each chapter to highlight with your students. In this case, more is not better; more is merely confusing.

The second section of the triangle, "Content for most students," is where you identify concepts and skills that most students will be able to master but which may be difficult for some of your students with more significant learning difficulties. For example, most kids will be able to learn about and remember the basic concepts behind the Sugar and Stamp Acts, but there may be some students with memory or comprehension deficits who never master and/or retain an understanding of these taxes. You will want to include these concepts in your teaching, being careful to always tie them back to the Big Ideas to which they are related.

Figure 5.1   The Triangle of Knowledge

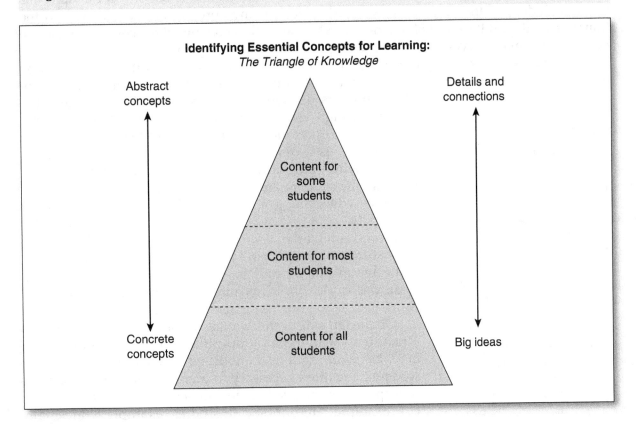

Identifying Essential Concepts for Learning:
The Triangle of Knowledge

Abstract concepts

Details and connections

Content for some students

Content for most students

Concrete concepts

Content for all students

Big ideas

In Practice

Mr. Brostowitz was using the Triangle of Knowledge to plan instruction for his 11th-grade English class, which was about to begin reading *The House on Mango Street*. He began by identifying one of the most important Big Ideas for this book: People who don't speak English are often relegated to the bottom rung of society in America. He thought that all of his students, including Jaime, could discuss this Big Idea.

As he began to think about the second level of the triangle, he identified some more difficult themes, such as Esperanza's struggle to gain power by learning to manipulate the English language. Suddenly, Mr. Brostowitz began to realize that Jaime was a lot like Esperanza. Jaime was bright and talented, but unfortunately he didn't have the facility with the English language that Esperanza had. His learning disability made it hard for him to read and write, even though his ability to understand concepts was as high as any student in the class.

As Mr. Brostowitz thought about his Triangle of Learning, he realized that he had to be careful not to limit his expectations for Jaime or any other student in his class. Although Jaime may not be able to write, he could probably understand concepts at the very top of the triangle. Mr. Brostowitz smiled—even *he* could still learn new things from reading *The House on Mango Street*.

Finally, the third section of the triangle, "Content for some students," is the content that only a few of your highest-achieving students may be able to master and retain. In our example, this might include how the Sugar Act decreased trade to many ports in the West Indies and the Canary Islands and the effect of that decreased trade on the economy of the colonies. (Okay, be honest—how many of you can answer that question? Hands up, please!)

Also, *please be aware of preconceptions*, as Mr. Brostowitz was in the *In Practice* box on page 65. Just because a student has a disability and can't do everything that all the other students do doesn't mean she won't understand the content at high levels. Our friend Jonathan Mooney (2008), author of *The Short Bus: A Journey Beyond Normal*, is a perfect example. He is extremely dyslexic, and because he couldn't read or write until sixth grade, it was always assumed that he was unintelligent and couldn't learn. Imagine everyone's surprise when he graduated with honors from Brown University, authored two books, and become a nationally renowned motivational speaker! Making assumptions about what students can and can't learn is a dangerous proposition, and often as not we may be wrong. Nevertheless, having a clear idea of the Big Ideas and important concepts that you want all kids to know is critical to effective teaching.

On the left side of the triangle are some things to consider for students with more significant cognitive disabilities, who may be working on a modified curriculum. For those students it is often necessary to identify one or two concrete concepts from the grade-level curriculum for them to learn. For example, in our social studies example you might identify "what is a tax?" as a concrete concept. Or, if that's still too abstract, some students might work on a concept as simple as "money" or "pay." You can see that even the very simplified concept of "pay" relates back to the standard identified previously. It also relates to the EQ: "How would you feel if someone took your money without asking you?" Remember, the level of response can and should vary based on the students' levels of academic ability. Differentiation in response is expected and encouraged, but all students are still focused on the same content standard, no matter what their ability.

Here is where collaboration becomes key. You don't need to make these decisions on your own—use the expertise of your colleagues to help you identify the Big Ideas and the concrete concepts that are appropriate for your learners. Do you have an English language coach or coordinator at your school? Ask that person for help identifying the Big Ideas most important for your English learners. Can't imagine what Big Ideas are reasonable for a student with Down syndrome or autism or learning disabilities? The special education teacher is the expert in curriculum and planning for students with disabilities and should be able to help you identify what content to include in the Big Ideas for the range of students in your classroom. Remember, there are different specialists in special education (teachers for students who have moderate to severe disabilities, mild to moderate disabilities, deaf and hard of hearing, speech and language issues, behavioral disabilities, and so on). Look at those individuals as more opportunities for input and collaboration; you don't have to make all of these decisions on your own. Talk to teachers at your grade level who may have experience teaching your subject.

Principal Points

Often teachers are afraid to prioritize the Big Ideas that are embedded in their textbooks because they believe if it's in the textbook, they are obligated to teach it. Administrators can help with this problem by providing professional development time for teachers to work together to identify the important Big Ideas or key standards that are in each of the units in a particular subject area. By working in grade-level groups to do this work, teachers begin to develop confidence in their ability to decide which parts of the curriculum are most important and that it is okay if they don't "cover" everything in the textbook. There is another plus side. Identifying and explicitly teaching the important ideas rather than a series of unrelated details helps raise test scores, too (Harniss, Caros, & Gersten, 2007).

Even your administrator is a critical cog in this process, as she may have ideas about what she considers critical curriculum and what you can leave out. Remember, you don't have to do it all yourself!!

UNIVERSAL DESIGN FOR LEARNING: HOW DO WE DESIGN OUR LESSONS SO EVERYBODY "GETS IT"?

Great work—you've identified the important stuff in your textbooks and the most important standards. (Believe me, once you do that you will find that you've relieved yourself of a LOT of pressure. As Marzano and Kendall [2007] reminded us, we don't have the time to actually teach every standard to mastery; add to that the range of student abilities and disabilities and it's easy to see that no one human being can teach all that different stuff to all those different kids!) Given that limitation, what's next? How do you plan your lessons to focus on those important ideas, while making that content accessible to all your students? The answer is Universal Design for Learning or UDL.

What is UDL? It's a method of lesson planning that helps you plan for *all* your students, so that your lessons are accessible to everyone in your class. Instead of trying to create modifications and accommodations for your students after the fact, UDL helps you be *proactive*, so your lessons are ready to go with approaches and strategies that will work for almost all of your kids.

Let's look at the facts. Usually when we are trying to make our curriculum accessible for struggling learners, we modify and accommodate the work *after* it's been planned. In other words, we plan the lesson that will work for the majority of our students, then we go back and think about what we need to change to make the lesson accessible for our special learners. That's not to mention all the other myriads of kids in our classes who have some kind of unique learning need and require personal attention. For each of these students, we might need to create an individual accommodation that allows him or her to participate in the activities and understand the content at the appropriate level of challenge. It's a daunting task, and for many teachers, it is one that makes them feel like there just aren't enough hours in the day.

> ### Key Concept
>
> *Universal Design for Learning vs. Differentiation*
>
> Clearly, UDL is related to differentiation, but it has several critical differences:
>
> - UDL is done proactively. Choices are built into the lesson plans in advance rather than making adaptations after the fact.
> - UDL asks you to provide choices to all the students. So instead of saying, "Jonathan, you can type your essay because I know it's hard for you to hand-write it," you give all students the options of hand-writing or typing. UDL recognizes that all students have unique and different learning styles and will benefit from differentiation strategies.
> - Because choices are provided to all students, the stigma related to having modified or adapted work is eliminated.

UDL takes a different approach to differentiation—it's a proactive strategy that helps you build differentiation into your lesson plans from the very beginning, eliminating the need for most of the accommodations we typically make after the fact. It's based on the principle of universal access, first developed in the field of architecture. Have you ever tried to drag a heavy suitcase into a hotel and been oh-so-thankful for the wheelchair ramp that keeps you from having to drag that suitcase up a flight of stairs? That's universal access! That ramp, which was designed to help people in wheelchairs, has also turned out to be invaluable to people with suitcases, moms pushing strollers, and even for Sally's very old dog Molly, who can't walk up stairs anymore. What was designed for a specific population, people in wheelchairs, has turned out to be helpful to everyone.

In a Nutshell
Universal Design for Learning (UDL)

Principle of UDL	*What is it?*	*What does it look like?*
Representation (sometimes referred to as **Content**)	**How we teach the content** As we know, all students learn differently, and if we consistently present new information in one way, through lecture or reading, for example, we will only be allowing access for some of our students.	Choices in the way we present information, such as the following: • Using multiple modalities (visual, oral, and hands-on) • Using formats that can be adjusted (enlarged text, amplified sound) • Using graphic organizers to organize the important ideas • Using mnemonic devices to aid memory • Highlighting key ideas, transition words, etc. • Preteaching complex concepts and vocabulary • Activating background knowledge • Chunking information into manageable bits • Using checklists, sticky notes, and other tools to help retention • Using text reading programs and devices • Using videos and technology to show models, examples, and real-life applications
Expression (sometimes referred to as **Product**)	**How the kids show us what they learned** Our traditional learning tools, such as textbooks, pens, paper, and even computers, are not accessible to all students. If you have students with reading disabilities, physical impairments, or deficits in an executive function, they might not be able to use these traditional tools effectively. If that is their only option, we may never be able to tell what they really know or can do.	Choices in the way students can interact with the materials and present their outcomes, such as the following: • Options for output, including videos, posters, drawings, models, speeches, debates, storyboards, comics, music, and so forth • Dictation programs and devices • Alternates to traditional keyboards • Access to spell-checkers • Individual white boards • Use of calculators • Word prediction software • Sentence starters • Software for outlines and graphic organizers • Differentiated models and feedback • Individualized learning goals, prompts, and checklists
Engagement (sometimes referred to as **Process**)	**How we motivate our learners** Each of our students responds differently to different types of learning opportunities. If all of your activities were game-based, for example, some students would be highly motivated, and others would be turned off by the	Choices in the way students complete their work and interact with the curriculum, such as the following: • Different types of rewards and feedback • Choices in sequencing of work and activities • Different levels of challenge • Curriculum that is personalized and relevant to students' lives

Principle of UDL	What is it?	What does it look like?
	competition. Some students like the challenge of individualized, long-term projects, while others prefer predictable daily routines. It is up to us to provide students with a variety of experiences that allow them options to work in their preferred manner and to give them choices that empower them as learners.	• Age-appropriate materials and activities • Gender- and culture-appropriate options • Opportunities for reflection and feedback to the teacher • Reduced distractions in the classroom • Varied levels of risk and novelty • Options to use headphones or screens to reduce distractions • Varied work periods with frequent opportunities for breaks if desired • Chances to work alone, with partners, or in groups, and choices about those options • Emphasis on process over product • Positive learning communities and classroom cultures • Use of positive behavior support to encourage desired behaviors • Feedback that encourages persistence and effort

Not surprisingly, that's the principle behind UDL, too. By designing your lessons to make them accessible to students with special needs (including those who are gifted), you end up helping everyone in your class. By creating lessons that work for students with reading differences and cognitive differences and physical differences, what we end up doing is creating lessons that are more comprehensible to all our kids. *This is universal access to learning for everyone.* What could be better?

Here's how it works, in a nutshell. (And speaking of nutshells, take a look at *In a Nutshell* on pages 68–69, which goes into more depth on each of these components of UDL.) There are three things you need to think about when you are planning to use UDL: How will I *teach* the content to make it accessible? (*REPRESENTATION*) How will the students *communicate* what they learned? (*EXPRESSION*) And how will I *motivate* all my learners? (*ENGAGEMENT*) Those three concepts are the keys to planning for all students. Let's give it a try.

UNIVERSAL DESIGN FOR LEARNING: HOW DO I USE IT?

In this section, we walk you through the process of using UDL to plan a lesson. Because we want to "get inside your head" as the teacher, we put this section in first person. And because we are real teachers, with real experience in real classrooms, we are telling you up front that this walk-through is a "best-case scenario" type of deal. We understand that you don't always have time to create the perfect, engaging lessons that you'd like, so what we're offering you here is a chance to fantasize about the ideal universally designed lesson. So relax, close your eyes . . . play along with us as we pretend to be you and use UDL to plan your lesson. Can you feel it? Are you with us?

It's Friday, and I'm planning a science lesson about earthquakes and their relationship to plate tectonics for next week. I just took a workshop on UDL, and I want to try it out next week. In the past I might have planned to have the students read from the text-book, do a brief whole-class discussion on the content of the chapter, look at some diagrams or videos of the movement of plates, then answer the questions at the end of the chapter. A nice, comfortable, old-school science lesson.

(*Authors' Note:* And dare we say it . . . boring? If we don't, the kids sure will! Our mantra is . . . and you may want to write this down because it's so brilliant . . . "Boring is bad." We know. Thought-provoking. But profound.)

As I think about the way I used to plan, a variety of students come to mind, for example, Carolyn. Carolyn has dyslexia and can't decode at grade level, so she can't really follow along in the textbook, and although she has good oral comprehension, she's liable to miss many key points. Not only that, her writing is so poor that answering the questions is really problematic for her. Although I know this lesson doesn't really meet Carolyn's needs, I could plan to sit with her to help her complete the written work. I also could pair her up with a stronger student or put her in front so I can help her follow along as we read. All of these strategies are a little stigmatizing, but they help Carolyn keep up with the rest of the class.

Gio, my student with attention problems, just can't seem to stay focused when we're doing whole-class reading. He would probably cause a disruption by playing with his pencil loudly or wriggling around in his seat, and there is a high likelihood for behavior problems when he is answering the questions, too (a nonpreferred task for Gio). I know I would have to do a lot of redirection with him throughout the lesson and would probably have to stop teaching several times to get Gio back on task. Although I'm used to doing this, it doesn't seem to be helping Gio overcome his attention problems—it really isn't getting any better.

Ulysses is a totally different story. He's a hard worker, motivated, and never causes any trouble. Unfortunately, as a second language learner, his English vocabulary is still pretty basic, so a lot of the science content is incomprehensible to him. He's willing to give it his best shot, but his work shows confusion on the concepts, and English writing is very difficult for him. I could pair Ulysses up with a strong student to answer the questions, but I know that a lot of the time the other student will do most of the work while Ulysses just does his best to follow along.

Want more info?

Check out the website of the Center for Applied Special Technology, http://www.cast.org, for great ideas, tools, and technology related to UDL.

Then there's DeMarq. DeMarq is an extremely high-functioning student who is bored by repetitive tasks that don't challenge his higher-level thinking. Although he is not a behavior problem, I often worry that I'm not giving him the opportunity to move ahead as quickly as he can. On this particular lesson I know he will do a good job, but he could probably process this content on a much higher level if I gave him the opportunity.

I also have a student with Down syndrome named Christopher. Christopher is a good-natured young man who is well liked by his peers, but his comprehension of ideas is significantly delayed. To be honest, I don't always know what to do with Chris, so lots of times I will give him something to color that is related to the lesson. He loves that. He also likes to be the teacher's helper, so I will give him opportunities to pass out papers, collect work, and so forth. Although I know he isn't always involved in the content, at least he's happy and busy.

And finally there's Yolanda. Most classrooms have lots of Yolandas—students with no identified learning problems but who are disenfranchised and at risk of dropping out. Yolanda hates science, and she doesn't see any reason why she should learn the content I am supposed to cover. Most of the time I just cross my fingers that Yolanda will come along for the ride and not cause disruptions or put her head down and sleep. I don't have any good strategies for getting Yolanda to learn my science content, and frankly, if she doesn't care, why should I?

So what can I, as a lone teacher, do to help this diverse group? Well, according to the workshop I just took, a great way to help them is to plan my lessons using UDL. UDL asks me to identify ways to get all my students involved from the very minute I begin to plan, and it uses the three principles of *REPRESENTATION, EXPRESSION,* and *ENGAGEMENT* as its guidelines.

First, let's consider the teaching part of the UDL equation—*REPRESENTATION.* What can I do in my teaching (how I *represent* the material) that will make the content more accessible to Carolyn, Ulysses, Gio, DeMarq, Christopher, Yolanda, and all the other kids? Starting with the basics, I know that Ulysses and Chris (and many of the other kids) need help with the vocabulary, so I'm going to use **cartoons** to preview some of the vocabulary and make it more accessible to them. I will carefully choose four or five vocabulary words to **preteach** that are critical to understanding the main concepts from the text, and I will make that content interesting by using cartoons and pictures as I teach. (The book *Vocabulary Cartoons* by Sam Burchers [2007] is a great source of fun, cartoon-based mnemonics for vocabulary instruction.) That's one of the principles of UDL—**using mnemonics** and other memory devices to help kids remember new information. For example, in my plate tectonics lesson, I know I'm going to teach about convergent plate boundaries so I've decided to teach that by showing students that convergent plates crash. I'll write Convergent = Crash and emphasize the **C**s in both words to help students remember that term. I'm pretty sure that these strategies I've planned will help all the kids understand and retain the vocabulary better. Chris may not master all the words, but if I'm careful to include at least one concrete, practical word (like *earthquake*), the vocabulary cartoon strategy will help him learn and understand that word.

I also know that UDL supports **activating background knowledge** as part of *REPRESENTATION.* We could do a KWL chart identifying what kids *know*, *want* to know, and have *learned*, but I'm pretty tired of that and I suspect my students are too, so instead we're going to play a quick game of Jeopardy to review the concepts we've learned related to this lesson. The KWL would have taken me about 10 minutes, so I'll plan on using that amount of time for Jeopardy. I know that games are really motivating to Gio and Yolanda and to lots of my other kids who don't really like "boring book stuff." Even DeMarq enjoys the opportunity to show off what he knows in a game format. There are several free Jeopardy games available online, and all I need to access them is PowerPoint. I'll just Google PowerPoint Jeopardy and I know I'll find some websites where I can get the game. Because this is easily accessible for me and the students, I won't feel overwhelmed by the setup or feel like I'm losing valuable instructional time. If I set up the game in teams, Chris can participate as a team member, even though he may not remember a lot of the content. His teammates can help him identify the questions he does know. Because Jeopardy by nature includes information at a variety of levels (100-point questions vs. 500-point questions), this can also allow me to differentiate my content questions by what I want all students to know (100 points), most students to know (200–400 points), and some students to know (500 points). I may be amazed by what they actually know!

Before we read the textbook, I'm going to show my kids a great video on YouTube about earthquakes. I'm going to use that to catch their interest and to present the content in a visual way. One of the principles of *REPRESENTATION* is to **provide content in other modalities** besides just orally. Technology is a great way to do that. I know that lots of my kids have trouble getting meaningful information out of a video, though, so we're going to watch it in chunks. After each section of the video we'll go into the text and read about that particular topic. For example, when the video talks about plate motion, we'll stop and read the corresponding part in the textbook. That makes the content come alive for the kids and supports comprehension for everyone. For Carolyn, that type of front-loading really helps her decoding, and for Yolanda, the video helps her understand the concepts that often elude her. The short bursts of instruction also support the attention of Gio and Yolanda, both of whom get disengaged quickly. To support all the students, I will prepare some simple graphics on charts. These will be particularly useful to Chris, who is focusing on the Big Ideas.

In order to give all my students the chance to interact with the content a bit more, I'm next going to give them a **graphic organizer** (*REPRESENTATION*) that covers the main points in the text and ask them to outline the information on the graphic organizer after we go through the text and the video. I know that UDL wants me to motivate my learners by **giving them choices** (*ENGAGEMENT*), so I'm going to give them options about how to complete the graphic organizer: alone, with a partner, on a laptop, or cutting and pasting prewritten answers into the organizer. They can even choose to make their own graphic organizer if they wish—that's a great challenge for a kid like DeMarq. I can also give the class choices in where they get the information to add to the graphic organizer. In addition to the textbook and video, I can have alternative resources available: the Internet, books about geography, and scientific articles. These may also provide a challenge to DeMarq and any other students with specific interests in this area. (And I don't want to presume that only gifted students will want to delve deeper.) Another important way to *ENGAGE* my students is by making the learning meaningful to them. This is particularly important for my kids who are at risk like Yolanda. In this case, I know that Yolanda has relatives in California, so after we watch the video, I'm going to ask her to share what she knows about their experiences with earthquakes. I'll talk it over with her the day before so she can have time to prepare. This will also reinforce the key word that Chris is focusing on today; he'll be particularly interested to hear his peer, Yolanda, talk about it. A pictorial graphic organizer for Chris will help him understand the concept as she talks about it.

Now I need to think about how the kids can *EXPRESS* what they have learned, again focusing on the UDL principle of **providing choices** to the students. I know that answering the questions will work for a lot of the kids, but frankly, it seems a bit boring, and many of my students do this kind of work poorly. Yolanda and Gio will rarely attempt it at all. I want them to show me that they've learned the Big Ideas I've identified using my Triangle of Knowledge chart and that they can answer my EQ for the lesson ("How do we get earthquakes?").

Want more info?

Check out the strategies at the end of the chapter and at http://www.corwin.com/diverseschools for information on text-to-speech and voice recognition software for your classroom.

I'm going to let them choose how they want to do that. They can do any of the following: write a skit, poem, rap or blog; make a poster, PowerPoint, or oral presentation; answer the questions in the textbook by writing, typing, or dictating into a tape recorder or voice recognition software . . . I could go on for days, but I think that's enough options for this assignment. These options, given to all students, allow Chris to show what he's learned as efficiently as DeMarq. Although De Marq may have acquired a lot more understanding than Christopher, both could make a poster or a poem to show their acquisition of concepts. Students can choose to use their textbook to help them find the information, or they can use a number of good websites or other resources I've identified for them. That should give all my learners enough options that they can successfully complete the final assignment. All my students know how to use the text-to-speech function on the computer, so Carolyn can use the computer to access and organize the content quite effectively if she chooses that option. She can also use Dragon Dictate to transcribe her answers onto the computer or even on my iPhone if I don't have enough computers available. (And hooray—Dragon Dictate is a free iPhone application! We'll tell you more about it later.) For students who have trouble concentrating, we have a variety of options including noise-canceling headphones and private work areas that any student can use. Some will work in groups; others will prefer to work individually. I'm fine with that in my class, since I know that as adults we make these choices all the time.

By giving them choices in how they *EXPRESS* their learning, I am jumping right over Gio's attention problems and Carolyn's writing problems. Even Yolanda is likely to participate when she is given meaningful choices like this, because she can pick an option that plays to her strengths and affinities. It's also important to note here that by building these choices into my lesson plan, I've now differentiated for my gifted learners too. DeMarq just loves to write long, complicated limericks about topics we are learning. The choices ensure that I'm able to provide the breadth and depth on the topic to challenge and interest him. I've built that option right into the lesson plan for any student to choose and for any student to implement at his own level of understanding. (Are you worried about how you might grade all these choices? Don't fret—we discuss that in Chapter 8!)

I'm also going to give my class the option of working with a partner or small team. I've found that this is very motivating for many of my students, and I use it consistently as a kind of informal peer support strategy. I read some information about how, though the United States is considered generally an "individualistic" society, many of its members come from "collectivistic" societies (Trumbull, Rothstein-Fisch, Greenfield, & Quiroz, 2001). What this means for me as a teacher is that I have to realize that some students may prefer to work together based on their cultural backgrounds. The personalities of my students vary yearly, but I consistently find that a percentage of my class will choose to work with a partner on tasks such as this, and it seems clear that the students are learning from each other as they collaborate. It took me some time to build an effective classroom climate for group work, and I started small, with interactive, one-minute, cooperative activities such as Think Pair Share (Lyman, 1981) and Numbered Heads Together (Kagan, 1995), but over the first couple of months of school they grew to love cooperative activities, and most of them are proficient at group work now. (You can get more info on these cooperative strategies in Appendix II.) Like any other skill, I had to teach, scaffold, and give feedback on its use. You know, I'm actually getting kind of excited about this universally designed lesson. . . .

PLANNING WITH UNIVERSAL DESIGN FOR LEARNING: IS IT ROCKET SCIENCE?

Thank you for letting us step inside your head and plan for a few minutes. As you can see, planning with UDL is *not* rocket science, but it *does* require a basic understanding of the different technologies, tools, and options that are available to make learning more accessible to all the kids in your classroom. We aren't saying it's child's play—we know that creating true universal access can seem overwhelming at first. Nevertheless, some of it is just basic good teaching—using visuals, creating graphic organizers, and showing videos are all things we learned about in our teacher preparation programs. However, *how* we use them is critical, and the choices we give to students about how to implement them are key to UDL. In fact, if we had to boil UDL down to one simple definition, we'd say it is *proactively planning lessons that use a variety of strategies to present information and that give students options for how and with whom they complete their work.* This is a gross oversimplification, but it gets to the point. It's obvious that by using the principles of UDL, we've not only made a lesson more accessible to learners with special needs, we've also made it a heck of a lot more interesting. That's what UDL does—it asks you to broaden your thinking about your lessons so that you get out of the old "read, lecture, worksheet" teaching and into something that's more engaging for everyone.

Because we are two very practical and classroom-oriented authors, we've chosen to provide you with some other examples of interesting, universally designed lesson plans that you could use or adapt for your classroom. In the appendices you will find concrete examples, created by skilled classroom teachers, of how you might use UDL to plan some common lesson types in a variety of classrooms (see Appendix I, available online at http://www.corwin.com/diverseschools, for UDL Lesson Plans). As you read through them, think about our

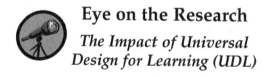

Eye on the Research
The Impact of Universal Design for Learning (UDL)

Issues	*What has the research found?*
Student Achievement	• UDL can help increase academic engagement and positive behavior in students with disabilities (Morrissey, 2009).
Testing	• UDL can be used to make testing more accessible to all learners (Dolan, Hall, & Banerjee, 2005; Salend, 2009).
Students With Moderate to Severe Disabilities	• UDL can be used to involve students with multiple disabilities in meaningful literacy activities (Browder, Mims, Spooner, Ahlgrim-Delzell, & Lee, 2008).
Accessibility	• Adolescents with reading deficits can access and use technology in a UDL model as effectively as students with higher reading levels (Marino, 2009).

For more research in this area go to http://www.corwin.com/diverseschools.

students—Gio, Carolyn, Christopher, Yolanda, DeMarq—and all the students who are difficult to plan for in your classroom. Stop and think about how the principles of UDL modeled in these lessons meet their needs. What specific choices could you build in for *your* students? What would you add or change? Remember, there isn't one correct way to plan lessons with UDL. It's all about knowing your kids and knowing your content, then providing opportunities for choices and options that any student could implement. With a little practice, anyone can do it!

And by the way, we know that in the real world, it isn't always like this. We know that sometimes . . . maybe even most of the time . . . you haven't done the type of proactive planning that you'd like to do in a perfect world. Hang on. The next chapter will help you through this very real-world problem of what to do when you just don't have time to plan the ideal lessons you'd like to have!

TAKING UNIVERSAL DESIGN FOR LEARNING OUT OF THE ABSTRACT

Strategies for providing multiple means of representation

- Use text-to-speech options for books and computerized materials. Recording for the Blind and Dyslexic has almost 60,000 titles available for registered users (http://www.rfbd.org). Bookshare is another source of thousands of digital books (http://www.bookshare.org), and CAST (The Center for Applied Special Technology) also is a source for free digital books (http://udleditions.cast.org).

- Help students learn how to organize their thinking by modeling and teaching the use of graphic organizers. One source of free online graphic organizers is Webspiration: http://mywebspiration.com.

- Use captioning software such as InqScribe or the beta-test captioning on YouTube to create captions for your videos before you show them. Not only will students who are deaf and hard of hearing have access, but it will help many others as well.

Strategies for providing multiple means of expression

- Not only is it important to give students choices about how they display what they learned, but it's also important to give them models of the different choices that are available to them. Once you've made some model posters, sculptures, skits, and so forth, you will find that you can use them over and over. After a while, you'll also have excellent student models to share as well.

- In terms of monitoring time, the use of visual and auditory timers can be very helpful for many students who may have difficulty gauging the passage of time. One very easy-to-use timer, which graphically depicts the amount of time left in a given task, is the Time Timer: http://www.timetimer.com. The Kagan website also provides multiple online timer options (http://www.kaganonline.com).

Strategies for providing multiple means of engagement

- Increase student autonomy by teaching them to set and reward their own goals and giving them the freedom to shape classroom activities as much as possible. Allowing students to choose the order in which they complete nonpreferred tasks, for example, can increase engagement and motivation.

- Create virtual communities of learners based around areas of common interest, then make sure your students have access to the technology they need to participate. (Don't forget that they may need speech recognition software, text-to-speech options, and other assistive technology!) For example, you might create a blog for students interested in video games, another on movies, and one on rap artists. Students would be assigned writing projects, but they would get to choose which topic they would blog about.

- Share lesson plans on a districtwide website so that all teachers with common subjects, students, and challenges can benefit from one another's work.

On the web

For more strategies for providing multiple means of representation, expression, and engagement go to http://www.corwin.com/diverseschools.

THUMBNAILS OF RESOURCES ON THE INTERNET

The following elements can be found on the companion website for *Collaborate, Communicate, and Differentiate!* at http://www.corwin.com/diverseschools.

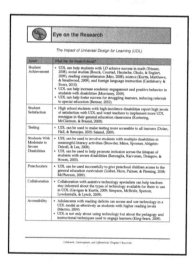

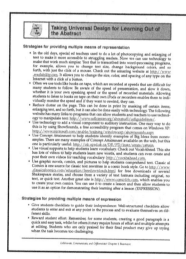

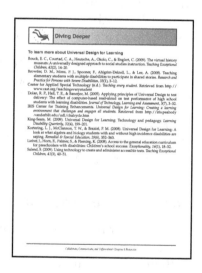

6

Modifying and Accommodating to Reactively Address Student Needs

Voices From the Field

"We don't have the schedule or personnel to allow me to be in any one class on a regular basis. A lot of time I find myself going into a classroom and just asking, 'What are we doing today?' I know it's not best practice, but it's all the time I have. At least I know when I'm in there, I can quickly provide some on-the-spot accommodations and modifications for the students who need them."

Eunice K., special education co-teacher

"I'm with Brandon in the general education classroom every day as a classroom assistant. Although the special education teacher is responsible for most of his accommodations, from time to time things come up. How can I make sure that Brandon is truly part of the classroom activities, even when we haven't planned in advance?"

Zulema S., paraprofessional

THE BIG PICTURE

In the last chapter, we discussed the need to be proactive. We emphasized how designing a lesson for universal access is far more effective than trying to retrofit an existing lesson. We stressed the importance of proactive planning. **77**

All of this is true and we want to underscore that our very first choice is to have you be proactive about your collaborative efforts to help kids. That said, though, we are also realists. There are times when you aren't able to be proactive, for whatever reason. In those situations, you need to know what some second-best choices are. What are accommodations and modifications and how can we embed those in the curriculum when universal design isn't possible? How might we use assistive technology to help students? And finally, if we are not able to work directly to co-plan or co-teach with colleagues (a topic we explore in depth in subsequent chapters), what can we do indirectly to still collaborate? This chapter addresses these questions.

In this chapter we do the following:

- Clarify the difference between accommodations, modifications, and adaptations and give examples of when to use them.
- Share information on assistive technology and how to access it for student learning.
- Provide collaborative strategies for supporting students through monitoring, consulting, and indirect services when direct support is unavailable.

Read on!

ACCOMMODATIONS AND MODIFICATIONS: WHAT ARE THEY AND WHEN DO WE USE THEM?

Should we proactively plan for the needs of all learners? Sure, we know you're for it philosophically and theoretically, but we also bet that now you're wondering if your authors have not been in actual schools for a while. Don't we know that most educators barely have enough time to get through their day? Of course we know that. We also know that classes run most smoothly when they have been planned in advance. But what happens if a fire drill occurs during our planning period or you're away at staff development for three days or a related service specialist is only able to drop by once a week for 30 minutes with no proactive planning? What can you do in those cases? What are some acceptable *on-the-spot* adaptations that can help students be successful?

We also know that some of you are probably not totally convinced that *any* kind of adaptation is required or appropriate. So in addition to determining what is acceptable in the classroom, we also want to address the very real differences of opinion some educators may have related to providing said adaptations. (See *Frame of Reference* on page 80.)

First, let's clarify some terms. Adaptations are any accommodations or modifications that are provided to a student or group of students to help them access the curriculum, exhibit improved behavior, or learn social skills. Though the words *accommodations* and *modifications* are frequently used interchangeably in schools, there is a subtle but important difference between them. An *accommodation* is any change from the typical expectation that does not alter or lower the standard. For example, if students are completing 10 math problems that range from easiest to hardest, a student who struggles with task completion and needs more time may be asked to only do the odd problems. This would be an accommodation—he is still demonstrating that he can do the work from easiest to most difficult, but he simply did not have to do as much work as his peers. His work was still meeting the same standard.

On the other hand, a modification is a change from the typical expectation that *does* alter or lower the standard. In the same example, if the student was asked to do the first five problems, that would be a modification. The first five problems are the least difficult; by not working through the remaining problems, the student has not been able to display that he can meet that standard. Another child might do five problems focused on an easier skill; that would also be a modification. Although both accommodations and modifications can and might be appropriate in different instances, it's important for you to be aware of whether you're making accommodations to the material or *modifying* the expectations when you give a student different work.

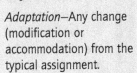

Key Terms

Adaptation—Any change (modification or accommodation) from the typical assignment.

Accommodation—A change that does not alter or lower the grade-level standard

Modification—A change that alters or lowers the grade-level standard

Students with identified disabilities may have both accommodations and modifications written into their IEPs. However, providing these adaptations in the classroom can be difficult on numerous fronts. First, anything done differently from one student to the next may result in the oft-heard complaint, "That's not fair!" This argument seems to come just as often from teachers as it does from students. Students may want what their peers have, and to get beyond that, it's up to you as the teacher to create a classroom climate that is accepting of different people doing different work. On the other hand, some teachers disagree philosophically with providing different options for some students when the others do not receive those options. (See how UDL helps alleviate that problem? Another reason to be proactive!) We address the "That's Not Fair" conundrum in the next section. However, even those educators who are amenable to providing accommodations and modifications in the classroom may struggle with identifying possible options and figuring out how to implement them. Don't worry—we won't leave you hanging. We'll help you out with lots of great strategies for that problem later on in this chapter.

THAT'S NOT FAIR! HOW CAN I DO IT FOR ONE AND NOT FOR ALL?

"That's not fair!" How often have you heard this complaint? How often was it *you* making it? C'mon, be honest. Doing something different for one kid can often cause stress and friction. This can be particularly problematic between individuals who are supposed to collaborate. If one person believes philosophically in the adaptations and the other struggles to see how it is fair to the other students, conflict can occur. Check out the *Frame of Reference* box on page 80. Both teachers clearly care about the students, but they also had to work through their differences of opinion to come to a consensus. Because they were willing to communicate, share, and even agree to disagree for a while, they ended up as a stronger team—and more important, the student's needs were met.

FRAME OF REFERENCE

Mrs. Hutchinson is an English teacher who felt that, in an English class, her student Del needed to do the essay assignment. She stated to her co-teacher, Ms. Zikel, that there were no other options. Ms. Zikel disagreed. In her opinion, Del's writing disability was so bad that she didn't believe it was appropriate to have him physically write a five-page paper. She advocated to Mrs. Hutchinson that they should allow Del to do the paper another way instead. Ms. Zikel believed that Del could still be responsible for doing the research, organizing the content, planning the argument, and making sentences that are grammatically correct and provide sufficient detail. He just wouldn't have to do it on paper. As a veteran English teacher, Mrs. Hutchinson wasn't convinced, but she agreed to disagree because she respected Ms. Zikel as a fellow professional educator. Imagine her surprise when Del turned in a well-researched and well-articulated paper that he had organized using Inspiration and then dictated into Dragon Dictate. Because Del did it differently but still met the same standards as the other kids, her frame of reference on adaptations changed. From then on, she was much more willing to accept Ms. Zikel's suggestions for student accommodations.

Special education professionals are taught through their coursework to see students as unique individuals. They are taught to differentiate, modify, accommodate, and otherwise meet the students' varying needs. This emphasis on individualization is often not a part of training for general educators, administrators, or even parents. Thus, we may come into our conversations about adaptations from very different frames of reference. To understand why accommodations and modifications are a valid, and often necessary, part of instruction in today's inclusive settings, consider the following examples. (You may want to use these with your own students or colleagues!)

That's Not Fair—Example #1. A mom took her twins to the department store. She bought her daughter a beautiful pink party dress, complete with rhinestones and sequins. As they started to leave, her son complained, "That's not fair! You didn't buy me anything." So she bought him one too.

That's Not Fair—Example #2. Two students are at the top of a black diamond ski slope. One is a champion skier; the other has never seen snow. Is it fair to push them both and say, "Go!"? Of course not; it might be lethal. What then could you do to make sure this is "fair" to them both? Consider the following:

1. Different starting points—one goes down the bunny slope and one does the black diamond run.

2. Direct instruction—both skiers get lessons, but one is focused on the basic "wedge" while the other is learning to ski backward.

3. Peer support—the strong skier helps the weaker one, provided later they go surfing so that the nonskier has an opportunity to shine as well.

4. Alternate pathways—let the weaker skier go down the hill on his bum or give him a snowboard.

5. Extra time—put a time limit on the stronger skier but not the weaker one

That's Not Fair—Example #3. At your next staff meeting, ask all the individuals who are wearing glasses to stand up. Then ask those individuals who are standing to get in one of three groups based on their vision without glasses: mild disability (can see but will squint and get a headache), moderate disability (can see close but not far or vice versa), or severe disability (effectively blind). Usually, there will be a few folks in each of the three areas, just as there are in any typical inclusive setting. After discussing how ludicrous it would be to deny these individuals their accommodation (glasses, in this case), also talk about how silly it would be to take them all out in the hall and give them the *same* glasses (akin to "pulling out" kids with disabilities to read them all the same test). Now find out how many educators are wearing contacts in the large group. Have those individuals stand up to represent children with "invisible disabilities"; we may not be able to see the contacts, but without that accommodation, the person is now unable to function with the rest of the group.

These types of activities enable educators, parents, and students alike to talk about what it means to be different. They also clearly point out that, while differences may make things challenging, they can also often be addressed by simple accommodations. What is not acceptable is to treat everyone exactly the same. To be fair is to treat everyone differently. To be fair, everyone must get what he or she needs (Welch, 2000).

You may be wondering how Universal Design for Learning interacts with modifications and accommodations, especially given our emphasis on the need to proactively plan for all learners using UDL. There are two good reasons that adaptations are still necessary, even with a strong emphasis on UDL. The first is that there are some times when an adaptation is necessary for one or more students, whereas the rest of the group doesn't need it and may even be more confused by it. For example, while you may use UDL principles to make visually accessible handouts in a larger font, the student who is totally blind will need a copy in Braille. By proactively planning for instruction, you may have already collaborated and communicated with the Braille transcriber and you have that Braille copy available; however, you certainly wouldn't give it to the whole class. The second reason is that no matter how well intentioned we are during planning, there will always be times when we as teachers decide to go to "Plan B." If a student isn't accessing the information or appears overwhelmed or confused, despite your prior planning and consideration of her special needs, you may still need to try something else. For example, you and your co-teacher have collaboratively developed a packet of work on photosynthesis that you both believe is universally designed. After explaining the directions, the students begin to work. You notice after a few minutes that Bobby is beginning to shut down. He states, "It's too much. I can't do all this!" You quickly remove the packet, pull off the first page, and give it to him. You see him visibly relax when you say, "Here. Just do this page. When it's done, raise your hand and either Ms. G or I will come over to see how it went." Even if you have every intention of giving him every page in that packet, you have just used an accommodation (one page at a time) to address his special need. Good for you! Did everyone else need that? No. Did Bobby? Yes. And so he got it.

ADAPTATIONS: A NICE IDEA, BUT WHERE DO I START?

So how do you start coming up with ideas for accommodations and modifications that you can use at the drop of a hat? Our *In A Nutshell* on page 83 is designed to provide for you just a taste of what is out there. Try these out but be sure to seek out even more ideas on your own. You can also take a look at Appendix III (available online at http://www.corwin.com/diverseschools), where we have examples of modified work that can give you ideas of where to start.

But be careful—we urge you to consider thoroughly the special requirements of *your* particular students. Avoid the "one size fits all" approach. As we said before, pulling all the kids with IEPs out in the hallway to read the test aloud is neither equitable nor appropriate. What may be a reasonable and necessary adaptation for one student is a waste of time for another.

To get you started, we have also included another handy *In a Nutshell* chart on page 84. This one gives you nine ways to approach adapting curriculum, derived from the work of Cole et al. (2000). These should be especially helpful when you have to be on your own to make these decisions on the spot without any wonderful colleagues around with whom to collaborate.

As you are using the chart to make your choices, try the least intrusive choices first. For example, simply increasing the amount of time a student has to complete a task, or decreasing the amount of work expected (choices 1 and 2), can be easy to implement and unobtrusive in the classroom. *It's critical, though, as you make these adaptations, that the student is still held accountable for the work!* The worst way to adapt work is to say, "Just complete as much as you can." By saying that, you have communicated to the child that if she works more slowly she can get away with less work. You also may have communicated that you have low expectations in terms of her ability to complete the work. When adapting curriculum, it is important to make your expectations concrete and hold the student accountable: "Carolyn, I'm going to have you do only the odd numbers on this assignment. I know that you can do the work; it just takes you a bit longer for each problem. However, even though you have fewer problems, they are still the same difficulty as everyone else and if you don't turn them in, you will lose points for classwork, just like everyone else, so let's get to work!"

Another critical element to consider is that of student independence. The third choice on the list is increasing the level of support. Although this is a perfectly viable option, you want to be aware that the more adult or peer support you consistently use with a student, the less likely he is to develop strong independent work habits. Students can develop something called "learned helplessness" and that's something we *don't* want. Whenever possible, use more support as an adaptation of last resort. It's usually better to adapt the work so a student can complete it independently rather than rely on an adult or a peer to help him with it.

Notice that, of the nine adaptations provided, only one is automatically likely to be a modification (change in standard), and that is "Substitute Curriculum." Depending on how they are used, the others may be modifications *or* accommodations. How do you choose which to use? How do you decide whether you need an accommodation or modification? We wish we could provide you with a step-by-step chart for making those decisions, but it really, truly, is individual to the child, and it may be specified on the IEP. It's that whole *individualized* program thing. You may have two students with the labels of "Learning Disabled," but we promise you, they will look very different and have very different needs. Labels are helpful in that they provide us with general information, but be wary of looking to labels for information on the child. Instead, we recommend you get to know all of your students—those with and without labels—and that you learn not just their areas of weakness or disability, but even more important, their areas of strength!

In a Nutshell

*Examples of Easy-to-Use Adaptations**

Area of Difficulty	Type of Adaptation	How to Do It
Writing: Student struggles with the fine motor aspects of writing.	Output	Have name/date on labels to be attached to papers, instead of student having to write own name each time; allow student to audiotape or type assignments instead of writing them down.
Reading: Student is overwhelmed by large amounts of text.	Input	Fold the paper in half so the student only sees half of the work or use a "mask" (manila folder cut so that only one part is folded back for students to see).
Reading: Student struggles to decode words in math problems.	Input	Rewrite math word problems using simplified language. This can be done without changing the math content, and it allows the student to complete work independently. Alternatively, you can have a student with extra time record tomorrow's word problems on an iPod.
Behavior: Student tends to talk out of turn or get out of her seat.	Input	Create a stoplight and use a clothespin to indicate if talking is allowed (green), limited to when hands are raised (yellow), or not allowed (red). For many students, a visual reminder can help keep them on task and behaving appropriately.
Behavior: Student does not participate orally or doesn't like to give up the floor when he gets it.	Output	To increase—but still limit—oral participation, use a Koosh ball that lights up. When you toss the ball at a student, it means he needs to respond. However, he is only allowed to respond for as long as the ball is lit (typically 20 seconds).
Memory: Student has very poor short-term memory.	Input	Provide mnemonics (memory tricks) for students and allow the mnemonic device (acronym or picture) to be displayed in the room.
Attention: Student cannot sustain attention for a long amount of time.	Participation	Provide student with cards to take self-initiated brain breaks; student can stand or sit in a previously identified part of the room as she continues to listen.
Organization: Student loses papers or can't follow multiple-step directions.	Output/ Participation	Provide checklists whenever possible; as student completes one part, grade it and collect it rather than having student responsible for all parts; allow student to e-mail work so it can be kept electronically rather than on a hard copy.

*Please note: These are accommodations, not modifications. They do not alter any standards. Also, ALL accommodations and modifications should be kid-specific. Not all strategies work for all kids. Most important, know your students!

In a Nutshell

Nine Ways to Approach Adapting Curriculum

What to Adapt	Explanation	Example in Practice
Amount of Work	Change the number of items the student is expected to complete	Carolyn, who has a learning disability, will be given only 5 of 10 problems to read because it takes her much longer to decode than her peers.
Time	Change the time allowed to complete the task, assignment, or test	Carolyn will also be provided with additional time to complete the work and won't be graded down if it's late.
Level of Support	Change how much help this student is getting	Ulysses, who is an English language learner (ELL), will be provided additional support in his native language by an ELL teacher.
Input	Change the way this student is being taught the material	Gio, who has ADHD, is going to be able to listen to a podcast of a lesson as he moves around, rather than sitting still during a lecture.
Difficulty	Change the skill level, problem type, or rules	DeMarq, who is gifted, is going to be given five problems, just like his peers, but his problems are more conceptually challenging. Chris, who has Down syndrome, will be given three pictures on a concept from which to make a choice when asked a question. The teacher will then use these pictures to extend the discussion for the rest of the learners.
Output	Change the way the student shows you what he learned	Del, who has a writing disability, will do his research project by dictating it rather than handwriting or typing it.
Participation	Change the degree to which or the manner in which the student participates	Yolanda, who doesn't have a disability but is highly at risk, will be encouraged to work in small groups when desired since it increases her motivation.
Alternate	Change the goals or expectations for the student while using the same materials	Instead of showing his work on math problems, DeMarq will be asked to provide a possible application of each type of math problem to a real-world situation.
Substitute Curriculum	Change the instruction, materials, and goals for the student in order to be more appropriate	Chris, our student with Down syndrome, is going to receive an adapted version of the science text and will cut and paste parts of a plant and the plant cycle, instead of answering worksheet questions related to photosynthesis.

Source: Adapted from Cole et al., 2000.

In fact, we think focusing on students' strengths is one of the best ways to approach adapting curriculum. A **strength-based perspective** is one in which teachers use students' abilities and affinities to help coax out their best work. To do this, you need to first learn about your students' different learning styles, multiple intelligences, and interests in order to motivate them and engage them in the lesson. For example, if Yolanda is your student who doesn't have a disability but doesn't regularly get engaged in the lesson, what can you do about that? It is simply unacceptable to give up on her! You may want to start by reading Rick Lavoie's (2008) book *The Motivation Breakthrough: Six Secrets to Turning On the Tuned-Out Child*. Then you may want to give a quick in-class assessment to find out what students in your class identify as the things that interest them outside of class. Make it a checklist if you think writing is a nonpreferred activity for many kids. Then, after you see that Yolanda has checked "movies, going online, hanging with friends, and TV," try to engage her in a conversation to find out what types of movies she likes, what she does online, which friends she has, and what TV shows she watches. The more you learn, the more you may be surprised. You may find out that her favorite movies are horrors, that she blogs incessantly, that two of her best friends are in your other class periods, and that she loves CSI because she wants to be a crime scene investigator herself. You are now armed with information! Check out these adaptations for Yolanda:

- *Social Studies.* Class assignment is to report on one aspect of the Civil War. Provide Yolanda with the task of learning about the types of gory deaths that occurred during the war because "you are one of the only students who I think can handle that kind of horror."

- *Language Arts.* Class assignment is to write a persuasive argument. Tell Yolanda she can blog hers and you'll read it tonight.

- *Math.* Class assignment is to create problems to give to peers to solve. Allow Yolanda to create problems for her best friends in other class periods and offer to deliver them.

- *Science.* Class assignment is to learn about DNA. Instead of the typical lecture, you contacted the local police department and a crime scene investigator has come out to do a guest lecture. Yolanda is enraptured!

Making adaptations for students is not about doing something different when you have to. It is about doing something different because that is what is right, that is what the student needs, and that is what will help the student learn the content and be successful. Even if you have a caseload of 150 students, it behooves you to learn as much as you can about each of them. As we said in a previous chapter, we believe this kind of up-front work can actually reduce your workload later on—the connection you make with Yolanda now will prevent you from having to meet with her parents at the end of the semester. This book is about improving student learning through collaboration, so collaborate with your students and their families to find out their strengths, their needs, their concerns, their desires, and how they can help you teach them. Not only will you find it easier to connect with them in your teaching, but you'll start to enjoy your job a bit more, too. You know, once you get to know 'em, those kids aren't half bad!

> **Want more info?**
>
> The book *Just Give Him the Whale!* (Kluth & Schwarz, 2008) offers many creative ways of using a student's interests and passions within your lessons. See our *Diving Deeper* section on the web for the whole citation.

USING TECHNOLOGY: DO I REALLY HAVE TO LEARN ALL THAT STUFF?

Technology is a critical tool for adapting instruction in today's world, and it is an important means for making last-minute adaptations in the classroom. Do you want a powerful reminder of our need to include technology in today's classroom? Consider this: *Students today are digital natives, while most teachers are digital immigrants* (Prensky, 2001). It is simply unacceptable that some teachers will staunchly state that they don't "do e-mail or PowerPoint." They use the fact that they are "old-school" as an excuse to avoid even the most basic of technology. How would you feel if one of your teachers said she didn't "do calculators" and wanted you to use an abacus? Or she said she didn't "do pens and pencils" and wanted you to scratch your essay on a stone tablet? Geez, folks. We are in the 21st century, and part of that—like it or not—includes technology.

Before we get into *assistive* technology, which is technology directly related to individuals with special needs, we want to emphasize the need to use *any* kind of technology. Technology makes curriculum more accessible for kids—it's as simple as that. We know that you aren't all equal in your abilities to use technology, so here is a great place for collaboration. If you are a "techie," offer your services to your peers. If you are one of the "old-school" types described earlier, ask for help. You might offer to share your years of expertise with a colleague who can share her knowledge of technology with you. (e.g., "If you help me create a PowerPoint presentation on the Civil War, I'll help you create a cooperative learning activity that will really engage your students.")

Just as we model collaboration in our interactions, so too can we pair students so that one student is stronger in content and one is stronger in the technological skills. The use of technology also helps us address students' kinesthetic and tactile learning modalities. We can collaborate to prepare our students by creating real-world activities, which are interdisciplinary, integrated, and project-based, while concurrently addressing those skills identified as critical for the 21st-century learner: collaboration, critical thinking, oral communication, written communication, technology, citizenship, career orientation, and content-based learning (see http://www.21stcenturyschools.com). Having said that, not only do you need to learn how to use technology, but if you have students with disabilities in your classes, you will need to have some working knowledge of assistive technology as well. Let's take a look at what it is and how you can use it. It's not as scary as you might assume!

Key Term

Assistive Technology—Any device, tool, or software designed to help provide access to instruction.

ASSISTIVE TECHNOLOGY: WHAT ARE THE TOOLS AND HOW DO I USE THEM?

Assistive technology sounds more daunting than it is. Many teachers hear the term and immediately assume we are talking about expensive equipment or software. Not so. Did you know that a fuzzy pencil wrap in the shape of an animal might qualify as assistive technology? Crazy, eh? But it's true. Assistive technology is simply any device, tool, or software whose purpose it is to help individuals have access to instruction. Officially, "the term 'assistive technology device' means any item, piece of equipment, or product system, whether acquired commercially off the shelf, modified, or customized, that is used to increase, maintain, or

---

In Practice

Ms. Chung looked at the file again. She had been fine when she heard she was getting a new student in the middle of the semester, even one in special education, but no one had told her Evan had significant disabilities. She thought she was just getting another student with a learning disability or ADHD. But the file said Evan had cerebral palsy, was in a wheelchair, couldn't write or talk, and used assistive devices to communicate. Assistive devices?!? Ms. Chung sat down heavily, wondering what she was going to do.

৵৶

One week later, Ms. Chung smiled to herself as she looked at Evan interacting with some of his peers. The students had moved their chairs over to his adapted desk and they were asking him questions about his Dynavox. As each child asked a question, Evan would slowly move his hand and type the answers to their questions. Ms. Chung would never have guessed her sophomores could be so patient, but she realized that the technology was a real draw for them. The technology helped them to see past Evan's disability and learn more about this new student who joined their class. Even though the Dynavox was still a bit intimidating, Ms. Chung could clearly see how having Evan in her class was a chance for all her students to develop empathy, tolerance, and a broader worldview. Plus, the technology was cool! And ya know, so was Evan.

---

improve functional capabilities for individuals with disabilities" (IDEA, 1997). There is an amazing array of assistive technology available to teachers to help them address the needs of students, and it doesn't have to be daunting. There is a continuum of technology, from simple tools to highly technical and specialized devices, and the entire spectrum in the middle. Learning about assistive technology can be informative and fun.

Think about the student who has poor handwriting due to a fine motor problem that makes it hard for him to accurately grasp a writing utensil. Without thinking about it, you provide him with a fat pencil for his draft and then make sure to have him work on the computer to type his final draft in lieu of writing it all out. Guess what? You just used assistive technology. Well done.

Granted, we admit it's not always that easy. There are some communication devices and software that are expensive, complex, and require training to use. But typically, if these are needed, there is someone who has been trained in using them. Check out the *Adaptive Products and Services* box in Appendix IV (available online at http://www.corwin.com/diverseschools). As you can see, getting support for the use of assistive technology is key. Teachers need to be open to the wide variety of assistive technology services and products available. When you are willing to see what's out there, you will often be able to find others willing to collaborate with you to ensure their use.

Technology is a very real part of today's society. Students today are drawn to technological advances. When assistive technology such as communication devices, software, and electronics are used to support students with more specific or significant disabilities, other students may be interested in learning about the assistive technology and may even want to help in its use (see *In Practice* above). This is a wonderful opportunity for increased inclusive practices and social interactions for students. Other less high-tech assistive technology devices, such as white boards, dictation software, or portable keyboards, may be easy to obtain, use, and incorporate into the classroom. They may also end up being very appropriate for use with all students, not just those with disabilities.

The need for technology might even result in an assignment that ends up including all students. For example, Rance is a student who doesn't communicate orally. The history standards say that students need to be able to understand the concept of services and products in a global economy. In the past, you had students role-play different scenarios in class, but you know Rance can't do this. Rather than being frustrated or throwing out the whole idea, you go and talk to a special educator, a speech/language specialist, and Rance's parents. Through this collaboration, you learn a variety of ways to recreate the assignment that will include Rance, while engaging the other students as well. Now, the biggest difficulty you have is choosing from the following excellent options:

- Have students go online to identify as many examples of products and services as they can in five minutes.
- Preprogram responses into Rance's assistive communication device so that he can participate in the role-play in a preidentified section.
- Ask students to create PowerPoint presentations that demonstrate various services and products.
- Provide all students with a class set of Flip video cameras to walk around the school and see what services and products are being used.
- Create a class blog where students can discuss the different services or products they have seen in the last 24 hours.
- Challenge students to work in teams to create a products and services WebQuest for the other teams to complete.

Want more info?

Check out the website of the Annual International Technology & Persons with Disabilities Conference at http://www.csun conference.org

Some of you reading this love technology; some are scared by it. We understand. That's why we are emphasizing the need for collaboration. You do not have to be a technological expert; what you do have to be, however, is willing to learn, willing to ask others, and willing to try. If a student is struggling in your class, whether or not she has an identified disability, it is possible that the use of technology in some form may help. As educators, aren't we committed to helping students succeed *in any way we can?* That way may include technology. Take a baby step from wherever you are technologically, and then try to keep moving forward.

MAINTAINING CONSISTENCY AND COMMUNICATION: WHAT DO I DO WHEN I'M ALL ALONE?

There will be times when it is necessary for reactive measures to be taken and your collaborative partners are not around. Perhaps you are the special educator or speech therapist and you cannot physically be in each classroom at all times given your large and spread-out caseload. Or perhaps you are the general education classroom teacher and, despite your willingness to collaborate with others, you still feel a bit overwhelmed and at a loss when kids are struggling in your class and there are no other adults around with whom to share ideas or strategies. Fear not! While we certainly think that two adult heads (and as many hands as we can get) are better than one in a classroom, we are also very practical and know this is often not possible. So, what do you do? Communicate! Following are some strategies for maintaining communication regarding differentiation strategies, modifications and accommodations, and tracking progress, even when you are not able to work directly with your collaborative partners—because we know that as much as you want to, you may not be able to collaborate in person all the time.

First of all, establish a communication system with your partners. What works best for you all? For some, this will be a simple e-mail system. For those who don't tend to check e-mail much, a hard-copy communication system may be preferred. Some teachers already employ home–school communication books or journals that go between parents and teachers; these can also go between general and special education personnel. Take a look back at the form we gave you in Chapter 2 (available online at http://www.corwin.com/diverseschools). Using a simple form like that one can make the work of collaborating to create adaptations a whole lot easier. We must emphasize, however, despite the tendency to get overwhelmed with work and day-to-day requirements, it's important to establish a consistent and structured routine for communication, whether that is daily, weekly, or monthly. Otherwise, the communication breaks down and some partners are left feeling "out of the loop," while the struggling student continues to struggle. Set up something you all feel you can live with, and then *stick to it*. This holds true for all of us, on both sides of the collaboration.

Would you like more useful strategies for meeting students' needs when time together in person is not available? How about cheat sheets and folders?!? Let's face it—no matter how much we care about each student—it can be difficult to remember each individual IEP goal or objective, the accommodations allowed, and the strengths and needs of each child. However, if a student is struggling in the class, the general educators need a tool that reminds them quickly of disability areas ("Does the student have difficulty with visual or auditory processing?"), strengths ("The student loves motorcycles and using his hands."), and possible adaptations ("extra time; visual cues; fold paper in half"). The IEP is a wonderful document but can be overwhelming to many teachers and is not easily accessible in many classrooms. On the other hand, developing a cheat sheet like the "Student Profile" offered in Appendix V (available online at http://www.corwin.com/diverseschools) helps all educators remember important information when working with students. If one of these is created for each student with a special need, then disseminated among all team members and kept in confidential classroom folders, teachers can refer to them as needed.

Other helpful folders can be developed to help students work on their specific, individualized goals and objectives. When classroom teachers have time for students to work on individual or independent work, they can pull out a folder that has a student's goal-related work in it. For example, in a middle-school English class, students have time to start on their homework or finish up a project in the last 10 minutes of class. Instead of having Jeremy do that, however, Mrs. Sunderland provides him with a worksheet from his folder that provides Jeremy with additional instruction on the use of adjectives (a goal that is on his IEP but that they are not currently working on in class). Special service providers (Title I teachers, English language learner teachers, special education teachers, speech/language pathologists) can work closely with general educators to create these folders so that they are ready to go in the classroom. This also helps to ensure that students are still working on their IEP goals and objectives even when service providers cannot be physically present.

All right, we admit it. There is a very real likelihood that you may not always be working in close proximity with another adult in order to collaborate in person. And we are just now realizing that the majority of the suggestions we've provided for tackling this sticky problem are, well—let's face it—*proactive* strategies. What can we say?!? We are diehard "proactivists." (Editor—please ignore your spell check telling you that proactivists is not a word. We know that. But we like it anyway.) The truth is, the more you can acknowledge and plan for the needs of kids in advance, the better off you and they are. If you have taught for a year, you know that

Principal Points

Cheat sheets are a really useful tool that can help your general educators keep up to speed on how to help their students with special needs. However, it's important to remember that the information on a cheat sheet is still protected by rules of confidentiality. We know of one teacher who left her cheat sheet sitting out on her desk, only to have a parent come in and read it. As you might imagine, this led to a lot of trouble for both the teacher and the administrator. Make sure you train your teachers in all aspects of confidentiality rules concerning special education.

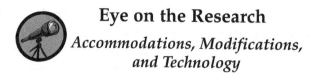

Eye on the Research
Accommodations, Modifications, and Technology

Issues	What has the research found to help students?
Accommodations and Modifications	• Studies suggest that the more training educators have on students with disabilities and their needs, the more comfortable they are with providing various accommodations, modifications, and adaptations (Harvey, Cotton, & Koch, 2007). • The provision of curricular modifications can result in more engaged student responses, fewer negative student behaviors, and less need for teacher classroom management redirection (Lee, Wehmeyer, Soukup, & Palmer, 2010).
Assistive Technology	• The use of assistive reading software improved the academic self-perception and functional task performance of high school students with learning difficulties (Chiang & Jacobs, 2009). • Assistive technology is critical for some students with disabilities to access educational materials, demonstrate high academic achievement, and compete academically with nondisabled peers (Alper & Raharinirina, 2006).

For more research in this area go to http://www.corwin.com/diverseschools.

while it is not possible to plan for everything, there are certain truths in education we can count on:

- Some kids will not do their homework, no matter how fun it is or how much you plead.
- Some kids will have a hard time paying attention.
- Some kids do not like to read. Or write. Or do math. Or sing. Or dress for PE. And so on.
- Some kids have behavioral problems. Big ones. Those children are never absent.
- Some kids have parents who seem not to care; others have parents who seem to care too much; few have parents who care "just right."

Given these and similar truths, we simply can't help thinking that the only way to keep ourselves sane as educators is to take them in stride and plan accordingly. Ah, plan. There's that word again. . . .

TAKING ADAPTATIONS OUT OF THE ABSTRACT

Strategies for providing accommodations, modifications, and assistive technology

- Send a quick survey home to parents to ask them about their impressions of their children's areas of ability, strength, and weakness. Sometimes parents can share information on skills their children have that you may never have known, but that you can incorporate into the classroom.

- The iPad has a lot of fun, interesting applications that can make learning more accessible for everyone. In particular, check out Proloquo2go—this application makes the iPad into an adaptive communication device for students who can physically manage it.

- Create student profiles (such as the one in Appendix V) at the beginning of the year and keep a copy electronically. As kids change, the profiles can be updated and next year's case managers can merely "tweak" the profiles before sharing them with team members.

- Identify a place in the school for all teachers to obtain class sets of materials to help with accommodations. For example, "masks," Koosh balls, colored overlays, and WhisperPhones may all be available in boxes in a particular closet. That will only be helpful if all teachers (a) know the materials exist, (b) know how the materials can be useful, and (c) know where the materials are housed.

On the web

For more strategies for accommodations, modifications, and assistive technology go to http://www.corwin.com/diverseschools.

THUMBNAILS OF RESOURCES ON THE INTERNET

The following elements can be found on the companion website for *Collaborate, Communicate, and Differentiate!* at http://www.corwin.com/diverseschools.

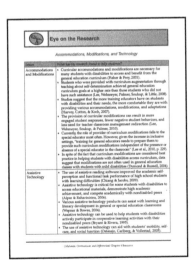

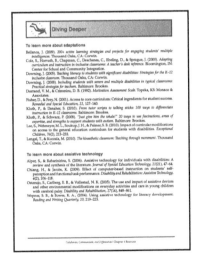

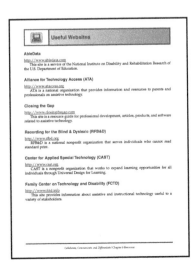

7

Improving Student Learning Through Co-Teaching

Voices From the Field

"Sure, I've co-taught before. I hated it. All I did was walk around and check that my students had their homework or paid attention. I was a glorified aide, at the mercy of whatever the general ed teacher wanted me to do."

Lisa K., special education teacher

"Co-teaching? No thanks. I don't really see the benefit of having another adult in the room if he or she doesn't know the content. Plus I hear horror stories of co-teachers always coming late, leaving early, or missing class altogether."

Manuel L., general education teacher

"We love it! It's great having a partner to bounce ideas off of, and to share the work, stresses, and successes. The kids really benefit! We know we are lucky that we work so well together. We don't want to go back to teaching alone."

Amy G. & Kevin W., seventh-grade co-teachers

THE BIG PICTURE

Co-teaching is the new big thing. Okay, if you've been doing it for years, you may question that statement, but let's face it—co-teaching is definitely growing in popularity. Two of the major reasons for this newfound support for co-teaching were described in Chapter 1. *Can you name the two laws that mandate individualized supports while also emphasizing standards-based curriculum and assessment?* If you said IDEA and NCLB, give yourself a pat on the back. Essentially, IDEA and NCLB let teachers know that most students—even those with identified disabilities who may previously have been educated in a self-contained or pull-out setting—are now going to be taught in the general education classroom. At the same time, we are also being expected to ensure that all children are receiving standards-based instruction with high expectations and common assessments. No surprise, then, that we've asked experts in special education and general education to collaborate not just out of the classroom, but now in the actual classroom as well. And voilà: co-teaching!

In this chapter, we clarify what co-teaching should and should not look like, when it should be used, and with whom you can co-teach. We also explain both the benefits and potential pitfalls of co-teaching, as well as the components of *effective* co-teaching. Keeping with our focus on practical strategies for collaboration, we provide tips and techniques for co-instructing (one of the three keys of true co-teaching). Tips for co-planning and co-assessing (the other two keys of true co-teaching) are provided in the next chapter.

In this chapter do the following:

- Define co-teaching and explain why it may be a desirable service delivery option for kids.
- Clarify the necessary components for effective co-teaching and explain what to do if you don't have those components.
- Describe people you can co-teach with and what it would look like in the classroom.
- Emphasize how co-teaching can improve student learning.

But wait!
There's more . . .

COLLABORATIVE TEACHING: WHY ARE WE HEARING WEDDING BELLS?

One of the frequent misconceptions about co-teaching is that simply putting two adults in the same room accomplishes this task. Not so, we say! Like in the *Voices From the Field*, too often we hear teachers complain that they are treated like glorified aides, like Lisa, or that they don't see the point, like Manuel. Often that's because someone in a position of authority told someone else that co-teaching needed to be happening, and the trickle-down effect resulted in teachers who were thrown together and told to go forth and co-teach. No training, no explanation, no getting-to-know-you period. Nothing. And what do you get? A bunch of unhappy teachers, like Lisa and Manuel. Let us address that by explaining what really good co-teaching is supposed to look like.

Key Term

Co-Teaching—Two or more professionals sharing the planning, instructing, and assessing of students.

What do we want to see in a co-teaching relationship? We think there are several critical components (originally outlined by Friend & Cook, 2009) that are essential to making a successful co-teaching experience, and we briefly discuss each of those here. Without these components in place, you may not be getting the maximum effectiveness from your co-teaching experience. So here is what we'd like to see in your co-taught class:

Three key elements. We want to see two trained teachers who share in the **planning, instructing,** and **assessing** of all the students in a meaningful way (Murawski, 2010). Since good teaching involves planning what you are going to do, doing it well in the classroom, and then assessing what worked and what didn't, good co-teaching involves the same key elements—but shared. This ensures that we are both able to bring our areas of expertise to the relationship and that we both feel like equals. Which brings us to the next component. . . .

Parity. Parity means equality. There is nothing worse than feeling like your time is wasted, that a colleague doesn't respect your expertise, and that kids are struggling when you could be helping them. Yet this is exactly what happens when two teachers are put in the same classroom and one acts as a superior to the other. We want to see equality between teachers, an understanding that neither teacher has more power than the other. In the classroom, that means that while you may know the math content better than I do, you also respect that I know more differentiation strategies than you do that will help us more effectively *teach* that math content.

Sharing the kids. In addition to sharing responsibilities, we should also be willing to share the students. In an effective co-taught classroom, we would see two people who believe that all of the students in the classroom are their responsibility jointly—not "my kids" and "your kids." The special educator would never announce that he was going to take "his kids" to "his room" to read the test to them, just as the general educator would never tell a student who had her hand raised, "Sorry, I can't help you. You'll have to wait until Ms. V is free."

Ongoing collaboration and frequent communication. Co-teachers recognize that a good classroom partnership isn't easy. Neither is "raising" kids. When we hear partners talking in the halls about their shared successes or jointly brainstorming solutions to some of their shared difficulties, we know that these are two adults who are truly committed to improving student learning. If you and your partner are having difficulties with each other or a student, remember—use your words. Talk it out. If you two are really struggling with an issue, feel free to bring in outside help. Often a colleague can act as a nonbiased "counselor" or another brain to help figure out strategies for improving student learning and attention. The best part of collaboration is . . . you are not alone in this!

The power of sharing. How is the co-taught classroom different than the solo-taught one? It should be evident by taking a peek into the class itself. In an effective partnership, we would see two individuals who are more dynamic together than either could be alone; two people who are not afraid to try new strategies, who respect student learning differences, who get students in small learning groups as well as teach using whole-group instruction, and who recognize that universally designed and differentiated instruction (DI) is the goal for all inclusive classrooms. Above all, we would see students who are succeeding, who are mastering content, and who have been truly included into the social and academic fabric of the classroom because of the collaborative efforts of their co-teachers. Does this sound daunting? It shouldn't. It's the expectation of all classrooms; the beauty of co-teaching, though, is that you have a partner to help you manage it all.

No doubt many of you have seen—or even experienced personally–what co-teaching should *not* be. It shouldn't be a class where one teacher is king while the other feels like he has to ask permission to use materials or go to the bathroom. We shouldn't hear teachers complaining that their time is being wasted or that they can't "really help" students this way. Above all, we shouldn't have students who are failing, who are embarrassed by their failures, who aren't motivated, or who are falling between the cracks because their teachers aren't doing a good job of working together. Remember when we talked about Essential Questions? Well, our EQ for co-teaching is this: ***What is it that these two teachers are doing together that is substantively different and better for students than what one teacher would do alone?***

We subscribe to the analogy of co-teaching as a marriage (Murawski, 2009). Think about it: we have two people who will work together on a daily basis, sharing the decision making and responsibility for the education, social skills instruction, discipline, and self-esteem building of children. Sounds like a lot of marriages to us! And just like a marriage, we also believe that any time two individuals are going to share this type of responsibility, they need time to get to know one another, to share beliefs, to problem solve, and to communicate their own needs. Marriage takes work, and so does co-teaching. The result, however, can be well worth the effort.

So what does this thing called co-teaching look like in the classroom exactly? For co-teaching to occur, both teachers need to be sharing the instructional workload throughout the co-teaching process. There are several ways to do this, generally referred to as the co-teaching "models" or "approaches."

CO-INSTRUCTION AND STUDENT LEARNING: HOW DO WE AVOID STEPPING ON EACH OTHER'S TOES?

Friend and Cook (2009) identified five models for co-instruction that teachers can use when co-teaching. (They have since identified a sixth approach, "One Teach–One Observe," but we believe it is best subsumed within the original five so we have opted not to include it here.) Descriptions of each of these five approaches are in this chapter's *In a Nutshell* (see page 97). These approaches are a great way for new co-teachers to start talking about how they would like to work together in the classroom. They are certainly not the only approaches available; other options are described in some of the articles listed at the end of this chapter's materials (in the *Diving Deeper* section on the web). What we want to emphasize here is that teachers need to proactively communicate and plan how they would like to work together in the shared classroom and that their approach to instruction *needs to change regularly* to take full advantage of having two teachers in the classroom. Sure, some material lends itself to whole-class instruction, but based on the research, we would argue that too many teachers rely on that approach exclusively (Murawski, Boyer, Melchiorre, & Atwill, 2009; Weiss & Brigham, 2000; Weiss & Lloyd, 2002); conversely, the research supports the use of cooperative learning groups, small-group instruction, flexible grouping, and differentiation for improved student learning, especially for students with special needs.

Seem complicated? It's not. First, look at the approaches themselves. Remember, these are the basic models—we call them the "Volkswagens" of co-teaching. You'll be able to adapt them and make them your own as you become more comfortable with your partner. Do you want to have a better idea of what a lesson would actually look like? Check out how two teachers might work together using a variety of these co-teaching approaches to improve student learning (see *In Practice* on page 99). We have also included in Appendix VI (available online at http://www.corwin.com/diverseschools) a few example lessons that demonstrate the use of the various approaches. Check them out. As you will see, these models can be used

In a Nutshell

Commonly Used Co-Teaching Approaches to Instruction

Co-teaching Approach	Class Setup	Quick Definition
One Teach, One Support (OT/OS)	Whole Class	One of you is in front of the class leading instruction. The other is providing substantive support (e.g., collection or dissemination of papers, setting up labs, classroom management). Both are actively engaged.
Team Teaching	Whole Class	Both of you are in front of the class, working together to provide instruction. This may take the form of debates, modeling information or note-taking, compare/contrast, or role-playing.
Parallel Teaching	Regrouping	Both of you take half of the class in order to reduce student–teacher ratio. Instruction can occur in the same or a different setting. Groups may be doing the same content in the same way, same content in a different way, or different content.
Station Teaching	Regrouping	Students are divided into three or more small, heterogeneous groups to go to stations or centers. Students rotate through multiple centers. Teachers can facilitate individual stations or circulate among all stations.
Alternative Teaching	Regrouping	One teacher works with a large group of students, while the other works with a smaller group providing reteaching, preteaching, or enrichment as needed. The large group is not receiving new instruction during this time so that the small group can rejoin when finished.

throughout the instructional time to add variety, intensity, and individualization to your teaching and to take full advantage of having two teachers in the classroom. The key things to ask yourselves and each other as you co-teach are these: "Is what we are doing making a positive difference for students?" "Could we do the same thing alone or is there a reason there are two of us here?" (Murawski & Dieker, 2004; Wilson, 2005). Go back to the Essential Question. If what you are doing is *not* substantively different and better, then you need to figure out how to make it so!

One Teach, One Support (OT/OS). In this model, one teacher is up front leading the instruction while the other is supporting that instruction. This approach is the most commonly used approach in co-teaching, but that's not necessarily a good thing. Many teachers feel comfortable with this approach because one teacher takes the lead in providing direct instruction in front of the class while the other merely provides whatever support is needed. This may involve taking roll, disseminating/collecting papers, using proximity control for behavior management, observing and collecting informal assessment data, helping individual students, and the like. Sound familiar? Of course it does. It's not that much different from a typical classroom, is it? That's exactly why we want to caution you about this approach—it's *too* much like the typical classroom. While this may very well fit within your comfort zone, it's not going to result in extraordinary instruction for those students who don't do well in typical, whole group–style instruction. Use this approach occasionally, but don't let yourself get too comfortable with it. Remember that merely taking turns leading the class is not likely to result in improved student learning. While this is a useful model to use once in a while, and a good way to "get your foot in the door," good co-teaching needs to go much further than this.

Team Teaching. In this approach, both teachers are in front of the students, demonstrating that they respect one another and can "share the stage." However, the kids are still in the same whole-group format. Therefore, though students may benefit from the fact that teachers are now able to model information, demonstrate different ways of accomplishing the same task, debate one another, or role-play to gain interest, the students are still stuck in their traditional rows or classroom configurations and are not working with their peers. The student-teacher ratio is not improved or reduced in any way. Thus, co-teachers should use this approach judiciously as well.

Parallel Teaching. This is the first of the three regrouping approaches. By regrouping, we mean that this is a time when the students are actually working in small learning groups, as opposed to seated in their individual desks, awaiting whole-class instruction. In parallel teaching, teachers divide the class into two heterogeneous groups (not necessarily randomly; we all know there are times we simply do not want two particular kids in the same group). The teachers can choose to teach (a) the *same content in the same way* in order to reduce the student–teacher ratio (for example, reading a book to elementary students or discussing a novel's themes with secondary students), (b) the *same content in a different way* in order to address different learning profiles (for example, while one group of students looks at a flat map to learn about the path of migrating animals, another group looks at a globe), or (c) *different content* (for example, one group stays in the classroom to learn how to organize a research paper using a graphic organizer, while another group goes into the computer lab to learn how to utilize a search engine). This approach creates smaller groups that allow you to better focus your instruction, individualize lessons, scaffold questions, and improve student learning. This approach can also be used for cooperative group activities, where each teacher supports half of the class.

Station Teaching. Also known as "centers" (especially in elementary classrooms), this approach encourages teachers to get students in even smaller groups for more focused instruction. Once in small groups, students rotate from station to station until they have completed tasks at all stations. The rotation is what differentiates stations from teachers merely having cooperative learning groups in their class. Kids working together is wonderful, but just putting them in a group is not considered station teaching. Co-teachers can work at one discrete station or they can circulate, facilitating multiple stations. When stations are used, content is "chunked" for better learning, kids are able to have built-in brain breaks, social interaction, and kinesthetic movement as they rotate, and teachers are able to individualize instruction for different learners.

Alternative Teaching. In this approach, there is typically one large group and one or more small groups. There are a variety of ways for teachers to use alternative teaching. For example, one teacher may be reviewing homework with the large group, while the other teacher takes a few advanced students to provide them with a more challenging problem to solve, using the same concepts as last night's homework but at a much more complex level. Or, as the large group works on beginning a writing project, both co-teachers work with small groups of students who need help getting started. Or, as one teacher works with the large group providing guided practice on a newly taught concept, the other teacher works individually with a student with a more significant disability, providing him with more appropriate modified instruction. It is important when using this approach that it doesn't become a de facto large group of general ed students and a small group of students with special needs (special ed/at risk/ELL/slow learners). That is not its intent. It is also important that new content is not provided to the large group when a small group is separated, otherwise teachers will find they have the same problems that the old pull-out situation created; kids will keep falling further and further behind.

With all of these approaches, you really need to make a concerted effort to work outside your comfort zone. Are you and your partner doing a great job with OT/OS and Team teaching? Congratulations. Now challenge yourselves to regroup students into different configurations.

As you can see from the *In Practice* box below, Shawntee and Brendon worked together to take full advantage of having two teachers in the classroom. When the co-teaching models are used effectively, everyone benefits. The students get opportunities for small-group and one-on-one interactions, the teachers are better able to individualize, and everyone gets more involved in the content with the chance to do hands-on activities and have increased movement in the classroom. Remember, the focus of our book is collaboration and its ability to improve student learning. Co-teaching is an excellent example of how this can play out. When you are both committed to making the most of your co-teaching, it's a win–win situation for everyone.

In Practice

Shawntee and Brendon are co-teaching ninth-grade science. They spent an hour and a half last week planning for all this week's classes. They both already knew what they needed to teach based on the school's pacing plan (Chapter 6: The Cell), so they started by determining the big picture (what do all kids need to know?), then they determined a general lesson plan (start together, break into groups, pull back together), and then they broke the lesson into parts so each could separately plan a different part of the lesson. They came together again to share

(Continued)

(Continued)

their plans and to determine what additional differentiation would be required for the students with special needs. The following is one of their lessons for the week:

1:00–1:05	OT/OS	S. collects homework while B. takes roll.
1:05–1:10	Team	S. & B. role-play the upcoming activity related to the cell so students will know what to do.
1:10–1:15	Parallel	S. takes one group and provides them with pictures of parts of the cell. B. takes other group and gives them descriptions of parts of cell.
1:15–1:25	Team	S. & B. circulate as students walk around, finding their matching partners.
1:25–1:45	Parallel	S. works with one half of the class at the microscopes, helping students identify parts of the cell. B. works with the other half of the class at their desks, helping students identify parts of the cell in a textbook/worksheet activity. (Tomorrow, students will be in the opposite groups.)
1:45–1:55	Altern.	S. reviews the homework assignment for the large group, giving them a model to work from and circulating to help those with quick questions. B. works in a small group with two students in the class with cognitive impairments, who have modified work related to identifying parts of the cell. All students are dismissed at 1:55.

CO-TEACHING PARTNERSHIPS: WHO ARE OUR POSSIBLE PARTNERS AND HOW MIGHT PARTNERSHIPS VARY?

Hopefully we've convinced you that co-teaching is something you want to try, and your administrators, teachers, and all your stakeholders are on board to let you give it a shot. The next question is, with whom can you co-teach? Well, the answer is simpler than you might think: pretty much any two equal partners who are willing and able. Notice that we say "equal partners." This can be two special educators, two general educators, a general and a special educator, or even a teacher and a specialist (speech or math or English language learners). Any time two professionals come together, bringing various areas of expertise, they are able to co-plan, co-instruct, and co-assess for the benefit of the students. That's co-teaching! It's important to keep in mind, though, that while there are many student teachers, paraprofessionals, interns, and adult volunteers who may be very adept at helping teach in the classroom, these individuals do not typically have the same "power" in the classroom and thus, there is a lack of parity between adults. In addition, these individuals may not have the same training as a certified teacher or related service professional and likely will not share the planning and assessing of a group of students. So when you're talking about volunteers, paraprofessionals, or teaching assistants, while you should be able to collaborate beautifully, you will not be truly sharing the responsibility as you would in co-teaching.

How, then, do you get to the idyllic marriage you want? Believe it or not, the research tells us that one of the best strategies is to volunteer to work together (Murawski et al., 2009).

Want more info?

(?)

Though teachers don't co-teach with paraprofessionals, they do indeed collaborate with them. Check out Mary Beth Doyle's book, *The Paraprofessional's Guide to the Inclusive Classroom: Working As a Team* (2008), for useful tips and strategies.

While this may not have been your first choice, take a minute to think about it. When you volunteer, you are more able to have a voice in what you co-teach and with whom you will collaborate. It's like choosing a partner instead of being placed into an arranged marriage. Rather than waiting to see if this will happen to you, go to your colleagues in special or general education and talk about the possibility of collaborating in a co-teaching scenario. Identify people who would be willing to be your work wife or husband, and then go talk to an administrator about the possible benefits to the students you would share. Two people with different frames of reference and different areas of expertise volunteering to work collaboratively to address the varied needs of all kids in the shared classroom—who could argue with that?

GETTING STARTED: WHAT DO WE DO AFTER THE HONEYMOON?

You've chosen a partner, and you're ready to begin. How do you set up your schedule? Do you need to co-teach all day long? No. Often schedules will not permit such a luxury. Instead, many special and general education co-teaching teams will only co-teach a group of students for one subject or period each day. It is even possible for individuals to co-teach one lesson (e.g., the special educator and school nurse teach one lesson about health issues to a group of at-risk students), a unit (e.g., two fourth-grade teachers join classes to teach a unit on space, culminating in a field trip to an observatory), or part of a class (e.g., the special educator joins a block-scheduled secondary English class for the second half of the period once a week). That said, while these are all possible options and excellent "baby steps" to ongoing co-teaching, the goal of co-teaching is for improved student learning; for that, two professionals need to share the group of students in a more consistent manner. Both teachers need to be able to adequately plan for those students' academic, behavioral, and social needs. Remember, there is something to be said for starting slowly. It could be that "baby steps" are more appropriate to the situation than jumping right in to full-blown co-teaching.

To co-teach most effectively requires both of you to really know your shared kids; it is hard to do that if you are only teaching one lesson or unit together. In addition, if you are only sharing part of their instruction, it is very likely that the students will see one of you as the "real teacher" and the other as the "glorified aide." Consistency is key. Choose a time every day or, at minimum, every week when you can reliably teach co-planned lessons using the models of co-teaching described earlier, and you will be on your way to a first-rate partnership like the happy newlyweds you are.

In Practice

Belize is a special ed teacher in a K–12 school. When she first started co-teaching, she didn't realize how important consistency was. She was frequently pulled out of her co-taught classes for IEPs, parent meetings, discussions with other teachers, and even to substitute classes. It really hurt the relationship she had with her co-teachers and even more with the kids. When she finally was able to work collaboratively with her administrators to create a schedule that let her co-teach consistently, she realized the impact it had on her ability to improve student learning. Because she was there every day, she knew what was needed and she was able to deliver. As she states, "Without a doubt, all the kids did better when my co-teachers and I were both there consistently to help them out."

THE BENEFITS OF CO-TEACHING:
WHY IS THIS MARRIAGE SO IMPORTANT?

We know, we know. Sharing the planning, instructing, and assessing sounds way simpler than it is. Any time we are talking about two or more people trying to collaborate, we have a variety of issues, as we've discussed in previous chapters. Now we are asking you to up the ante by collaborating daily, on an ongoing basis, and in the same classroom. Why in the world would we do that? Simple. Students benefit. Adults do too, by the way, but our primary focus is on the kids. Also, let's face it—dating may sound like more fun, but in the educational arena, it really results in some teachers who are running around, trying to work with too many people, and ultimately feeling like chickens with their heads cut off. Not a pleasant sight.

So, what kinds of benefits do students and adults receive through this type of intense collaboration? We have provided a quick synopsis of some of the major benefits for you in our *Eye on the Research.* Simply put, when two teachers work collaboratively in the same classroom, kids with and without special needs are able to improve in their academics, behavior, self-esteem, and social skills. While these are critical, we thought it would be silly not to mention some of the practical benefits as well. Let's face it: sometimes it's the practical benefits that make the rest fall into place (e.g., bathroom breaks = happy teachers ⇒ happy teachers = more likely to differentiate instruction to meet individual student needs!).

Speaking practically, we also recognize that there are some serious issues related to co-teaching. Some of the major issues you may have already identified for yourself have been recognized in the research as well. These include personality conflicts, loss of control, scheduling and staffing, planning, administrative support, content knowledge, collaborative skills, and naturally, time (Scruggs, Mastropieri, & McDuffie, 2007). These have also been addressed in the *Eye on the Research* on page 103 and continued on the web at http://www .corwin.com/diverseschools. Notice that we encapsulated the aforementioned issues into four major categories: personalities, logistics, training, and time. These are described in the next section on potential pitfalls. Not co-teaching yet? Pay attention, then, so you can either make sure these issues don't happen at your school *or* so you can recognize the issues when they do come up and you can try to address them right away before they grow.

FACING THE POSSIBLE PITFALLS:
WHAT AM I GETTING MYSELF INTO?

We could write a whole book on co-teaching—in fact, Wendy wrote two! But even if you follow every brilliant tip, what it all boils down to is the fact that the two people in the classroom need to be willing to work cooperatively together. They need to recognize that their collaboration is about benefiting students, and they need to be able to put aside differences and work through issues. Most of us (ourselves included) have great ideas for how to teach. To give up that control to another person is very hard to do. To give it up to someone who we think may not know our content, grade-level curriculum, organizational methods, or students as well as we do is even more difficult. We recognize this, and we appreciate the struggle. But take a look back at the research—the outcomes are worth it. Good co-teaching can be one of the most effective ways to present and individualize content to meet the needs of the whole range of students in your classroom, from gifted kids to typical kids to English learners to students with disabilities to . . . well, all your kids!

Eye on the Research

Research-Identified
Benefits of Co-Teaching

Benefits of Co-Teaching	What has the research found?
Academic	• Students in co-taught settings may benefit from improved academic performance, increased emphasis on cognitive strategies and study skills, increased emphasis on social skills, and improved classroom communities (Murawski, 2006; Walther-Thomas, 1997; Weichel, 2001). • Teachers in a co-taught setting are more likely to use differentiated instructional groupings, hands-on activities, flexible and varied assessments, and other strategies, which result in the provision of individualized instruction (Adams & Cessna, 1993; Cross & Walker-Knight, 1997; Giangreco, Baumgart, & Doyle, 1995; Murawski, 2006; Murawski & Dieker, 2004; Walsh & Snyder, 1993).
Behavioral	• Research studies on co-teaching have found that the value added by having a special education teacher in the room to co-teach resulted in more individual attention for students, more on-task student behavior, and more interaction with teachers (Boudah, Schumaker, & Deshler, 1997; Murawski, 2006; Zigmond, Magiera, & Matta, 2003).
Social	• Students in a co-taught setting reported improved social skills and self-concept and stronger peer relations through the reduction of pull-out situations (Bahamonde & Friend, 1999; Jones & Carlier, 1995; Salend & Johansen, 1997; Walther-Thomas, 1997).
Practical	• Teachers who co-taught successfully found that they were more energized and creative, were able to trust one another, used humor more often, and had more fun teaching (Adams & Cessna, 1993; Gately & Gately, 2001; Murawski, 2003).

For more research in this area go to http://www.corwin.com/diverseschools.

The pitfalls of co-teaching can be compounded if we are expected to co-teach with someone who isn't someone we really want to work with, due to conflicting personalities, teaching abilities, student connections, or just because, well, we just don't want to. The main way to resolve this issue is to make sure that teachers have a voice in choosing the individual with whom they will co-teach. Teachers and administrators should work together to identify potential partnerships and then preface any co-teaching situations with training on the importance of parity, respect, and shared responsibility. That's critical to the success of the partnership, and it needs to be done early—scheduling and training of co-teachers is best done before the beginning of the school year or semester, so that the needs of individual students may be considered in class placement decisions and so that teachers have a chance to get to know one another.

Another critical area for training is on the actual techniques of differentiation and co-instruction. Two well-meaning teachers may like one another, work well together, and even want to help students, but without instruction in specific methodology, they won't maximize their co-teaching potential. We have both heard many teachers say, "I've been teaching for 10 years, sometimes even with a partner, and I never knew these strategies existed. We could have done so much more for the kids!"

Principal Points

There is a critical point here for administrators, so we want to emphasize it again. Research has repeatedly shown that co-teaching is most successful when teachers volunteer and when they get to choose their partners! What does this mean for administrators? At first, when a co-teaching program is just getting started, teachers should be recruited voluntarily to work together, have a voice in choosing their co-teachers, and have extra incentives (such as an extra planning period, more aide time, or first choice of classrooms) to help them with the extra work and stress that inevitably happens in a new partnership. In situations where there are few special educators and little choice in partnerships, build in other opportunities for volunteering. These may include letting them select partners within a department or grade level, letting them select when to co-teach in the day (morning or afternoon), or letting them select ways to get planning time (common planning period, stipend for afterschool planning, sub once a month, etc.).

All too often teachers are thrown into co-teaching situations with no training or understanding of what should be occurring, and the result is often two individuals who continue to work within their own spheres, or frames of reference. Both generally do what they have always done, but as they are often unsure of each other's roles in this new relationship, the result can be less than desirable. Some special educators don't feel they have a role in the classroom, so they come late, leave early, and wait to be asked to do something; conversely, general educators may not know what special educators bring to the situation so they continue to teach as usual, leaving the students with disabilities to the purview of the special educator. This reoccurring pattern (aka "same ol,' same ol'") continues as each teacher feels unhappy with the status quo, but doesn't know what to do to change it. Sound familiar?

Finally, we must also address the issue of *time*. There is no question that, in order to truly impact student learning, teachers must spend time thinking, talking, planning, and implementing strategies together. Coming up with the various methods of differentiation will not come naturally to many teachers and they will need to research, collaborate, and experiment. This all takes time. Teachers already feel inundated with the demands of their classrooms; to have to share ideas with another overburdened teacher on a daily basis may seem impossible. But, ask yourself, how else will change occur? Despite the very real constraints on our time, we always manage to find the time to do the things that are genuinely important to us. So, ultimately, we need to make sure that this type of paradigm shift is seen as important—first by ourselves, then by other teachers, by parents, by administrators, and by all our other

FRAME OF REFERENCE

The general ed teacher may be thinking she's solely responsible for planning and instruction, while the special ed teacher may be thinking he's solely in charge of all the kids with special needs. These different frames of reference can lead to a lack of shared roles and responsibility, and they ultimately can lead to a lack of true co-teaching.

stakeholders. If we value our co-teaching, we will be able to use our time more effectively. If we don't, the demands for collaboration, above and beyond our other daily responsibilities, may overwhelm us. It's as simple as that.

But take heart! Dieker (2001) found that *veteran* co-teachers only needed 10 minutes to effectively co-plan for a week's worth of instruction. Although it will no doubt take more time in the beginning, if you can make it through that first difficult year, you will find out that co-teaching can actually save you time in the long run. And remember, it can be fun *and* good for kids! How cool is that?

TAKING CO-TEACHING OUT OF THE ABSTRACT

Before co-teaching begins

- Start a "Co-Teaching Focus Group" to learn more about co-teaching best practices before trying to put it into place. Do a book study on co-teaching. (Can we subtly recommend Wendy's books? Purely unbiased recommendations, of course!) Have group members become experts on certain aspects of co-teaching. Be sure that your focus group includes representatives who are general and special education teachers, administrators, parents, other specialists, district or board members, and even students if possible.

- Limit the number of students with disabilities in your co-taught classes to less than 30% (20% is preferable). The majority of those will be students with high-incidence disabilities such as LD, but any given class might also include one or two students with more significant challenges such as severe autism, Down syndrome, or a significant cognitive disability. Be careful: classes that end up with all the kids with learning issues aren't inclusive! We call that *tracking,* ladies and gentlemen, and around here that's a dirty word.

- Keep your co-teaching sacred. Create a schedule of your co-taught classes and give it to all administrators and teachers. At the top write, "Co-teaching time is sacred. Please do not disturb!" Identify on the schedule times that you *are* available for consultations, IEP meetings, and so forth.

Once co-teaching begins

- Create verbal and nonverbal cues to communicate with one another. Signals for we're behind (tap on the wrist?), need to talk (tap head?), it's too noisy (pull on ear?), explain more (circle finger in the air?), and others can make the day go much more efficiently and won't interrupt instruction. Also, the kids will see that you two are always communicating, so they'll be less likely to play "parents" against one another.

- Consider the use of two-minute "brain breaks" to check in with your co-teacher. Brain breaks are important for students as well (the research tells us that kids can pay attention for about one minute per year of age when they are not internally motivated). So, if you need a moment to check content with your partner or to prep some materials, tell the students that they have a two-minute brain break to talk, process, or discuss the content just learned.

- Ask to have your classrooms moved closer together. If one teacher has to walk for 15 minutes to co-teach with the other teacher, that is going to reduce your time to do other things such as plan and debrief. Don't forget to use other options for quick communication, like instant messaging, texting, online chatting, and the like. These can't replace face-to-face planning, but they are a great augmentation.

- Put both teachers' names on all papers and communications home and on the door to the classroom or the white board. That communicates the importance of your co-teaching and your parity to the kids, the families, and the school personnel.

On the web

For more co-teaching strategies go to http://www.corwin.com/diverseschools.

THUMBNAILS OF RESOURCES ON THE INTERNET

The following elements can be found on the companion website for *Collaborate, Communicate, and Differentiate!* at http://www.corwin.com/diverseschools.

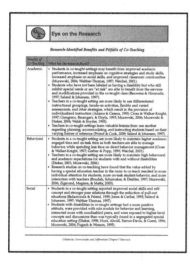

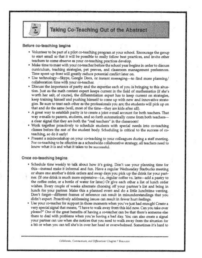

8

Collaboratively Planning and Assessing

Voices From the Field

"I keep hearing how important proactive planning is, but when exactly is that supposed to happen? I simply don't have time to meet regularly with other teachers."

Fatimah J., ELL educator

"I'm fine with sharing instruction in the classroom. But my partner and I had serious problems when we talked about assessing and grading. We simply didn't have the same opinions on how to grade."

Brian K., 10th-grade English teacher

THE BIG PICTURE

You've read over and over again how critical it is to be proactive, to collaborate with others, to plan in advance how to meet the needs of students. You are totally on board theoretically and then you step out of the clouds and into the real world and think, "When?" and "How?" You visualize the other adults at your school and imagine talking to them about various ways to assess and grade. You blanch at the thought. No worries, friend. (May we call you "friend"?) This chapter concentrates on exactly those issues.

In this chapter we do the following:

- Describe the role of collaborative planning and ways to do it more efficiently.
- Share the "What, How, Who" approach to quick and dirty collaborative planning.
- Share tips on how to discuss assessment and grading issues, especially when they become tricky.
- Discuss ways to differentiate for assessment and grading with students with special needs.

Read on!

COLLABORATIVE PLANNING: HOW CAN WE DO THIS MORE EFFICIENTLY?

As Fatimah in our *Voices From the Field* aptly noted, collaborative and proactive planning is critical to effective differentiated and universally designed instruction, and yet time to actually plan with a colleague seems to be nonexistent. Experts on co-teaching have noted time and time again that without co-planning, teachers tend to continue to teach as usual, with no real differentiation strategies and just a One Teach/One Support approach (Murawski, 2010; Weiss & Brigham, 2000; Weiss & Lloyd, 2002). A key benefit of inclusive education is that when special service providers and classroom teachers collaborate, there is a ton of shared expertise. General educators often have the knowledge of standards, curriculum, and content. Combine that with the Title I teachers' knowledge of research-based reading strategies, or the special educators' knowledge of differentiation strategies, accommodations, and disability information, or the English language specialists' knowledge of SDAIE (specially designed academic instruction in English) strategies, and we're golden! Truly, the result can be impressive.

> **Key Term**
>
> *Co-Planning*—Including multiple frames of reference and expertise in the planning process; making sure lessons are no longer "the way we've always done it."

However, without time for sharing this expertise, teachers resort to what they do naturally—teaching a class the way they have been taught to teach it alone. (And we already know that doesn't work for many of our kids.) If nothing different is done in the classroom, we can't expect any different outcomes, either. Kinda stands to reason.

Clearly, all of the research and all of our own experience is telling us that time is critical to effective co-planning (and thus to effective co-teaching, too). So, what can we do to find and use time more efficiently? Here are some suggestions.

Establish a regular time to plan collaboratively. Teachers never have enough time to do everything they need to do, and this includes planning for instruction. Having to meet with another teacher and figuring out a schedule to do this is complicated. For this reason, it is important that if you are supposed to collaborate or co-plan with someone, you two find a time that works for both of you and then hold that time sacrosanct. This may end up being once a week during lunch, or twice a week before school, or three times a month during a common planning period. Depending on the level of collaboration needed, it may be more or less. For example, co-teachers may need to meet a few times a week, whereas teachers who are merely consulting regarding a shared student may only need to meet once every two weeks. The most important tip here is that this planning time should be held regularly; if you are trying to dig up time each week and fit it into an already tight schedule, it will never happen. On the other hand, if a meeting is scheduled as a regular occurrence and considered as important as a department or grade-level meeting, you can respond to requests for other meetings by saying, "Oh, I'm sorry. I already have an appointment on Wednesdays after school from 3 to 3:30. What other time can we meet?"

Select an appropriate environment without distractions. Classrooms are the typical place for teachers to meet and plan, but they aren't always the most efficient spot. Why? Because classrooms come with telephones that never stop ringing, ungraded papers that taunt you from the desk, and students who stop by with incessant questions. (Darn those students! Wouldn't our jobs be a lot easier without them?!? Joke intended, of course.) If you are going to use a classroom for planning, be sure to shut the door with a sign saying "Unavailable," turn off the phone, and sit together so you are not facing any other distracting elements. If not the classroom, where else might you meet? The school library, an open conference room, a testing office, the lunchroom or auditorium, or the unused classroom of another teacher are all possibilities. In addition, for meetings before or after school or on weekends, coffee shops, restaurants, local libraries, parks, and each other's houses are all possibilities. We even know one co-teaching team who met on a boat! Those teachers were seriously thinking outside the box . . . and having fun while doing it. Again, though, be aware of outside distractions such as noise, traffic, seagulls, and interruptions.

Have an agenda. And snacks. At the beginning of every planning session, do a quick recon to determine what needs to be accomplished in this session. For example, "We need to talk about Annette's lack of homework, Julian's behavior, and the major research project coming up that many kids may struggle with." Having a quick checklist related to what needs to be accomplished helps the "Type A" collaborators feel better that there is a plan, and it helps both teachers be on the same page in terms of discussion and time. It also helps reduce digressions. Keep a piece of paper handy to write down any additional related, but not critical, issues that come up that you want to discuss at the end of your planning session. That way, if time runs out, you know what is left to be discussed at a later time—either in person, by e-mail, or on a phone conference. Speaking of time, it is equally important to make sure your agenda identifies how long you have for this planning session. If someone needs to leave in half an hour, you want to note that right away so time isn't wasted. Whatever time you scheduled for this planning session, try to keep it to the time you planned. If you keep finding yourselves running out of time, analyze your sessions to see if you have been chatting a lot or wasting time in other ways (getting materials you forgot, answering phones, both working on material that could have been divided). Too often, planning sessions become gripe sessions or share sessions. Thirty minutes have passed and participants have only discussed their spouse's mishaps, their own children's recent accomplishments, and their frustrations with a new administrative mandate. If you keep to your allotted time, you may find yourselves using time more efficiently and keeping to your agenda better. By the way, the snacks suggestion isn't really research based. It's just that your authors simply enjoy planning more (and are typically more agreeable) when we have a Diet Coke and a snack in front of us. Depending on when, where, and how long you are planning together, you may consider making sure there is a refrigerator or vending machine available or just take turns bringing snacks to the planning meetings. We consider chocolate mandatory, but you can make your own decisions. . . .

Determine regular roles and responsibilities. As we have clearly established, time is at a premium. Adults know their own strengths and preferences, just as they know the areas in which they are not as strong. Save time by discussing these educational and personal characteristics in the beginning of your collaborative relationship (Murawski & Dieker, 2004). There are certain tasks that happen frequently that you and your partners can identify as your own "roles," thereby saving time as you won't have to discuss them each time you meet to plan. Once tasks are determined, they can be divided and attacked separately. For example, if you are co-teaching, one of you may always be responsible for coming up with warm-ups and journal topics, while the other will be responsible for making copies of handouts and updating the agenda and homework boards. On the other hand, if you are meeting with a team to discuss a student's progress, one team member can always be responsible for bringing copies of grades, one can be responsible for bringing any disciplinary information, one can be in charge of contacting the parent prior to each meeting for home updates, and one can bring the snacks. (Yeah, we know. We're into snacks. Sue us.) The more regular responsibilities and roles collaborators can identify and delegate early on, the fewer things to worry about at each planning session.

In Practice

Ms. Stark looked around the room at the other seven members of the Professional Learning Community (PLC). They were all bickering, disagreeing, and raising their voices at one another. "This is professional?" Ms. Stark thought to herself. She raised her hand and waited. After a moment, one of her colleagues noticed her and stopped talking; the others slowly followed suit.

ॐ

When it was quiet, Ms. Stark calmly said, "This seems unproductive to me. I would like to suggest that we each take particular roles when we come to these meetings so that we don't keep wasting time like this. Barb, you seem to be most concerned about students' behavioral infractions. How about coming to each meeting with a list of three to five students you'd like to discuss? Alfred, you seem to typically want to discuss how new administrative or union issues will impact us. Could you take the lead on bringing those to each meeting for a quick discussion or update? Is anyone else interested in making an agenda for each meeting or should I do that part?"

Document your planning and save it for future reference. Teachers are always planning. They pick up paper rulers when shopping at Ikea to use in a math activity at school; they go on a date and think about how to tie the movie's plot into the theme they are teaching next week; they hang on to empty toilet paper rolls to use for a craft activity. The issue isn't that teachers don't plan; it is merely that we do not always plan formally, sitting at a desk, and we do not have a lot of time to plan collaboratively. A major problem with planning between teachers is that it often occurs "on the fly" (or as Beninghof [2003] aptly called it, "Bathroom Stall Planning"). This results in a lesson that either (a) is not well thought out, or (b) ends up being great but can't be duplicated the following year because teachers are not really sure what they did. Special educators often end up collaborating and co-teaching with various partners in the same year, and general educators may be expected to collaborate with a special education teacher, a Title I teacher, an ELL teacher, a math coach, and a speech-language pathologist. While this can be overwhelming, much time would be saved if that collaboration happened once and was saved for future reference, rather than having teachers recreate the wheel every year. When planning is done, be sure to keep a copy of the plan for future reference and improvement. If a team creates a plan that successfully includes Mitzi, a student with Asperger syndrome, in the fifth-grade science lesson, that same plan may be helpful when the team has a student with similar needs the next year, to other fifth-grade teachers who have students with similar needs, and to Mitzi's sixth-grade teachers when she matriculates to the middle school.

QUICK AND DIRTY CO-PLANNING: WHAT? HOW? WHO?

While not everyone who collaborates is also co-teaching, those who are trying to plan co-taught lessons together may benefit from using the What/How/Who approach (Murawski, in press). The What/How/Who approach is a way to quickly plan a lesson that is based on state standards, addresses grade-level content in accordance with pacing plans, and yet still provides a good use of both teachers and their areas of expertise in order to effectively meet the needs of a diverse group of learners. Woo-hoo! By the way, the use of a timer as teachers plan each stage of the lesson will help keep the lesson focused, efficient, and effective.

Here's how it works: The first question asked is "*WHAT* needs to be taught in this lesson?" The person who should be leading this conversation is typically the general education classroom teacher. This information should be easy-peasy for the general educator to share. Set the timer for five minutes. In five minutes, the general educator should be able to identify the following:

- What standard the lesson is addressing
- What objective the lesson will have
- What kind of time frame teachers have for instruction
- What the Big Ideas and Essential Questions are for this lesson (go back to Figure 5.1 to think about the Triangle of Knowledge.)

The next item discussed is "*HOW* will we teach this lesson in order to make sure it is universally accessible for all students?" Both co-teachers should equally take part in this conversation. Try to answer the "HOW" question in 7–15 minutes (depending on the complexity of the lesson, the level of content knowledge of both teachers, rapport between the teachers, and so forth). After teaching together awhile, this time requirement should decrease. During this part of the planning session, co-teachers should be able to identify the following:

- How comfortable do we both feel with the new content?
- What co-teaching approach (i.e., Team; One Teach, One Support; Alternative; Station; or Parallel) will be most effective for the *beginning* of the lesson? The beginning of the lesson may include a warm-up, modeling, review, or "hook" for the new lesson. Most of these do not require equal content knowledge for both teachers. Consider multiple ways of engaging students' interest and motivation. Drills and boring warm-ups are not considered a strong choice for the beginning of the lesson, despite their frequent use. Think about it—what a great way to disengage kids right from the start! Instead, think of more

creative anticipatory sets (or "hooks") to get them interested in finding out more about today's area of instruction. Embed the "drills" or required reviews into an already interesting lesson.

- What co-teaching approach will be most effective for the *middle* of the lesson? Remember, brain research suggests that kids can pay attention for about one minute per year of age, so regrouping approaches (e.g., Parallel, Station, Alternative) may be a good way to keep students' attention. Consider how you can use UDL to represent information in multiple formats and media (Rose & Meyer, 2002).
- What co-teaching approach will be most effective for the *end* of the lesson? Clever ending activities can check comprehension, provide formative assessments, and help solidify today's new content. Consider the multiple pathways for students' actions and expressions (Rose & Meyer, 2002). Don't rely solely on standardized or formal paper-and-pencil tests to see what they learned.
- Based on the co-teaching approaches selected, what will the special service provider be responsible for related to materials, planning, implementing, and assessing?
- Based on the co-teaching approaches selected, what will the general education teacher be responsible for related to materials, planning, implementing, and assessing?

Keep in mind that once you guys determine who is going to do what, you don't need to do all the specific planning and preparation together. For example, by using Parallel Teaching, one teacher can take the lead in planning and prepping a writing activity while the other teacher takes the lead in creating the comprehension activity. Students will be able to participate in both parts of the lesson, but you only have to prepare half as much. Bonus!

The third, and final, question asked is "**WHO** may need additional consideration in order to access this lesson?" The person who typically leads this conversation is the special education teacher or special service provider. Try to answer the "WHO" question in 5–10 minutes (though this will certainly vary based on the complexity of the needs of the learners in your class).

The special educator should be able to identify the following:

- Who might struggle behaviorally, socially, or academically with aspects of the lesson
- How UDL can be more effectively implemented to meet those needs
- What accommodations or modifications might also be necessary
- What additional types of differentiation strategies would make the lesson more interesting, motivating, or accessible for all learners
- What additional materials may be necessary to help with the lesson
- What other experts may need to be consulted in helping make the lesson accessible (e.g., speech-language pathologist, occupational therapist, parents, Braille teacher, football coach)

When teachers have worked together for a while and are more familiar with each other and the content, it is more likely they will need the lower end of the time range (i.e., 17 minutes).

Principal Points

A lack of time to co-plan is one of the most significant barriers to effective co-teaching (Murawski & Dieker, 2004). As administrator, your job is to help identify ways for co-teachers to co-plan. If possible, offer options:

- Common planning time during school day
- Substitute coverage once a month
- Stipends for afterschool planning
- Release from lunch duty or other extracurricular duties
- Planning software or co-planner
- Paid summer planning time
- Administrative coverage

Teachers who are co-teaching for the first time or who are new to the content may need the upper end (e.g., 30 minutes). Your authors can attest to that. We have co-taught tons of times, and where we once sat and co-planned for hours, we now can knock off a great lesson in less time than it takes to finish our snack. (Yes, we really do have snacks.) Having an agenda, structure, and time guide will help ensure a much more efficient planning session.

Just to get you started, we've included a blank form to help you with the What/How/Who approach, as well as a completed one as an example (see Appendix VII online at http://www.corwin.com/diverseschools). Compare all the various lesson plans we've provided for you in the appendices. You have examples of lessons planned for universal design, lessons planned for co-taught situations, and lessons that were planned quickly and dirtily. (Go with us on that one.) See how these all tie in together? The "quick and dirty" approach gets you going but also helps you address standards ("what"), universal design ("how" and "who"), co-teaching approaches ("how"), and differentiation ("who"). Isn't it great when it all makes sense?

> **Key Terms**
>
> *Assessment*—The gathering of information to make decisions, which includes observation, measurement, evaluation, and grading.
>
> *Grading*—The conversion of those evaluations into symbols to communicate with students, families, and educators (Bowe, 2005, p. 353).
>
> *Co-Assessing*—Sharing in the gathering of data and the data-based decision making regarding evaluation and grading.

ASSESSING AND GRADING COLLABORATIVELY: WHAT IF WE DON'T AGREE?

Okay, you've collaborated with colleagues to create amazing universally designed and differentiated lessons. Kids are actively engaged, motivated to learn, and demonstrating understanding daily. All is well . . . or is it? The standardized test comes along and—bam! It looks like all your hard work was for naught.

We've been there. We feel your pain. But we have finally gotten to a place where we can comfortably say to ourselves that there are always going to be paper-and-pencil (okay, Scantron-and-pencil) tests and kids who simply are not good test-takers. We can't let that stop us from trying to teach those students. When you hear students talk about why rivers were so important in starting early civilization, or see them solve multistep equations as part of a group game activity, or watch them write impassioned (and grammatically correct!) letters to the principal begging for Battle of the Bands to be allowed again, you know they have learned. You know you have been doing your job well. Yeah, that doesn't make it easier when the school's test scores come back, but nevertheless it's true.

Check out the *Key Terms* box where we provide the definitions of assessment and grading. Why are these important? Because you need to realize—and more important, take to heart—that they are not necessarily the same thing. Sure, you should have conducted assessments in order to determine your grades, but assessment is a pretty broad umbrella. That end-of-the-year high-stakes exam is just one little part of a comprehensive assessment. As Schmoker (2009) writes, "Schools and even whole states could make steady gains on standardized tests without offering students intellectually challenging tasks" (p. 71). Yes, it is a big deal for the school when test scores rise, and yes, parents will use those results to see if their children are learning and if you are able to teach them. But the schools that are able to point out students' successes in Odyssey of the Mind, local science and art fairs, published writing pieces, debates, and other concrete activities will be able to demonstrate in real-world accomplishments what their students are learning. When parents hear their child read for the first time, or see their kid get a job due to a strong oral interview and good work habits, or hang an award-winning picture their youngster created, or read an article their offspring wrote for the school newspaper, they have proof positive that their child is learning. What we need to do as collaborative educators is recognize the importance of *differentiated* assessments; how can we truly get at what kids are learning in a variety of ways?

FRAME OF REFERENCE

Parents and teachers may have very different frames of reference regarding grading. For example, Claudia Baldwin had significant fine motor difficulties resulting in dysgraphia. Writing with a pen or pencil was physically painful for Claudia, and her mother was advocating for various accommodations. After much discussion and many meetings, it was determined that Claudia would be on a 504 plan so that she could have reasonable accommodations related to writing.

Despite all of this, the general education English teacher balked at the request to let Claudia use a keyboard to type her writing assessments, stating, "Well, I can't wait to go back to the classroom to tell the rest of the students that Claudia gets to type and they don't. This is really not fair to the other students."

From Mrs. Baldwin's perspective, her daughter wasn't being allowed to show what she could do. From the teacher's perspective, Claudia was getting an unfair advantage. In order to work together as a team to help Claudia, they will have to work through these issues and come to an agreement about how to allow Claudia to show her learning.

This, however, is where conflict may arise. Many educators have very strong feelings about the use of formal tests or standardized measures. A high school math teacher may argue with a special education teacher that it doesn't matter that the student can solve a problem with a calculator; the state test doesn't allow a calculator, so it's simply not right/fair/okay for that child to be allowed to use a calculator in class. A school psychologist may argue with a parent that her findings on the formal academic tests indicate a disability, while the parent insists her son didn't even try so the results are invalid. A school board votes to implement merit pay for teachers based on test results, while those teachers with the largest numbers of English language learners and students with disabilities argue that they are then put at a disadvantage. All of these are issues of standardized versus nonstandardized assessments. So, what can we do about all this?

First of all, these issues need to be made transparent. Don't ignore them or just keep venting about them in the teachers' lounge. Address them proactively. Review Chapter 4 on communication skills and then read on to Chapter 9 regarding how to deal with conflict. Educators need to have conversations, sometimes many, many, many conversations, about their beliefs related to assessments. These conversations need to occur with one another, with parents, with administrators, with district personnel, and with the community at large. We need to do a better job at highlighting the various ways students demonstrate competency, not just the final scores on standardized tests.

Grades themselves are a sticky issue. To fail a student who has shown tremendous effort in class seems unfair, while passing a student who has not mastered the standards also seems inappropriate (Guskey & Jung, 2009). Add to that the requirement that IEPs are supposed to ensure that students with disabilities are able to pass classes and advance from grade to grade (a requirement of *Board of Education v. Rowley, 1982*), and there is a volatile issue at hand. Communication is important here, folks; we need to talk about these issues before they become a problem!

We believe that resistance to differentiated assessments or adapted grading is natural; people's beliefs about "what is fair" differ. This can be particularly problematic for students with *invisible disabilities.* "Teachers may be particularly reticent to make individualized adaptations for students with learning disabilities whose differences are not obvious and who are not likely to require an alternative curriculum" (Munk & Bursuck, 2004, p. 6). Given that learning disabilities account for the majority of identified disabilities, this is a pretty major issue. You can battle resistance to grading accommodations with concrete artifacts that prove student learning; these artifacts can illustrate how allowing for various assessment options increases the ways in which students can demonstrate their understanding, even for those students with invisible disabilities.

> **Want more info?**
>
> Check out Rick Wormeli's (2006) book called *Fair Isn't Always Equal: Assessing and Grading in the Differentiated Classroom.*

One veteran math teacher we know argued strongly that students who received any accommodations in her class should not be allowed to receive the same high school diploma that the other students received; in her words, "it wasn't fair to the others." After much debate with a special education colleague, she agreed to allow one student to present his solutions to math problems in an alternative format. She watched this student with a severe learning disability do his assignments by using a calculator and simply writing the answers without writing the problems out (a *must* for other students); afterward, she quizzed him about his problem-solving process and his results (all of which were accurate). She was impressed. Now, that same teacher is a staunch advocate for accommodations when needed. Again, in her words, "I finally see that those changes didn't water down his work. They merely changed the way in which he was showing me what he knew." Discussions often are not as powerful as examples; make obvious to others the ways in which differentiated assessments have improved student learning and the demonstration of that learning. We are all here to help students—even when we have different frames of reference regarding what that help looks like.

DIFFERENTIATING ASSESSMENT AND GRADING: WHAT ARE SOME OF OUR OPTIONS?

Understandably, some teachers and administrators may worry about the legalities of making certain adaptations when it comes to assessment and grading. IDEIA allows

In a Nutshell

Options for Differentiated Assessment/Grading

Type of Assessment	Description	Pros & Cons
Use process vs. product grading	The student receives one grade for the amount of effort put into an assignment and another grade for the actual product. The grades are then combined and the average is the grade for the assignment.	*Pros*—good for when you can observe a student's process; good for when students' input may not always be evident in the output (product) *Cons*—grading "process" may feel subjective to some teachers
Report progress on IEP goals	The student is assessed based on progress on goals and objectives on an Individualized Education Program.	*Pros*—individualized; specific to students' needs; good for students with more significant disabilities *Cons*—does not represent progress on standardized or grade-level content
Measure progress over time	Grades are based on where the student started and where she is now; "A" would indicate "exceptional" progress over time for that student.	*Pros*—individualized; specific to student; includes effort and hard work; recognizes individual progress *Cons*—may not represent progress on standardized or grade-level content unless strongly linked to content standards
Prioritize some assignments or content differently	This allows for different assignments to be made more/less important in context for the student (this allows teachers to help certain students know what to focus on first).	*Pros*—individualized; emphasizes work that is more important for student progress (e.g., do this particular assignment before you begin working on project or chapter reading) *Cons*—can be more work for teacher to keep up with
Create menus of options	Assign different points to various options so that students can select a different combination to add up to the required number of points (e.g., 100 pt. assignment = students can choose to do a research paper [100 pts.] or a position paper [50 pts.] and a PowerPoint presentation [50 pts.] or a poster [20 pts.] and a graphic novel [40 pts.] and a blog [40 pts.]).	*Pros*—individualized; allows for choice; lets students use their own strengths; motivating *Cons*—can be more work for teacher to keep up with; teacher should have models and rubrics for each option
Consider indicators of effort or behavior	This recognizes the work that students put into an assignment, rather than solely focusing on outcome.	*Pros*—validates students' work; increases motivation to put in effort *Cons*—does not represent progress on standardized or grade-level content
Modify the weights or scales for grading	This puts more emphasis on some assignments over others for grading purposes (e.g., tests weighted at 10% of the grade instead of 50% like other students).	*Pros*—individualized; emphasizes work that is more important for student progress; students still do all work *Cons*—can be more work for teacher to keep up with

students with identified disabilities to receive adaptations in the areas of content, methodology, service delivery, and evaluation. We've already addressed the first three in previous chapters—content (modifications and accommodations), methodology (UDL), and service delivery (co-teaching). *Evaluation* relates to the specific adaptations that will be implemented when the student's learning outcomes are judged—in other words, grading. These adaptations may include alternate tests, testing formats, grading adjustments, and so forth (Crim, Desjean-Perrotta, & Moseley, 2008). Keep in mind, however, that the use of strong curricular and instructional adaptations may make some grading adaptations moot. Simply put, if you are able to provide the student with content in such a way that he is able to access it like his nondisabled peers, then the assessment might not require any modification at all.

Remember how we said we are "proactivists"? That holds true for grading and assessment as well. We believe that the more proactive you are in determining possible grading adaptations collaboratively (with parents, students, co-teachers, or other folks who have a stake in this), the better off you'll be. Take a look at the various grading adaptations offered on page 116 (*In a Nutshell*). We think this list of options is practical and realistic, and it will provide a great jumping off point for your discussion. Get together with your co-teachers, department, or grade-level partners, and talk about each suggestion and grading option. Are there ones you are already doing? Are there ones you feel uncomfortable doing, and if so, why? Are there some new ones you'd like to try? Be sure that you have multiple frames of reference present at your discussion—for example, a special educator, general educator, administrator, and family member may all have different perspectives on these suggestions and on various grading adaptations. This may make for a lively—and at times, uncomfortable—discussion, but we promise that the results will be worth it.

Planning, assessing, and grading collaboratively is difficult. We're not going to lie. It's way easier to throw something together yourself the morning of class and to create one test that everyone takes at the same time and in the same way. But would you want to be in that class? Wouldn't you rather be in a class where your personal strengths and needs had been considered, where you were allowed to get copies of the PowerPoint presentation, or turn

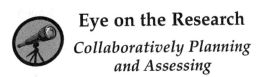

Eye on the Research

Collaboratively Planning and Assessing

Issues	What has the research found to help students?
Planning	• Co-planning enabled teachers to create more uniform instructional plans that were able to be differentiated to meet the needs of all students in an inclusive setting (Fennick & Liddy, 2001; Murawski & Dieker, 2004; Thousand, Villa, & Nevin, 2006). • Daily planning time was found to be more effective than weekly planning time (Scruggs et al., 2007).
Assessing	• When Bursuck and colleagues (1996) surveyed 368 elementary and secondary general education teachers on the use and utility of grading practices and adaptations, the results indicated that while number and letter grades were most commonly used, teachers found the less often used adaptations of pass/fail grades, checklists, and written comments were actually more helpful for students with disabilities. • Reviewing exemplary models of classroom assignments and assessments helps students understand teachers' grading expectations (Whittaker, Salend, & Duhaney, 2001).

For more research in this area go to http://www.corwin.com/diverseschools.

in an assignment electronically instead of as a hard copy, or where you received more time on an assessment that required you to use your least-preferred learning style? Inclusive classes by definition mean we're going to have students with all different kinds of skills, strengths, and needs. These require adaptations in our planning, instructing, and assessing (see Figure 8.1). Collaboration is the key to identifying and implementing the right assortment of adaptations for the right kids, at the right time, and in the right way. This is too much to do alone.

Figure 8.1   Strategies for Dealing With Assessment Issues

Level of Issue	Suggested Strategies
Child (e.g., Brandon is not passing his classes)	Pull together a meeting of the individuals who will have input on the child's assessment (family, general education teachers, special education teacher, school psychologist, related service providers, educational therapist, coaches, etc.). This may be an SST meeting, an IEP meeting, or just a more informal discussion, but the focus will be to discuss the child. Be open to different frames of reference; include the child when possible, and discuss the overall goals (*what* do you want to see demonstrated) before talking about how assessment will occur.
Classroom (e.g., co-teachers disagree on assessment methods)	Both teachers independently list all the various methods of assessment with which they feel comfortable and the ones with which they don't feel comfortable, then discuss them. See where there is disagreement and where there is overlap. Determine the assessment methods both can live with.
School (e.g., math department selected one method of testing)	Create a list of acceptable accommodations and modifications to the standardized method of testing so that all teachers know that there are options for students with special needs. Discuss as a group ways to check if a student learned the content, and come up with possible alternative options for assessment for those who do not test well on standardized formats.
District (e.g., school improvement decisions are based on student test scores)	Form a group comprised of parents, community members, students, teachers, and district personnel, and use the group to determine ways to share with the community other areas of achievement beyond the student test scores. Invite media representatives to attend the group meetings.
State/federal (e.g., laws require all students to take similar tests to demonstrate content mastery)	Write letters to Congress about the need for various uses of assessment data. Join national organizations (such as the Council for Exceptional Children) that are working toward ways for alternative assessments to be recognized. Support lobbying efforts for changes to laws that do not appear to support all children.

TAKING COLLABORATIVE PLANNING AND GRADING OUT OF THE ABSTRACT

Strategies for collaborative planning

• If collaborative planning is between co-teachers, consider using products that will provide structure and ease of use. These include Dieker's *Co-Teaching Lesson Plan* book (http://www.cec.sped.org/resources) and the Co-Teaching Solutions Systems (CTSS) Co-Teachers' Toolbox software (http://www.coteach solutions.com). The CTSS software allows co-teachers to e-mail, modify, and save their co-planned lessons.

- Use technology! The Track Changes feature in Microsoft Word enables users to send each other material and give feedback without losing the original document. Google Docs provides an opportunity for participants to share documents and give one another feedback, and we've seen it work beautifully for remote co-planning. The conferencing site http.www .gotomeeting.com allows team members to meet and plan together on the web from the comfort of their own home, office, or hotel room. Skype lets participants do webcam meetings without having to find time to get to the same location as well. All of these options can increase the active participation from those who may otherwise have not been able to help with planning.

- Did we mention snacks?

- Recognize and validate differences in planning styles. Some folks are "Type A" and will want to plan out each minute or aspect; others are "Type Z" and would prefer to simply discuss information globally rather than worry about the details. When these differences are noted, participants can talk honestly about how to come to a happy medium. For example, tasks can be divided so that Type A can do his right away and check it off his list, while Type Z can wait until the night before it is due and still manage to have it ready to go at the appointed time.

Strategies for collaborative grading

- Identify the situations in which you would be comfortable providing students with choices in how they demonstrate their learning. In which situations would you not be comfortable with providing students with choices? What is the difference between the two situations or types of situations?

- Include a statement similar to this one in your letters or syllabi home at the beginning of the school year: "I am always looking for better ways to assess your child's learning. I will incorporate a variety of these ways throughout the year, to include projects, tests and quizzes, discussions, use of technology, hands-on projects, and writing assignments. If you have suggestions on how I can better assess your own child or additional strategies I can use in the classroom for checking comprehension and learning, please feel free to share those ideas with me."

- Work with colleagues to come up with various menus of assessment options. While you may easily be able to think of papers, worksheets, and posters, you may not have even considered offering voice threads in PowerPoint presentations, webquests, poetry, or podcasts . . . especially if you teach math! Collaborating with others can help you come up with a real variety of options to engage learners and give them multiple ways to show you what they've learned.

On the web

For more strategies for collaborative planning and grading go to http://www.corwin .com/diverseschools.

THUMBNAILS OF RESOURCES ON THE INTERNET

The following elements can be found on the companion website for *Collaborate, Communicate, and Differentiate!* at http://www.corwin.com/diverseschools.

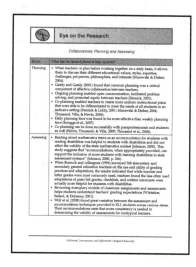

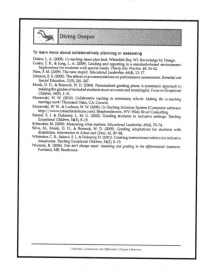

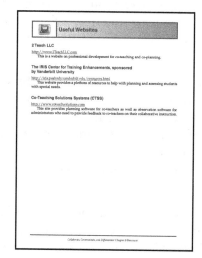

9

Addressing Conflict and Engaging in Problem Solving

Voices From the Field

"I have been a high school math teacher for more than 15 years. This year my principal assigned me to be a coach to the other faculty in our math department. I've been very vigilant about keeping a strict schedule and showing up for my coaching appointments on time and ready to work.

The other day I showed up in Mr. Cruz's classroom, ready to do a model lesson as we had previously arranged. When I got there, Mr. Cruz's students were finishing a project from the previous day that he wanted them to complete in time for Back to School night. Although I could understand that, it was impossible for me to reschedule my appointment or it would mess up my schedule with all the other math teachers. Mr. Cruz absolutely refused to let me do my model lesson, and I left the classroom very angry and frustrated. This was not the first time he had done this. My schedule for the rest of the month is now ruined! Later, Mr. Cruz went to the principal and told him that he doesn't want to work with me anymore. He said that I am inflexible and intolerant. When the principal called me into the office, I told him that Mr. Cruz is flaky and undependable and I urged him to reprimand him. Sadly, he didn't—he just reassigned me to another room.

I've been avoiding Mr. Cruz ever since. But I've heard rumors of what he's saying about me behind my back, and one teacher even came to me to try to intervene. I told him I wasn't interested. How am I supposed to collaborate under these conditions?"

Mr. Santibanez, ninth-grade math coach

THE BIG PICTURE

There's a good chance that this situation is familiar to you. Two educators, both with the best of intentions, end up in a conflict situation that seems unsolvable. Neither party is working with the other, and conversation about the conflict is only happening behind people's backs. The bad feelings are just getting worse! The principal's efforts to solve the conflict have been completely ineffective, and it seems that no one has the means or the will to make this difficult situation better.

Sadly, situations like this one are all too common, particularly in today's collaborative schools. Collaboration requires people working together. To work together effectively, one must communicate. When people communicate, there are bound to be times of miscommunication or differing goals. This can lead to conflict. To resolve conflict takes strong skills in problem solving. If you always liked proofs in geometry, you are probably a step ahead of us in realizing that we just determined that Collaboration = Potential Conflict = Need for Problem Solving. This chapter tackles the difficult issue of what happens when adults don't play nicely together and how we can move forward to more proactive (there's that word again) and effective problem solving.

In this chapter we do the following:

- Identify common areas for conflict between individuals who are collaborating and common causes of conflict in schools.
- Share tips on how to avoid conflict and how to address it when unavoidable.
- Review the steps of problem solving and how to facilitate the use of the process with others in problem-solving meetings or groups.

Don't stop now!

CONFLICT: WHAT CAUSES IT AND HOW CAN WE AVOID IT?

Let's start with the second half of that question first. The bad news is, if you work in a collaborative school, you probably can't avoid conflict. Frankly, when you collaborate with other humans you encounter the possibility of conflict—it's as simple as that. The only way you can avoid conflict with adults is to avoid the adults themselves; in other words, no collaboration. But there's good news, too. Conflict can be a positive thing. In fact, when conflict is resolved constructively, it can lead to stronger outcomes with more buy-in from all concerned parties (Friend & Cook, 2009; Somech, 2008). Conflict is often the way we work through our stickiest and most controversial educational issues. The good news? When we come out on the other side, we often have built stronger relationships and better solutions to our problems.

Schools can be like little petri dishes of conflict, particularly as they become more collaborative. When teachers worked alone, as the kings and queens of their classrooms, conflict was much less likely to occur. Now that teachers are being asked to work together, the likelihood of conflict has greatly increased. Researchers have identified a whole bunch of reasons why conflict occurs in schools. For example, our old friend frame of reference can be responsible for a lot of conflict. Different professionals from different disciplines often come into educational situations with different norms and goals, which can be the breeding ground for conflict (Fast, 2003). Other causes of conflict in schools have been identified as poor leadership, teachers who are struggling with their workload or their classroom management, and ineffective partnerships with parents (Baer, 2010; Maxfield, 2009). Big surprise, huh? Here's another one: teachers who are stressed or who feel unsupported often end up in conflict situations.

Competition for resources, perceived inequality of treatment, or status and cultural diversity can also be robust contributors to the conflict-stew at your school site (Baer, 2010; Cai & Fink, 2002; Feldman, Masalha, & Derdikman-Eiron, 2010; Worchel, 2005). In fact, cultural differences, one of the primary contributors to frame of reference, is also often a primary contributor to conflict. The way diverse cultures perceive and resolve conflict can be really different, and this can have a strong influence on the success of collaborative interactions (Cai & Fink, 2002; Worchel, 2005).

FRAME OF REFERENCE

Mrs. Buchanan and Mrs. Atwood are intervention specialists. Recently, they had a strong disagreement about how to provide services to Katie, a student at their school who was struggling to read grade-level materials. They discussed it a little bit and agreed upon the possibility of having Katie come to the learning lab two days a week for reading intervention. Satisfied, Mrs. Atwood went out and began to arrange the intervention with Katie's mom and classroom teacher.

Later that day, Mrs. Buchanan found out that Mrs. Atwood had begun to make the arrangements for Katie, and she came to Mrs. Atwood very upset. Mrs. Atwood was shocked. As far as she was concerned, they had worked this all out earlier in the day. Mrs. Buchanan, on the other hand, felt betrayed and angry, and she felt like Mrs. Atwood had gone behind her back.

The next day, once the emotions had calmed down, the two teachers sat down to discuss what had happened. As they talked, Mrs. Buchanan revealed that she is a person who likes to take her time and think things over before taking action. From her perspective, they had just begun the discussion on how to help Katie. Mrs. Atwood, on the other hand, is a "get it done" kind of person. From her perspective, they had made a decision and were ready to move forward.

Having worked through this conflict, the two teachers now have a stronger relationship than ever. They are now able to work together while remaining sensitive to each other's needs. Mrs. Atwood feels that she benefits from having a partner who forces her to slow down and think carefully, while Mrs. Buchanan feels the advantage of working with someone who always gets things done in an efficient manner. Out of this conflict came a stronger partnership and a more productive working relationship for both parties.

Another primary trigger for conflict in schools related to students with disabilities can be IEP meetings. In fact, the Center for Appropriate Dispute Resolution in Special Education (CADRE) reports that in the school year 2007–2008, more than 5,000 special education cases were mediated and there were almost 19,000 requests for due process hearings in the United States. That's one heck of a lot of conflict! There may be lots of reasons why this type of conflict develops in IEP meetings, but recent research identified poor leadership, schools that don't stay current with the law, and the exclusion of parents (either actually or effectively) as three of the prime reasons that IEP meetings often deteriorate into discord and end up in mediation or due process (Mueller, 2009). Whatever the reason, preventing and addressing conflict in IEP meetings is an important topic for proactive conversation in any school setting.

ADDRESSING CONFLICT: WHAT CAN WE DO TO KEEP OUT OF TROUBLE?

Set clear goals. As we said earlier, avoiding conflict entirely when you're in a collaborative profession is unlikely; however, there are steps you can take to lay the groundwork for smoother interactions. One of the underlying causes for many instances of conflict is that the people collaborating have different goals; if I want to get Javier out of my classroom and you want to figure out how to make the classroom work better for him, we have different goals. So right off the bat, clarifying our goals at the beginning of the collaboration could be very helpful. Hmm . . . didn't we say that in our chapter on teams? Right! In fact, many of these suggestions for avoiding conflict are also suggestions for *building* strong collaborative relationships. The process is one and the same! Clarifying goals before meetings and keeping them focused on the overall good of the students can be a beneficial guideline for school-based collaborations (Fast, 2003). This is true whether we are talking about conflict in an IEP meeting or conflict between two teachers planning a school dance—we need to make sure our goals are in alignment if we want a productive interaction.

Want more info?

For more information about cultural contributions to conflict, check out *Bridging Cultures Between Home and School: A Guide for Teachers,* by Trumbull et al. (2001).

Establish parity. We mentioned a while ago that parity is a critical component to successful collaboration, but sometimes we forget that when we're embroiled in contentious meetings. One way to establish parity is to make sure that everyone has equal opportunity to speak. This can be particularly critical at IEP meetings, where parents will often feel that they are less empowered than the educational professionals (Mueller, 2009). Giving everyone an equal opportunity to address every new issue can help establish a sense of parity and "teamship" (teamery? teamdom?). This can be accomplished simply by going around the table whenever an important issue is being discussed and giving everyone the floor to contribute their opinion. That will work equally well in IEP meetings or in grade-level meetings with that annoying person from across the hall. (Admit it—you know who we mean!)

Set an agenda. Again, this sounds really obvious, but conflict often results from one person going off on a tangent about something that is important only to him or her or not allowing others sufficient time to share opinions important to them. By setting an agenda and sticking to it, collaborative teams can avoid some of those stickier topics right off the bat. If a controversial subject arises, agree to discuss it at the end after everything else has been resolved. At that point, it's likely that a collaborative atmosphere will have been established, and the topic may be resolved more easily than it might have otherwise (Mueller, 2009). If the person who originally brought it up was agitated at the time, there's a good chance that he or she will have calmed down and can discuss it more rationally by the end of the meeting.

Look for common ground. When conflict rears its ugly head, one of the best ways to avoid being completely engulfed by it is to identify areas of commonality (Maxfield, 2009). Make a list on a white board, and make it big! List everything you can think of that you agree upon before you wade into the shark-infested waters of disagreement. If your meeting is about a particular student, you might even consider placing a picture of that student in the center of the table. A concrete reminder of why you're there can help everyone remember to compromise (Mueller, 2009). Imagine the positive message you are sending to parents if they see you do this!

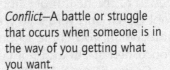

Key Terms

Conflict—A battle or struggle that occurs when someone is in the way of you getting what you want.

Negotiation—The resolution of conflict through mutual discussion and arrangement of terms.

Mediation—Getting help with the conflict when you can't effect a successful negotiation on your own.

WHEN IN DOUBT, NEGOTIATE: HOW CAN WE FIND COMMON GROUND?

Speaking of compromising, it's important to mention here that digging in your heels and refusing to budge on your position is rarely productive. Most of the time it's important to give as well as demand, and that can be difficult when you're in the middle of a conflict situation. One of the most important things to keep in mind when you're trying to negotiate through conflict is to avoid doing it when you are feeling very emotional (R. Fisher & Shapiro, 2006). Emotions affect our ability to think clearly, and they can't be ignored. The best strategy for negotiating when you are emotional is simply not to—get up, ask for a break, and come back when you're calmer. You may even need to reschedule your meeting, and that's okay. It's better to reschedule than to try to work through a conflict when you are highly agitated or upset. Don't get hung up on the fact that this meeting took a while to schedule or that you have a busy month coming up.

Fisher and Shapiro (2006), in their book *Beyond Reason*, suggest that negotiation will be most effective when you "take care" of all the parties at the table. How do you do that? Well, try to think how others might be feeling. Does everyone feel affiliated with the process, or are some people disenfranchised and unable to participate? If parties feel left out or unheard, it is likely to accelerate conflict. In addition, try to find out what people are worried about. If you are arguing over the class placement of a student, for example, it may be that the teacher feels unprepared to meet the needs of the student, or the parent is worried that the student won't be valued in that classroom. This sounds a lot like finding out about frame of reference, doesn't it? It should. Once the concerns are on the table, it's often much easier to work through them productively; without that information, those concerns just fester beneath the surface as unresolved emotion.

Finally, don't think in terms of winners and losers; think in terms of consensus-building (Fisher & Shapiro, 2006). Trying to "win" during a negotiation may prevent you from seeing areas where you can compromise. Most of the time, when we're negotiating conflicts, we have to be willing to give up some points in order to gain others. That said, it's important to mention that we are first and foremost educators, and as such, our responsibility is to the young people with whom we work. There may be times when it is absolutely critical for you to advocate on behalf of the health or safety of your student, and in those rare cases, we urge you to put your foot down and refuse to compromise. The welfare of your students must come first. Just be sure when you come to one of those difficult situations that it truly is the *student* you are concerned about and not your own welfare or peace of mind.

Seminal work by R. Fisher, Ury, and Patton (1991) in the Harvard Negotiation Project identified four key components of effective negotiation that can be helpful in any school conflict situation. Much subsequent work has been based on these four principles, so we'd like to spend a little time examining each.

1. *Focus on interests, not positions.* A position is a black-or-white stance in which you either win or lose. Instead, try to identify common interests from which a productive goal can be created. Consider the conflict situation in our *Voices From the Field* at the beginning of this chapter. The two teachers were arguing over one day's lessons. They totally lost sight of the bigger picture of how their work together benefited the students. By choosing intractable positions (either we work today or we don't), they set themselves up for failure and limited their ability to find a solution on which they could agree.

2. *Separate the people from the problem.* Again, using our previous example, after their initial disagreement, the teachers began to argue over each other's personality—"he's inflexible," "he's flaky." Their initial conflict turned into a much bigger issue of personalities, which is almost impossible to solve. By staying focused on the real problem, how they could continue to work together for the benefit of the students, they have a chance at creating a satisfactory solution to their conflict. And certainly, it's critical for them to avoid "talking out of school." If you want to talk about the conflict, do it with the person involved, not through a third party. Back talk and gossip have never made a conflict situation better. In fact, we suggest that the best thing to do if you walk into the teacher's lounge and there is gossiping going on is to walk back out again. Quickly. Before you get sucked in.

3. *Invent options for mutual gain.* In this case, we might bring up the old proverb of the children and the orange. Both children wanted an orange, and there was only one to be had. They agreed to split it, after which one child peeled her half and ate the fruit, throwing away the peel, while the other peeled her half, threw away the fruit, and used the peel to make a cake. The children focused on the easy solution instead of the alignment of their individual needs. In the case of our teachers, they need to avoid a quick solution, such as teaching today or not teaching today, and look for a creative alternative that could satisfy them both. For example, perhaps Mr. Cruz could have traded times with another teacher so that he didn't disrupt Mr. Santibanez's schedule. Or perhaps Mr. Santibanez could have adapted his model lesson to incorporate the Back to School project that needed to be accomplished.

4. *Insist on objective criteria.* This can be a tough one. If we were negotiating for the repair of an airplane, there would be no discussion—the most effective repair would be the one we would choose. Compromise would not be an option—nobody wants a repair based on compromise when they're hanging 20,000 feet in the air! When people's lives are at stake, we make our choices based on hard data. But sometimes in less objective situations, the criteria can be harder to determine. In our example, it might be necessary to sit down and see whether Mr. Santibanez's

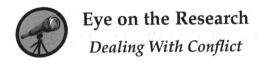

Eye on the Research
Dealing With Conflict

Issues	What has the research found to help us work through our problems?
Conflict and Culture	• Culture shapes an individual's perception and response to conflict, and cultural stories and myths will often dictate how conflict is handled and which groups are considered "out." In order to achieve peaceful resolution of conflict between different cultural groups, three elements are needed: acceptance of the group's right to exist, acceptance without fear, and the willingness to engage in cooperative interactions (Worchel, 2005).
Conflict in Schools	• Causes of conflict in schools include unsupportive or ill-prepared administration, struggling teachers, and student behavior problems. Suggestions for dealing with conflict include dealing with it before you become angry, asking humanizing questions, finding common ground, and avoiding monologues (Maxfield, 2009).
Conflict in IEPs	• After examining IEP and mediation documents, researchers found that the most common reasons for conflict in IEP meetings are lack of leadership, schools that are uninformed about the law, and parents being excluded from IEP meetings (Mueller, Singer, & Draper, 2008).
Conflict and Teams	• Successful teams know how to manage conflict. They should be both task interdependent and goal interdependent, and if one of these is low, conflict is likely to occur. When both characteristics are high, teams interact a lot and see the importance of the team functions; when both are low, team members work independently. Handling conflict in a team can give everyone a higher level of input into the solution and will allow the team to grow (Somech, 2008).

For more research in this area go to http://www.corwin.com/diverseschools.

schedule was really that inflexible, and if so, how could it have been changed to accommodate the needs of everyone involved? In any case, the point here is to make your decisions based on the objective facts, not on your emotions or your feelings about the person. Check out the reproducible form we've provided, titled "Negotiating During Conflict," at http://www.corwin.com/diverseschools; you may want to keep a copy of it handy in case of conflict.

Other suggestions for successful negotiation of conflict? The communication skills that we discussed earlier become critical here. Listen, listen, and listen some more, and then paraphrase important issues so you can be sure you got them right. Break down areas of concern into small, comprehensible items, and choose the least contentious to discuss first (Baer, 2010). Try not to vilify your partners—ask humanizing questions that will help you find common ground (Maxfield, 2009). And finally, avoid monologues at all costs. In fact, let's repeat the earlier point—listen, listen, and then listen some more!

Principal Points

Administrators are often asked to be the mediators in situations of conflict between two faculty members. Don't assume you have the skills to do this effectively. See the *Diving Deeper* section on the web to learn more about mediation, and use a checklist until you become proficient. (We've provided one for you at http://www.corwin.com/diverseschools; please see the four key components identified by the Harvard Negotiation Project on pages 126–127.) Mediation is not just a process of sitting down and talking it out—without the correct structure you could end up accelerating the conflict rather than resolving it.

WHEN NEGOTIATION FAILS: HOW CAN WE MOVE FORWARD WHEN WE'RE TOTALLY STUCK?

It's important for us all to acknowledge that sometimes it just isn't possible to work through conflict productively by ourselves. We've all been there, and we all know it's true. At that point, one of our choices becomes mediation. Mediation requires that we bring in a third party to act as a conciliator, to help us work through our issues to come to a resolution that works for everyone. As we mentioned earlier, IEP meetings all too often end up in mediation. The parties involved don't have the skills or the will to come to an understanding, and school districts spend tens of thousands of dollars a year bringing in outside help to resolve the issues in conflict.

The role of the mediator in any situation is not to be a judge, but to help the parties move away from intractable "positions" to a more mutually agreeable middle ground (Margolis, 1999). Participants must come in prepared to give information in an organized and unemotional way, and they should be allowed to present their point of view without interruption (Barsky, 2000). Once the parties' opinions have been clearly stated, and the parameters of the conflict have been sketched out, the principles of negotiation should be engaged under the guidance of the mediator. You can choose who you would like to have mediate your conflict situations, but choose carefully! If the party chosen has a vested interest in the situation, you may just end up with more conflict on your hands. In addition, sometimes teachers will be uncomfortable with an administrator mediating, especially if that individual is someone who is responsible for their regular evaluations. Instead, consider identifying a veteran teacher or other individual you both respect, and who is not vested in this problem, to act as mediator. If that person agrees to do it, you also need to agree to abide by whatever suggestions or decisions he or she makes.

PROBLEM SOLVING: CAN WE AGREE TO AGREE?

We do want to present you with one more viable (and valuable!) option for working through conflict. You and your colleagues can choose to work through a collaborative problem-solving process together. This is the best of all possible worlds. When teammates or partners choose to work through their problems in a collaborative and structured fashion, it is very likely that they will end up with a solution that makes them all happy and which they can all implement with satisfaction (Friend & Cook, 2009).

There have been years of research on consultative and collaborative interpersonal problem solving in education. Some of the most common applications for collaborative problem solving are to guide decisions regarding interventions and referrals for special education (e.g., Marston, Muyskens, Lau, & Canter, 2003) and to reduce problem behaviors in schools (e.g., Ervin, Schaughency, Matthews, Goodman, & McGlinchey, 2007). Problem solving is also a big factor in the implementation of RTI (e.g., Marston et al., 2003).

Each agency and school district that implements a problem-solving approach does it a little differently, but the basic components are usually quite similar. Jayanthi and Friend (1992) did a comprehensive review of the literature on interpersonal problem solving and identified five steps that were common to most studies.

Step 1. Clearly and succinctly identify the problem. This sounds simple, doesn't it? Just quickly write down what the problem is, and you can move on to Step 2. However, it's not as simple as it seems. The key to this step is spending the time to discuss the problem in depth. If you don't take the time to discuss all the components and think carefully about the true source of your conflict, there's a good chance you will identify one superficial component of the problem instead of the real underlying issues. For example, referring back to our old friends at the beginning of the chapter, it's highly likely that Mr. Santibanez would identify their problem as poor management on the part of Mr. Cruz, while Mr. Cruz might say the problem is Mr. Santibanez's inflexibility. Neither of these is truly the cause of the problem; they are more like symptoms. If we did a quick, superficial description of the problem and came up with these two issues, the problem becomes unsolvable. You can't change Mr. Cruz or Mr. Santibanez—they are who they are. So where does that leave us? Back in conflict! When identifying the problem for collaborative problem solving around a conflict situation, the best practice is to keep in mind the overall goals of the situation or the school. What would that be, you ask? Why, educating students to the best of our ability, we reply!

So in this case, with that overall goal in mind, we might be able to agree on a description of the problem along the lines of, "We need to meet the mandate for math coaching without sacrificing the other needs of the classroom or the needs of the students." Both teachers could agree on that, because both of their concerns are included in the statement. However, it may take us 20 minutes of conversation about the problem before we can weed out all the associated issues such as personalities in order to get to the heart of this problem—time management.

Please note here that our description of the problem is *simple.* We aren't listing all the factors involved or bulleting each teacher's concerns. Instead, we are trying to cut to the heart of the matter and create a description of the problem in one simple sentence. One important thing to keep in mind when doing this process (which is harder than it seems until you get the hang of it) is to avoid focusing on the individuals involved in the conflict. As soon as you focus on the teachers, it becomes an issue of personalities that is probably unsolvable. *Whenever possible, focus on the students or the big-picture issues involved in the conflict.*

There are a few other simple tricks you can keep in mind to help you define your problem. First, don't try to make it too narrow and specific, as you may end up limiting your possible solutions. In our example, a statement of "Mr. Cruz needs to get ready for Back to School Night" would not really address the underlying issues.

Second, if you're not sure you've really defined it well, try writing two or three other definitions of the problem and choose the best one. In our example, we might write the following definitions of our problem: "There isn't enough time to get everything done in the math class," "Mr. Cruz needs more time to get ready for Back to School Night," "Mr. Santibanez has too many teachers on his coaching caseload," and "Mr. Cruz and Mr. Santibanez can't agree on how best to use the time in math class." From those four, plus the one we wrote previously, it seems clear that "We need to meet the mandate for math coaching without sacrificing the other needs of the classroom or the students" is the most inclusive, descriptive, and comprehensive description of our problem. It is important to always try to consider the *cause* of the problem when you are defining it. In our case, the cause of our problem is the conflict between the need for math coaching and the need to get other things done in the classroom. By identifying the cause, we can more easily define our problem.

Let's take a quick look at another possible conflict scenario. Let's assume that a special education teacher, Mrs. Fayyazi, and her general education partner, Ms. Harvey, are discussing the needs of one of their students, Jackie. Ms. Harvey thinks that Jackie needs pull-out services for reading, while Mrs. Fayyazi feels that Jackie's reading needs can best be met with daily co-teaching between the two teachers. No matter how much they discuss it they can't seem to come to agreement. In this scenario, they might create a problem statement along these lines: "How can we help Jackie increase her reading skills?" There can be no disagreement with that statement—they both share that goal for Jackie—it's just *how they get there* that they can't agree upon. The cause of their conflict isn't their goals for Jackie, it's the means to achieve those goals. By focusing on the student and not on their disagreement with each other, they've created a problem description that they can both support. Once they've agreed on a problem description, they are ready to move on to the next step.

Principal Points

Administrators can also use the What/How/Who approach from Chapter 8 when helping facilitate problem solving with teams, departments, or the whole faculty. Ask participants the following:

- **WHAT is the problem or issue we need to solve?** During this time, make sure participants can agree on the issue and its components. A good follow-up question to make sure you are all on the same page in terms of goals is this: "What would success look like if we solved this problem?"
- **HOW are we going to solve this problem?** During this time, participants would brainstorm ways to address the problem. Be sure to write these ideas down so that you can determine which are the most feasible. Once a decision is made, move to the next step.
- **WHO is going to do what in order to solve this problem?** During this phase, roles are assigned and a timeline is created. Don't forget to build in a follow-up to make sure the problem was truly solved.

Step 2. Generate a variety of solutions. There are two critical components to this step. First, you want to create as many different solutions as possible so that you have a wide variety of diverse possibilities from which to choose. So the process should be one of throwing out as many ideas as you can, writing them down, and building on the ideas you've generated to come up with even more. There are lots of different methods for generating creative ideas, some of which are outlined in the *Taking Conflict and Problem Solving Out of the Abstract* section at the end of this chapter. Choose the one that works best for you and your team.

The second critical point is to delay your evaluation of the ideas until you are done generating them. If you stop to discuss or appraise your ideas as you go along, you are likely to stem the flow of creativity, and you won't come up with as many high-quality solutions (Jayanthi & Friend, 1992). This may sound easy, but in fact it's one of the hardest parts of the process. Believe it or not, humans are often highly critical beings. (No, really?!?) And our natural inclination is to talk about and judge every new idea that is offered to us as it comes up. If you've ever seen this happen in a meeting, you know what the outcome is. Two or three ideas are presented, they are picked apart, and discussed ad nauseam until the meeting time ends. Suddenly you are out of time, you have hardly any solutions to choose from, and you've already picked those solutions to pieces. No one ends up happy. So even though it's hard, and it may run contrary to your natural instincts, it's important to try to hold on to your feelings about the ideas until you are all done generating them. Just let those ideas flow. You'll have plenty of time to pick them apart in the next step of the process.

Step 3. Decide on a solution you are all comfortable with. Okay, *here* is where you get to be the critical, judgmental human that you were born to be! Take a good, hard look at the dozens of solutions you came up with in the previous step and identify the strengths and weaknesses of each of them. Make lists, cross things out . . . circle the ones you love and erase the ones you hate. This step is all about critical, thoughtful evaluation of your ideas until you've identified a solution that you all can agree upon. If you've done the previous two steps well, you should have at least one or two great ideas that can help you move forward to a resolution of your problem.

Step 4. Implement your solution. This step actually has two parts—creating a plan for implementation and then implementing that plan. Once you've chosen the solution you want to try, take the time to chart out how you will proceed with it. Identify who will be responsible for which parts, and create a timeline that is practical. Write down the materials or support you need, and who you want to bring in to help. Create a comprehensive plan about how you will proceed to make your solution successful. Make sure you include a description of what you are hoping to achieve—in other words, how will you know if you're successful? Create clear, simple criteria for success that all parties can agree upon.

Once you've done that, the next part is easy. Get to work implementing your plan! The important part here, of course, is that everyone fulfills the responsibilities to which they've committed, and if you have created a clear plan, that shouldn't be too difficult. Check in with one another every couple of days at first to see how things are going, and use each other for support if needed. Make notes and collect data on how the plan is going, so that you can review it in the final step.

Step 5. Evaluate your outcomes. If you are lucky, and you did a good job on the previous four steps, at this point your problem should be solved. You and your partners should be working productively toward your shared objectives. However, sometimes other problems arise, or our solution isn't successful. At that point we need to go back and determine why. If new problems have arisen, we may have to reevaluate and redefine our problem. It's also possible that the original definition just didn't do the trick, and we need to take another look at the underlying causes of our problem and create another definition. If that's the case, we start the process over from Step 1.

In other cases, it's the solution itself that isn't working, so we can just go back to our list and choose another one to try. If you did a good job with Step 2 previously, you should have a folder with a bunch of untried ideas that are ripe for the picking. In either case, though, the process hasn't failed you; you may just need to tweak it a little to arrive at your ultimate solution.

GROUP PROBLEM SOLVING: DO WE HAVE TO LEARN A WHOLE NEW PROCESS?

The simple and very happy answer to this question is "No!" The problem-solving steps we outlined earlier will work equally well with two people or a group of 12. We know one teacher who learned the process, showed it to her principal, and was asked to train her entire school in the process. They use it formally during their Student Success Team meetings and informally for a whole variety of smaller issues that come up around the school. You may want to share the *In a Nutshell* chart, titled "Important Considerations in Problem Solving," that can be found on page 132. Post it strategically in your school's conference rooms or maybe even in the teachers' lounge.

That brings us to another important point. The steps we've given you here, although very effective if you follow them formally, can also be used in a more casual manner. Any of the steps, in and of themselves, might be useful if you find yourself stuck for a solution to a less complex problem. For example, you may want to use the second step, generating solutions, when you and your teaching assistants are trying to figure out how to help Natasha complete more of her math work in class. You might walk through the process of clearly identifying the problem when you are trying to figure out why Yesenia has a meltdown around 10:00 every morning. The process is useful and effective, but it can be time consuming, so feel free to use it in a more informal manner when you need to.

In a Nutshell

Important Considerations in Problem Solving

		Things to Consider
Problem-Solving Step	**Identifying the Problem**	• Allow plenty of time to discuss the problem in depth before you define it. This step can take time as you try to ferret out the cause of the problem, contributing factors, etc. Don't forget to find out what has already been tried and found unsuccessful, as this is helpful information too. • Consider the big picture. With most problems there are things to discuss that are directly related to the problem and things that are less directly related. It's important to consider both before describing your problem. For example, if a child is having trouble in school, it is often valuable to discuss what is going on at home, too. Don't forget to ask, "What has already been done and what was the outcome?" • Don't make your problem description so narrow that it only gives you one or two solutions. For example, the problem, "Amy needs to be in special education," has only one solution—special education for Amy. Better might be, "Amy needs help to achieve grade-level reading skills." • Make sure you all share the same idea of what you want to accomplish. In the aforementioned example, it would be useful to describe specifically what Amy needs to accomplish in terms of her reading. Everyone needs a clear idea of what success will look like! • As much as possible, include a variety of perspectives in the discussion. People with diverse perspectives will often come up with diverse solutions that you otherwise might not consider.
	Generating Solutions	• Allow yourself the freedom to be silly when you are coming up with solutions. Sometimes the silly ideas that pop into our heads ("Let's try teaching him to bark like a dog.") will lead to some really good ones ("Let's try getting him a therapy dog."). • We said it before, but it can't be said too often. Don't evaluate your ideas as you generate them. Judging and evaluating will cause all creative thinking to come to a screeching halt! Positive comments are evaluative too and can stop the sharing just as effectively. • Go for quantity. The more ideas you can come up with the better. Don't cut yourself off too soon—if you come to a period of silence, wait it out. The silence can lead to another round of productive ideas.
	Deciding on a Solution	• First go through your list of solutions and cross off all the ridiculous ones or ones that you just aren't comfortable with. That will save you time as you go through the list. • Now go through the list again and circle the ones that you are particularly interested in. Those are the ones you should spend time discussing. • Once you've circled your favorites, go through and list the positives and negatives of each of them. For example, if the solution is, "do a functional behavioral assessment," a positive might be that it is thorough and will give you lots of information. A negative would be that it is very time consuming. • Once you've chosen the solution you are going to implement, make sure that it's manageable. If you choose more than one solution, make sure they work together as a functional unit. Having too many different things to implement is going to be unwieldy and will probably fail simply because you don't have the manpower, time, or will to use them with fidelity. • Make sure that the person who is going to have to implement the solution has the final say in what is chosen. If you try to force a solution on someone, it is unlikely that she will do a good job of implementing it.
	Implementing the Solution	• Create a plan for implementation by outlining all the necessary steps. • Identify a person or persons who will be responsible for each step. • Create a timeline that is reasonable, and stick to it! • Discuss how you will keep records to make sure the solution is implemented as it was intended. • Clarify what you are shooting for—what are your desired outcomes? • Schedule a couple of times to meet to discuss progress and a time to come back to evaluate the outcomes. • Don't be afraid to tweak your plan if it isn't working—this is a living process that can change and morph as needed.
	Evaluating the Outcomes	• Plan a time to meet to evaluate your outcomes, and stick to it. Even if the plan is working, it's critical to come together to discuss it, make changes or adjustments if needed, and plan next steps. • If your strategy isn't working, take the time to figure out *why*. This is where good record keeping and data collection will be invaluable. Things to consider: Was the problem defined incorrectly? Was the solution not a good one? Was the solution implemented as intended? Did you have all the information you needed to make a good decision? Is more information available now that should be added to the process? Are other individuals needed to help the problem-solving process be more successful?

TAKING CONFLICT AND PROBLEM SOLVING OUT OF THE ABSTRACT

Strategies for generating solutions

- Traditional brainstorming: In this strategy, participants work together to call out and write down as many ideas as possible as quickly as they can.

- Brainwriting (Madu, 2010): Another technique to encourage members who are less willing to speak up. Each member has a sheet of paper with the problem written at the top. They write an idea for a solution on the paper, then pass it to the right. As they receive a new idea, they read it, think about it, and generate another idea, perhaps building on the one they read. This process is repeated until each slip has five or six ideas on it. At that point, everyone makes a list of their favorite ideas, which are then discussed as a group.

- Slip writing: In this method, one that we frequently use without even knowing it, participants are asked to write all their ideas on little slips of paper for later consideration. This can be done with sticky notes, which are then put on a chart for organization and discussion.

Strategies for resolving conflict in IEP meetings

- Take some time to train teachers about the problems parents face in IEP meetings. Parents of students with special needs sometimes feel defensive, ashamed, uninformed, or just plain intimidated, and all those feelings contribute to the possibility of conflict erupting. Help faculty be responsive to these possibilities and teach them how to deal with families with sensitivity and compassion. An excellent book that addresses the frame of reference of both parents and professionals in an easy-to-read format is *Children With High-Functioning Autism: A Parent's Guide* (Hughes-Lynch, 2010).

- Make an effort to build rapport. Roger Fisher, director of the Harvard Negotiation Project, said it like this: "Personal ties bring human beings together and make them feel they're working together. And that changes the presumption of who we are—it changes us from being adversaries to being colleagues" (Adler, 2006).

Strategies for resolving conflict in schools

- Build partnerships. Find places where you can work with other stakeholders at your school and pursue those opportunities. Teaching can be a very isolating profession, so take the time to reach out to your colleagues and work together.

- Additionally, spend five minutes at every faculty meeting on some kind of icebreaker. Give everyone the opportunity to interact with and get to know the people sitting near them. Make sure to facilitate the activities so that everyone is working with new people each time.

- Have the whole faculty take a Conflict Resolution survey (e.g., Thomas Kilmann) and do activities related to those results.

- Have the whole faculty take a strengths survey and discuss how they could use those strengths to benefit the school and the students. Different websites offering strengths surveys (some free) are listed in the *Useful Websites* page on the web.

On the web

For more strategies for problem solving and resolving conflicts in IEP meetings and schools go to http://www.corwin.com/diverseschools.

THUMBNAILS OF RESOURCES ON THE INTERNET

The following elements can be found on the companion website for *Collaborate, Communicate, and Differentiate!* at http://www.corwin.com/diverseschools.

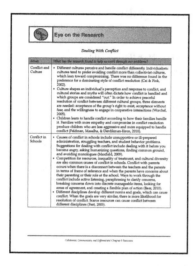

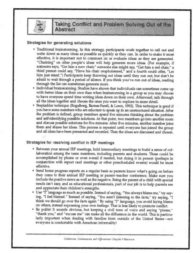

10

Creating a Collaborative School Culture

THE BIG PICTURE

Your IEP and SST teams are functioning like well-oiled machines. Co-teachers laugh in the halls as they reflect on a lesson that went really well. Grade-level and department meeting discussions include conversations about universally designed lessons and how to continue to provide high-quality, research-based instruction to students in their Tier 1 grade-level classrooms. Conflicts are solved by negotiation and conversation, rather than by yelling and throwing things. Families smile and talk to the media about the collaborative experiences they have with the school. And then you wake up. How do these dream schools come about? How do you integrate all the wonderful things you've learned in this book to create a truly collaborative school culture? The focus of this chapter is to help you pull it all together.

In this chapter we do the following:

- Describe a collaborative school culture.
- Explain how to create an IEP for school change.
- Discuss ways to pull together all the suggestions made in previous chapters.
- Give tips for institutionalization of these changes.

You know you can't stop now!

DESCRIBING A COLLABORATIVE SCHOOL CULTURE: WOULD I KNOW IT IF I SAW IT?

Ever heard of the American Association of School Administrators (AASA), the American Federation of Teachers (AFT), the Council for Exceptional Children (CEC), the Council of Great City Schools (CGCS), the National Association of Elementary School Principals (NAESP), the National Associaton of Secondary School Principals (NASSP), the National Association of State Directors of Special Education (NASDSE), the National Association of State Boards of Education (NASBE), the National Education Association (NEA), or the National School Boards Association (NSBA)? You've heard of at least one of them, right? Okay, well even if you haven't, you have to admit that this is a mighty impressive list! Just check out all those acronyms. Why are we impressing you with a list of associations? Stay tuned. This matters.

> **Key Term**
>
> *School Culture*—The unique quality that every school has that seems to impact every activity; based on the various norms, values, traditions, and beliefs held by teachers, families, and students over time.

In 1994, those 10 previously named national associations identified numerous schools that had become model sites for collaboration and inclusion. From these schools, 12 were selected to be part of a national Inclusive Schools Working Forum (Council for Exceptional Children, 1994). These schools were observed and researched in order to determine what common characteristics they shared. The 12 characteristics identified through these schools, though manifested differently at each campus, are ones that we can look to when envisioning our dream collaborative school. We know 1994 was a long time ago, but we maintain that these characteristics are still "the ones." Check them out in Figure 10.1.

Twelve characteristics. That's not that hard to achieve, is it? Hey! We saw you rolling your eyes. And you know what? We agree. This is brutal. But what those 12 schools (and the many others that weren't used for the research but were identified) have shown us is that it can be done. It simply has to be done thoughtfully, systematically, and . . . wait for it . . . collaboratively!

Before we move on, let's take a moment to discuss what we mean by *collaborative* school culture. The Center for Collaborative Education (2001) defined it this way:

> In a collaborative culture, members of the school community work together effectively and are guided by a common purpose. All members of the community—teachers, administrators, students and their families—share a common vision of what the school

should be like. Together they set goals that lead them toward this vision. In doing so, they create a culture of discourse in which the most important educational matters facing the school are openly and honestly discussed. Members respect each other, value their differences, and are open to each other's ideas. Even when there is disagreement, people listen to each other because they believe deeply that differences are vital in moving their school forward. (p. 3)

Figure 10.1   Characteristics of Model Inclusive Schools

Characteristic	Explanation
A Sense of Community	This provides a philosophy and vision that all children belong and can learn together. Diversity is valued. Self-worth, pride in own accomplishments, and mutual respect are developed.
Leadership	Responsibility is shared with the entire school staff in planning and carrying out strategies to make the school successful.
High Standards	High levels of educational outcomes and high standards of performance are established appropriate to students' needs. Levels of achievement, instructional content, and instructional delivery vary based on an individual's needs.
Collaboration and Cooperation	Students and staff support one another through collaborative strategies that may include co-teaching, student-assistance teams, cooperative learning, peer tutoring, and other collaborative arrangements.
Changing Roles and Responsibilities	Old roles for teachers, staff, and students are changed. Teachers facilitate more than lecture, students participate actively in learning, staff such as school psychologists and speech-language pathologists work in the classrooms, and so forth.
Array of Services	Services that include health, mental health, social services, and instructional services are all coordinated and collaborative.
Partnerships With Parents	Embraced as equal and essential partners, families of all kinds are actively involved in the education of their children.
Flexible Learning Environments	Individual paths to learning are expected and encouraged, rather than lock-step traditional approaches. Flexible grouping, meaningful individualized instruction, and appropriate content delivery are everyday occurrences.
Strategies Based on Research	Recognized as helping teachers obtain best practice ideas and strategies, research is used regularly to inform practice, rather than eschewed for being impractical.
New Forms of Accountability	There is less reliance on standardized tests and more reliance on forms of accountability and accessibility that demonstrate true student growth and progress toward individual goals.
Access	All aspects of the physical building are accessible to students and families, and technology is used to ensure that all aspects of learning and instruction are accessible as well.
Continuing Professional Development	Recognizing that learning is ongoing, professional development is designed and obtained to ensure continuous improvement by faculty and staff in meeting the needs of all students.

Source: Adapted from Working Forum on Inclusive Schools, 1995.

If, after looking at those 12 characteristics, you are still overwhelmed, then how would you feel about three? We're okay with starting small, as long as we're moving forward. If you prefer to boil down the necessary characteristics for change to the top three—the ones where you'll get the biggest bang for your buck, so to speak—then we would suggest you focus your energies on these:

1. Increased Collaboration (Did you think we would *not* put that one in?)

2. Quality Professional Development (Gotta help folks get the skills for change.)

3. Shared and Supportive Instructional Leadership (Can make it or break it.)

Waldron and McLeskey (2010) used their substantial research over the last decade or two to identify those three characteristics as key to comprehensive school reform. Their work has focused on reculturing schools in order to embrace and advance inclusive education efforts. They found a huge need to develop truly collaborative cultures in order to achieve school improvement. So, whether you'd like to undertake all 12 characteristics or just focus on the top three, at least now we all know what we're looking at doing. Next step—how do we actually do this?

In Practice

Everyone walked into the room as Miss Bettencourt, the principal, welcomed them and thanked them for agreeing to be there for the first meeting of the "Collaborative School Culture" Team (or CSCT). They knew they had each been hand-selected to represent the colleagues in their various areas.

❧

The meeting began and Miss Bettencourt asked group members to share their feelings on the present level of collaboration within the school. Mr. Lightfoot (the general education teacher representative) began by saying, "I think we are extremely collaborative. My seventh-grade team meets regularly; we talk all the time and we all seem to get along fine." As he spoke, the other members were thinking the following:

❧

Ms. Harding (special educator): Collaborative? Really?! Very few of them are willing to provide any kinds of accommodations for my kids.

Mr. Alpert (cafeteria supervisor): Collaborative? Really?! I doubt anyone here even knows my name, though I know every one of the kids in this school.

Mrs. Epstein (parent): Collaborative? Really?! Every time I ask for a meeting to discuss Bev's progress with Mr. Lightfoot or his team, I get the runaround.

❧

Miss Bettencourt smiled and said, "Well, that's refreshing. I guess we don't have very far to go then. Anyone else?" The room was silent.

CREATING AN IEP FOR SCHOOL CHANGE: WHAT KIND OF STEPS WOULD WE TAKE?

Ever heard the saying that writers should write "what they know"? We think educators should use what they know when tackling problems. We are going to take a process *that you are already familiar with* and use it to address the major issue of creating a collaborative school: the IEP process. We aren't choosing the IEP process because this is a special education process—quite the opposite—this process needs to be shared by the whole school, with the entire community in mind. We call it the IEP for School Change because it follows the same basic (although wildly simplified) steps of an IEP.

1. Determine what's going on currently (Present Level of Performance).

2. Determine where you want to be in a specified amount of time (Goal and Objectives).

3. Determine how you are going to get there, and who is going to do what and by when, in order to ensure you do so (Benchmarks).

Not bad, eh? In the next section, we walk you through the steps of creating your school's IEP for Change. And it begins with . . . surprise! Collaboration! (We're not really surprising you anymore with that, are we? We hope not.)

Getting started. You have now gathered a group to discuss how to create a school culture that will embrace all of the concepts we've been addressing in this book. Worried about how to provide incentives for folks to join yet another team? Just remind them that this team may ultimately be the group that ends up saving the school and the other school-based teams lots and lots of work. You will be celebrated and revered . . . or at least thanked, we hope. Instead of having team after team meet to talk about how to solve individual student or curriculum problems, this team will be focused on taking "a proactive and preventative approach by attacking the cultural and institutional basis of the problem" (Sue & Sue, 2003, p. 442). Who should you gather, by the way? Key individuals to represent the whole school! Don't forget families, community members, school staff (could be secretaries, maintenance, or cafeteria workers), itinerant teachers, and students. We know you'll remember the teachers, administrators, counselors, and other key staff.

Clarifying the purpose. On page 140, we've provided a step-by-step guide to conducting this very important process; however, there are a few steps we feel need a bit more explanation. The first thing to do is make sure you are all on the same page in terms of terminology (language), purpose of the meeting, and what it means to have parity (equality) as a team. Keep in mind that you may all have different frames of reference based on your own personal experiences with collaborative endeavors at the school. You may also need to discuss the fact that every time folks get together and talk doesn't mean collaboration is occurring (Friend, 2000; Friend & Cook, 2009). Look at our *In Practice* example on page 138; the beginning of that meeting does not bode well for future meetings. It's critical for you to create an atmosphere where people feel safe sharing their opinions and where everyone has an equal voice.

Step-by-Step Process for School Change IEP

Step	Description	Part of IEP Process
Agree upon norms for meetings	Logistics of meeting, job responsibilities, parity, other norms	Norm-Setting
Establish common language	Culture, school culture, collaboration, RTI, co-teaching, UDL	Norm-Setting
Do culture survey and interviews	Establish present level of performance (from multiple frames of reference).	Present Level of Performance
Determine goal; write mission/vision/philosophy statement	Use one overall goal over multiple time periods (e.g., What should this look like at the end of the 1st semester? End of the 1st year? End of 5 years? End of 10 years?).	Determine Goal
Determine smaller objectives (with specific measureable outcomes) that will lead to the overall goal	Consider various areas (instructional, environmental, social, behavioral, home–school, etc.); be sure to include various perspectives from all stakeholders.	Determine Objectives
Identify actions and timelines that need to be taken to accomplish objectives	Discuss responsibilities, specific actions, deadlines, materials needed, how you will know if success was achieved, and what to do in case of barriers.	Determine Benchmarks
Meet to share results and determine next steps	Share and celebrate areas of success; brainstorm ways to overcome areas of difficulty; evaluate outcomes to look for ways to institutionalize positive change; provide support where needed; determine how to disseminate results and build on successes; discuss present level of current performance and begin process again with next steps toward ongoing improvement.	Follow-Up, Share, Evaluate, Revisit

Setting norms. Once everyone is on board in terms of the goal of the team (i.e., to establish or enhance a collaborative culture at this school), then go over some basic logistical items. If you remember our chapter on teams, we emphasized that there is nothing worse than being on ineffective or inefficient teams. (Okay there are many, many things that are worse, but you get the drift). Talk about where meetings will take place, how often, when they'll start and end, norms for disagreeing or interrupting, and so forth (Center for Collaborative Education, 2001; Guskey, 2003a). We've included some helpful tips for you on pages 147–148. These team meetings are crucial; inefficiency in logistics can have a negative impact on effectiveness of content and team input. And, although we hate to admit it, this process will most likely not be quick. This could be the first of many meetings as you walk through this process. If you clarify your goals now, and create processes to help your team run smoothly, you will save yourself a lot of time in the long run.

> **Want more info?**
>
> McLeskey and Waldron have done substantial work on school change for inclusive education. Check out their work in the *Diving Deeper* section on the web.

Identifying current status. Once the team has agreed to norms and the overarching purpose, it is time to get to Step 1 of the IEP for School Change: *Determine Your Present Level of Performance* (or PLOP, isn't that acronym lovely?). Your job here is to collect data that tell you the current state of the collaborative culture (or lack of it) at your school. You will need to collect data on a wide variety of topics, including instructional practices, social culture, home–school collaboration, environmental factors, and any other critical areas you can think of. Your team members will certainly be able to share their various perspectives, but you may want to spread your net even wider for this particular step; it is truly important that your entire school have a voice in this process. Consider sending out surveys geared toward all the various stakeholders, having focus group meetings, collecting permanent product examples, and/or conducting interviews. We have included a *Needs Assessment Survey* to get you going at http://www.corwin.com/diverseschools; we absolutely encourage you to tweak it and make it suit the needs of your own school. Remember, each school has its own unique inclusive culture, so it's important to ask questions relevant to your specific school (McLeskey & Waldron, 2002b; Waldron & McLeskey, 2010).

Creating objectives. You've collected your data and everyone on the team shares consensus related to where your school is presently in terms of its culture. You are ready for Step 2 of the IEP for School Change: *Set Goals and Objectives for Improvement*. We know—you already established the goal of a collaborative culture, but don't forget how we keep harping on the fact that each school is different (McLeskey & Waldron, 2002b). Your "collaborative culture" may look very different from the "collaborative culture" of the school down the street; that doesn't mean it is any less collaborative. The objectives will help you specify where *your school* needs change.

In writing objectives, we have found that the best questions to ask are, "What do we want to see as a collaborative school culture?" or "What would success look like at our school?" Make sure that, once again, you do this in a variety of areas, such as families, teacher interactions, instruction, and so forth. Think about all the areas you might choose to tackle in order to get to a more collaborative overall school culture. Here are some examples:

- *PLOP—Families report having little regular connection to schools.* **Objective**—Develop both formal and informal ways for families to feel a connection and to be able to collaborate in substantive ways with faculty and staff.

- *PLOP—Teachers feel comfortable with the sharing that goes on with the same grade or department, but they report very little interaction outside of their own grade or department.* **Objective**—Find ways to increase the meaningful collaboration and articulation between teachers who are not in the same grades/departments.

- *PLOP—Reports from general and special educators, as well as family members, indicate that students with mild to moderate disabilities are more often included in general education classes and activities than are students with more significant disabilities.* **Objective**—Work with families, community members, staff, and teachers to improve the collaboration that occurs with all students, with a focus on students with more severe disabilities.

- *PLOP—Teachers and students do not have a real connection with support staff; support staff (maintenance, secretarial, yard, and lunch duty) report a division between them and faculty.* **Objective**—Identify ways in which support staff can be included in school culture in consequential ways.

- *PLOP—Faculty and staff are split in terms of their view of administrative style preference; some appear to want more input, while others feel they have been well-involved in decision making.* **Objective**—Create systems (e.g., site-based management team) that allow those individuals who are looking for more input to give it, without giving additional work to others.

These are examples of objectives, or minigoals, that may be created based on the Present Level of Performance your team identified in its triage survey and other data collection procedures. The more you know about where your school currently is collaboratively, the easier it is to identify objectives for achievement toward the overall goal. Your group may come up with tons of objectives; let the ideas fly! Once those objectives have been created in association with your present levels of performance, you may then need to work as a group (or even in small subcommittees) to prioritize them based on time, logistics, need, resources, and a reality check.

Creating a plan. Congratulations! You've worked through a thorough and time-consuming process to discover the strengths and weaknesses of your school in regard to collaboration, and you're ready to take action to make it better. You're anxious, aren't you? Ready to go to Step 3? We thought so. Step 3 is the specifics stage: *Determine Benchmarks (outcomes, responsibilities, and timelines).* This is where your group finally gets to decide what it's going to *do* to make change. You know where you are; you know what you want; now you have to take those critical concrete actions. In this step, you need to look at each of the objectives you identified in Step 2 and work as a team (yes, collaboratively) to figure out what concrete actions can be taken to achieve each objective. Let's take one of the previous examples and work it out (see Figure 10.2).

Example: Your group identified a real concern by families that they feel very little connection to schools (Step 1). Families reported not knowing what's going on or what the goals of the school are; they stated that they are not involved in decision making or other school activities. Team meetings such as PTA, SSTs, or IEPs are considered to be contentious, and families feel defensive. As a group, you all concurred that an important goal would be to improve that connectedness. You agreed to an objective stating that you will "develop both formal and informal ways for families to feel a connection and to be able to collaborate in meaningful ways with faculty and staff" (Step 2).

So we arrive at Step 3. Step 3 involves brainstorming ways to meet that objective. In other words, in our previous example, your team needs to come up with ideas to increase the connection between the families and the school. (During this step, go back to Chapter 9 and review the different strategies for generating ideas in *Hints and Tips* at the end of the chapter. Participants need to feel comfortable generating and sharing ideas without feeling embarrassed or constrained, and we've given you several ideas about how you can work through this process.) Once the group feels that sufficient ideas have been generated, go back to the ones you like the most and talk about who would be involved, what realistic timelines would be to accomplish that objective, and what some potential considerations or issues would be with that suggestion. If you don't talk about these logistical aspects right up front, it is unlikely the idea will come to fruition. You need to be sure that the group has considered the potential barriers and addressed them proactively. Are you all on board?

PULLING IT ALL TOGETHER: HOW CAN WE AVOID BEING OVERWHELMED OR HAVING ONE PERSON DO ALL THE WORK?

This book has provided you with numerous strategies for collaborating for various purposes. We've discussed Response to Intervention, teams, Universal Design for Learning, co-teaching, and home–school interactions—all for the purpose of improving student learning and success. Each of the tips taken individually may seem practical and doable. The difficulty arises when we look at these all together. Trying to do it all is daunting, and yet the only way true systemic change can take place is when all the pieces come together and don't feel like different and unrelated components.

Here comes the good news and it comes in two parts:

1. There is a lot of overlap in the various collaborative endeavors or instructional approaches we've been discussing (RTI, co-teaching, teams, UDL).

2. A major benefit of collaboration is that you are not doing all of this alone.

We suggest you use a small team of key individuals who represent all of the stakeholders in the school to spearhead this IEP process. Some of the areas will only impact teachers or in-class personnel, others will only impact certain areas of the school, while still others will impact the entire school and surrounding community. Once you identify these areas and the big questions surrounding them, divide and conquer. Get a group together that really wants to tackle the instructional issues (e.g., *How can we institutionalize collaborative planning that incorporates UDL, differentiation, and co-teaching without driving us to tears?*), while another group focuses on issues related to families (e.g., *How can we improve the communication between home and school that respects the time and expertise of both?*). A third group might address broader issues (e.g., *How can we provide our students with real-world content, skills, and practices that are beneficial to their future and to the future of our community?*). Set timelines for

> **Principal Points**
>
> Before beginning this process, take a good, hard look at your managerial style. Do you micromanage or do you "delegate" by telling others what to do? If you create and embrace collaborative teams, remember that parity and volunteerism are important components for success. If you are part of a team, you are just that: PART of the team—not *the* team or the decision maker on the team. Encourage and invite key people to be part of these teams . . . and then trust their expertise and input.

Figure 10.2 IEP for School Change: Example of One Area

- *PLOP—Families report having little regular connection to schools.* **Objective**—Develop both formal and informal ways for families to feel a connection and to be able to collaborate in substantive ways with faculty and staff.

Benchmark Ideas:

What could we do?	Who would be responsible?	What would be our timelines?	What are potential issues or considerations with this idea?
Institute a "Have Coffee With the Principal" activity once a month.	Principal; office secretary (set up); janitorial staff (clean room); PTA (get coffee and food)	Find and set dates for each month before school starts.	Need to publicize well; not all parents can come before school—also offer after school; check funding; watch time (45 minutes?); need interpreter; do we need child care?
Survey parents to identify areas of expertise and then incorporate them.	PTA could lead; teacher reps could help create survey and identify areas to use	Create survey by beginning of school year; give out in school packets; have electronic as well as hard-copy versions available.	Want good return rate; need Spanish version; follow-up phone calls; want to encourage all areas of expertise and suggest various areas for support (e.g., cooking, construction, technology).
Conduct professional development (PD) on teams and invite families to participate and attend.	PD team: School counselor, special educator, school psych; teacher rep	Use October PD date; need to get RSVPs by end of September; need to publicize in August or September.	Let faculty and parents know this is about IEPs, SSTs, etc.: give time for families to get time off work; include some parents as panel members; need to include info on addressing conflict.
Ask teachers to make positive phone calls home regularly; have interpreters available.	All faculty; need interpreters; ELL coach could help with cultural suggestions	Have sign-ups for interpreters/ELL; ask for five calls home each week all year.	Teachers run out of time; how do we incentivize and ensure this is occurring?

coming back together to the stakeholder team, not just to report progress, but also to share barriers or concerns, ask for suggestions, and reveal any achievements or accomplishments the team has made. Identify ways and times to share progress with the school community as well. Remember that while part of our goal is to transform our practices to become more collaborative, we also want to ensure the institutionalization of these changes. Isolated successes are not likely to be replicated. We need to celebrate our collaborative experiences and publicize our successes.

> ### In Practice
>
> It was his 20th year teaching, and Mr. De la Torre was excited about the new school year. However, when the principal had described the collaborative teams that would be tackling various issues in the school, Mr. De la Torre was skeptical. He didn't want to be told he needed to work with other people on a project he didn't care about. When the principal encouraged folks to share their own concerns or areas of interest, he had sarcastically offered, "How 'bout finding ways to get these kids to actually be motivated to learn for a change?" He didn't expect to be taken seriously, but the principal asked if he'd be willing to work on that particular issue. Now he was sitting across the table from a parent, two students, the school psychologist, two other teachers, and three community members: an aerospace engineer, a Starbucks manager, and a local author. All of them were energetically discussing ways to motivate students to learn. Mr. De la Torre leaned in and began to offer his own suggestions. This was worthwhile!

TIPS FOR INSTITUTIONALIZATION: HOW CAN WE MAKE SURE THESE CHANGES LAST?

How many times have you talked to a veteran teacher who has said, "It's all the same thing, just by a different name" or "I've seen it all before—the pendulum just swings back and forth"? Or perhaps you have been in education a while and you feel the same way. We need to recognize resistance to change as natural and even as a good thing. However, we also need to help our colleagues (and ourselves) recognize that when change is a result of a collaborative effort, there is more buy-in by stakeholders for that change to be meaningful (Irwin & Farr, 2004; Vaughn & Coleman, 2004; Walther-Thomas, Korinek, McLaughlin, & Williams, 2000). Think about it. Teachers get a mandate from the district office to incorporate more technology into the curriculum. Many teachers roll their eyes and continue doing status quo, because change is difficult and there is little buy-in. However, when a team consisting of a parent, student, vice-principal, Spanish teacher, special educator, math teacher, and paraprofessional get together and agree that technology needs to be better utilized to increase student motivation, family participation, and community involvement, it comes across as a true need and not just another idea from "top-down." Educational change is always more effective when it comes from within the school community.

Our *In a Nutshell* table on page 146 provides you with a variety of practical suggestions for ways to institutionalize collaboration in your school. Since collaboration is a "style for interaction" (Friend & Cook, 2009, p. 7), it's not something you can mandate. However, the more supportive people are of one another, the more teams work together to implement change, and the more successful these endeavors are, the more collaborative the school will become. True school change designed to transform curriculum and instruction, as well as the way we do things, means we have to not only commit to the reform, but we also have to make sure that we keep high expectations, have true instructional leadership, and engage in collaborative work. It is also clear that "change takes time and sustained effort and requires careful prioritization" (Borko, Wolf, Simone, & Uchiyama, 2003, p. 198). In fact, Borko and colleagues join other experts in school reform (e.g., Fullan, 2006, 2007; Waldron & McLeskey, 2010) in strongly recommending that schools that want to make real change in their school culture identify baby steps and realistic goals for doing so. The strategies we've provided in our *In a Nutshell* table demonstrate some very concrete methods for doing so. But don't smile too soon! Fullan (guru of all things related to change) said way back in 1991 that "simple changes may be easier to carry out, but they may not make much of a difference. Complex changes promise to accomplish more . . . but they also demand more effort, and failure takes a greater toll. The answer seems to be to break complex changes into components and implement

In a Nutshell

Strategies for Institutionalizing Collaboration in Schools

Strategy	Description of Strategy
Create a culture of expectancy	Create an atmosphere in which there is a bit of peer pressure to work with colleagues; expect collaboration by immersing the school in the concept; keep the concept out in front, and create multiple opportunities to collaborate around different topics/activities.
Increase sharing of information	Open meetings with faculty sharing successes and concerns; rotate through different departments, grade levels, or individuals; allow for personal sharing of successes and concerns as well as school-related ones; have faculty create a "central clearinghouse on students" with information gleaned by teachers regarding learning styles, grading preferences, parent feedback, multiple intelligences, etc. (avoid adding confidential information).
Encourage sharing of expertise	Help school members recognize and appreciate the shared expertise that exists; have an "expert in the lounge" day each week (with experts on anything from grading, foldables, skateboarding jargon, organizational tips, knitting, and working with parents); ask for newsletter articles; create an "Ask the Expert" website and include parents, staff, students, and community members as experts; ask teachers to conduct staff development programs so that it is not always experts from afar who are presenting.
Enable sharing of ideas	Have a folder at every photocopier in the school and ask teachers to make an extra copy of any good ideas or work they are doing to share with others; at the end of the year, compile a "best ideas" folder with open access; scan documents and create an Intranet folder for faculty access to good instructional ideas; encourage teams to share good lesson plans and avoid recreating the wheel; hold classroom walkabouts where teachers get to visit each other's rooms and share ideas.
Allow sharing of concerns	Create opportunities for roundtable discussions of ongoing concerns or issues; anyone who wants to can post an issue to discuss and a small group would get together to discuss and then share results for one hour or less; invite community members.
Promote sharing of knowledge	Facilitate book studies by ensuring multiple copies of books on differentiation, collaboration, and strategies; get funding for sending teachers and related staff to conferences (send individuals from different areas when possible); start Critical Friends groups or Action Research groups; make a connection with a local university's college of education and invite ongoing communication and collaboration with faculty there.
Model sharing of consideration, humor, compassion, and other positive personality traits	Regularly recognize the positive attributes of others and model them yourself; set up opportunities for rapport-building that don't have other ulterior motives (e.g., a family picnic that is not also a fundraiser); allow risk-taking, sharing of nontraditional ideas, and constructive criticism; laugh often and help others do so as well.

Source: Many ideas here were from Wormeli, 2006, and adapted to this concept.

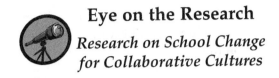

Eye on the Research

Research on School Change for Collaborative Cultures

Issues	What has the research found?
Professional Development	• Collaborative professional development is more time consuming and expensive (Lang & Fox, 2003) but also tends to be less fragmented, more long-term, more focused on student outcomes, and has higher levels of teacher buy-in, follow-up, and administrative support (Guskey, 2003d; Lang & Fox, 2003; McLeskey & Waldron, 2002a; Richardson & Placier, 2001).
Leadership	• School administrators who did not subscribe to distributed leadership, or who did not communicate regularly or support teacher leaders, were less successful in establishing a collaborative culture, building teacher trust, and having buy-in for change than those who did (Mangin, 2007).
Different Views of Teacher Collaboration	• *Teacher collaboration* and *collaborative cultures* are terms used differently depending on one's perspective. Five various discourses were identified on teacher collaboration in the research (Lavié, 2006). • Collaboration has been shown to be highly effective in including students with significant disabilities in general education classes (Downing & Peckham-Hardin, 2007).

For more research in this area go to http://www.corwin.com/diverseschools.

them in a divisible and/or incremental manner" (pp. 71–72). Hey, isn't that just what you've done? You identified your overall big goal, then your smaller objectives, and now you're working on the activities to achieve those objectives. Darn, you're good.

TAKING A COLLABORATIVE SCHOOL CULTURE OUT OF THE ABSTRACT

Strategies for creating a more collaborative school

• Put the word *collaborative* on the front screen at a faculty meeting and ask participants to write their own definition; share those definitions and select one as a group to be your school's definition of *collaboration/collaborative*.

• Once the definition of collaboration has been selected, ask stakeholders to share concrete examples of what they would like to see in a truly collaborative school. Ensure large amounts of feedback by doing the following: conducting surveys at faculty meetings, having a jar for ideas in the front office for faculty and parents, having a "tear-off and return" sheet in the school newsletter, putting an ad in the local paper, having an online survey available on the home page of the school website, having a school representative attend a Chamber of Commerce meeting to get feedback, having a booth for feedback at the school's sporting events, and asking students for their feedback during homeroom time.

• Value and celebrate different frames of reference—but also work to understand them. Just having a "Black Awareness Month," an "Autism Speaks Day," or a "Cinco de Mayo Celebration" doesn't help stakeholders understand different cultures or frames of reference. Add to these activities by asking participants to share their experiences and their preferred ways of communicating, learning, and dealing with conflict. Find out where there are differences and similarities.

• Keep reminding yourself why you are doing this. Pick one of these pithy quotes and have someone make you a beautiful sign of it. Put up your sign and look at it often. And overall, good luck! We're with you on this.

**“Coming together is a beginning.
Keeping together is progress.
Working together is success. ”**

—Henry Ford

**“ Alone we can do so little;
together we can do so much. ”**

—Helen Keller

On the web

For more strategies for creating a more collaborative school go to http://www.corwin .com/diverseschools.

THUMBNAILS OF RESOURCES ON THE INTERNET

The following elements can be found on the companion website for *Collaborate, Communicate, and Differentiate!* at http://www.corwin.com/diverseschools.

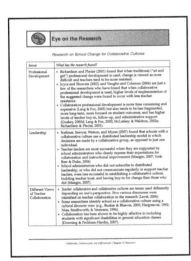

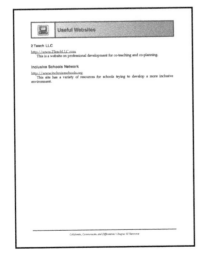

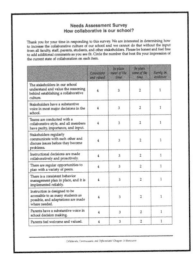

References

Achinstein, B. (2002). Conflict amid community: The micropolitics of teacher collaboration. *Teachers College Record, 104*(3), 421–455.

Adams, L., & Cessna, K. (1993). Metaphors of the co-taught classroom. *Preventing School Failure, 37*(4), 28–31.

Adler, R. (2006). Getting beyond "yes": An interview with Roger Fisher and Daniel Shapiro. *Dispute Resolution Journal, 61*(1), 40–43.

Adler, R. B., Rosenfeld, L. B., & Towne, N. (1995). *Interplay: The process of interpersonal communication* (6th ed.). San Diego, CA: Harcourt Brace.

Alper, S., & Raharinirina, S. (2006). Assistive technology for individuals with disabilities: A review and synthesis of the literature. *Journal of Special Education Technology, 21*(21), 47–64.

Anderson, M. (1917). *Education of defectives in the public schools.* Yonkers-on-Hudson, NY: World Book.

Aries, E. J. (1982). Verbal and nonverbal behavior in single-sex and mixed-sex groups: Are traditional sex roles changing? *Psychological Reports, 51*, 127–134.

Aries, E. J. (2006). *Sex differences and similarities in communication* (2nd ed.). Mahwah, NJ: Lawrence Erlbaum.

Arndt, J. S. (2008). Early childhood success: Recognizing families as integral partners. *Childhood Education, 84*(5), 281–286.

Baer, M. (2010). Conflict in schools: Reducing conflict and building community. *Independent School, 69*(2), 82–89.

Bahamonde, C., & Friend, M. (1999). Teaching English language learners: A proposal for effective service delivery through collaboration and coteaching. *Journal of Educational and Psychological Consultation, 10*(1), 1–24.

Barsky, A. E. (2000). *Conflict resolution for the helping professions.* Belmont, CA: Brooks/Cole.

Bauwens, J., & Hourcade, J. (1997). Cooperative teaching: Pictures of possibilities. *Intervention in School & Clinic, 33*(2), 81–85.

Bauwens, J., Hourcade, J., & Friend, M. (1989). Cooperative teaching: A model for general and special education integration. *Remedial and Special Education, 10*, 17–22.

Bellanca, J. (2009). *200+ active learning strategies and projects for engaging students' multiple intelligences.* Thousand Oaks, CA: Corwin.

Bender, W. N. (2008). *Differentiating instruction for students with learning disabilities: Best practices for general and special educators.* Thousand Oaks, CA: Corwin.

Beninghof, A. (2003). *Co-teaching that works: Effective strategies for working together in today's inclusive classrooms.* Bellevue, WA: Bureau of Education and Research.

Benner, S. (2010). *Promising practices for elementary teachers: Make no excuses!* Thousand Oaks, CA: Corwin.

Bennett, B., & Rolheiser, C. (2001). *Beyond Monet: The artful science of instructional integration.* Ontario, Canada: Bookation.

Blatt, B., & Kaplan, F. (1966). *Christmas in purgatory: A photographic essay on mental retardation.* Boston: Allyn & Bacon.

Blatt, B., & Kaplan, F. (1974). *Christmas in purgatory: A photographic essay on mental retardation* (2nd ed.). Syracuse, NY: Human Policy Press.

Bonebright, D. A. (2010). 40 years of storming: A historical review of Tuckman's model of small group development. *Human Resource Development International, 13*(1), 111–120.

Borko, H., Wolf, S. A., Simone, G., & Uchiyama, K. P. (2003). Schools in transition: Reform efforts and school capacity in Washington state. *Educational Evaluation and Policy Analysis, 25*(2), 171–201.

Boscardin, M. L. (2005). The administrative role in transforming secondary schools to support inclusive evidence-based practices. *American Secondary Education, 33*(3), 21–32.

Bouck, E. C., Courtad, C. A., Heutsche, A., Okolo, C., & Englert, C. (2009). The virtual history museum: A universally designed approach to social studies instruction. *Teaching Exceptional Children, 42*(2), 14–20.

Boudah, D., Schumaker, J., & Deshler, D. (1997). Collaborative instruction: Is it an effective option for inclusion in secondary classrooms? *Learning Disability Quarterly, 20,* 293–316.

Bowe, F. (2005). *Making inclusion work.* Columbus, OH: Pearson.

Browder, D. M., Mims, P. J., Spooner, F., Ahlgrim-Delzell, L., & Lee, A. (2008). Teaching elementary students with multiple disabilities to participate in shared stories. *Research and Practice for Persons with Severe Disabilities, 33*(1), 3–12.

Brown-Chidsey, R. (2005). Introduction to problem-solving assessment. In R. Brown-Chidsey (Ed.), *Assessment for intervention: A problem-solving approach* (pp. 3–9). New York: Guilford Press.

Brown-Chidsey, R., & Steege, M. W. (2005). *Response to intervention: Principles and strategies for effective practice.* New York: Guildford Press.

Bryant, B., & Rivera, D. P. (1995). *Using assistive technology to facilitate cooperative learning.* Presented at the Florida Educational Technology Conference, Orlando, FL. (ERIC Document Reproduction Service No. ED380975)

Bryant, D. P., & Barrera, M. (2009). Changing roles for educators within the framework of response to intervention. *Intervention in School and Clinic, 45*(1), 72–79.

Bryk, A., Camburn, E., & Louis, K. (1999). Professional community in Chicago elementary schools: Facilitating factors and organizational consequences. *Educational Administration Quarterly, 35,* 751–781.

Burchers, S. (2007). *Vocabulary cartoons: SAT word power.* Punta Gorda, FL: New Monic Books.

Bursuck, W. D., Polloway, E. A., Plante, L., Epstein, M. H., Jayanthi, M., & McConeghy, J. (1996). Report card grading and adaptations: A national survey of classroom practices. *Exceptional Children, 62*(4), 301–318.

Busher, H., & Bleaves, D. (2000). Growing collegial cultures in subject departments in secondary schools: Working with science staff. *School Leadership & Management, 20*(1), 99–112.

Cai, D. A., & Fink, E. L. (2002). Conflict style differences between individualists and collectivists. *Communication Monographs, 69*(1), 67–87.

Carnoy, M. (1999). *Globalization and educational reform: What planners need to know.* Paris: United Nations Educational, Scientific, and Cultural Organization, International Institute for Educational Planning.

Case, L. P., Speece, D. L., & Malloy, D. E. (2003). The validity of a response-to-instruction paradigm to identify reading disabilities: A longitudinal analysis of individual differences and contextual factors. *School Psychology Review, 32,* 557–582.

Castleberry, G. T., & Evers, R. B. (2010). Incorporate technology into the modern language classroom. *Intervention in School and Clinic, 45*(3), 201–205.

Center for Applied Special Technology. *Teaching every student.* Retrieved from http://www.cast.org/teachingeverystudent

Center for Collaborative Education. (2001). *Turning points: Transforming middle schools: Guide to collaborative culture and shared leadership.* Newton, MA: Author.

Chiang, H., & Jacobs, K. (2009). Effect of computer-based instruction on students' self-perception and functional task performance. *Disability and Rehabilitation: Assistive Technology, 4*(2), 106–118.

Colbert, R. D., Vernon-Jones, R., & Pransky, K. (2006). The school change feedback process: Creating a new role for counselors in educational reform. *Journal of Counseling and Development, 84,* 72–82.

Cole, S., Horvath, B., Chapman, C., Deschenes, C., Ebeling, D., & Sprague, J. (2000). *Adapting curriculum and instruction in inclusive classrooms: A teacher's desk reference.* Bloomington, IN: Center for School and Community Integration.

Cornille, T. A., Pestle, R. E., & Vanwy, R. W. (1999). Teachers' conflict management styles with peers and students' parents. *International Journal of Conflict Management, 10*(1), 69–79.

Council for Exceptional Children. (1994). *Creating schools for all our students: What 12 schools have to say.* Reston, VA: Working Forum on Inclusive Schools.

Crim, C., Desjean-Perrotta, B., & Moseley, C. (2008). Partnerships gone wild. *Childhood Education, 85*(1), 6–12.

Cross, L., & Walker-Knight, D. (1997). Inclusion: Developing collaborative and cooperative school communities. *Educational Forum, 61*(3), 269–277.

DeLaTorre, W., Rubalcava, L. A., & Cabello, B. (Eds.). (2004). *Urban education in America: A critical perspective.* Dubuque, IA: Kendall/Hunt.

Dieker, L. (1998). Rationale for co-teaching. *Social Studies Review, 37*(2), 62–65.

Dieker, L. A. (2001). What are the characteristics of "effective" middle and high school co-taught teams? *Preventing School Failure, 46*(1), 14–25.

Dieker, L. A. (2007). *Demystifying secondary inclusion: Powerful school-wide and classroom strategies.* Port Chester, NY: Dude Publishing, National Professional Resources.

Dieker, L. A. (2008). *Co-teaching lesson plan book.* Whitefish Bay, WI: Knowledge by Design.

Dolan, R. P., Hall, T. E., & Banerjee, M. (2005). Applying principles of Universal Design to test delivery: The effect of computer-based read-aloud on test performance of high school students with learning disabilities. *Journal of Technology, Learning and Assessment, 3*(7), 3–32.

Downing, J. A. (2008). *Including students with severe and multiple disabilities in typical classrooms: Practical strategies for teachers* (3rd ed.). Baltimore: Brookes.

Downing, J. A. (2010). *Academic instruction for students with moderate and severe intellectual disabilities in inclusive classrooms.* Thousand Oaks, CA: Corwin.

Downing, J. E., & Peckham-Hardin, K. (2007). Inclusive education: What makes it a good education for students with moderate to severe disabilities? *Research and Practice for Persons with Severe Disabilities, 32,* 16–30.

Doyle, M. B. (2008). *The paraprofessional's guide to the inclusive classroom: Working as a team.* Baltimore: Brookes.

Durand, V. M., & Crimmins, D. B. (1992). *Motivation Assessment Scale.* Topeka, KS: Monaco & Associates.

Dymond, S. K., & Russell, D. L. (2004). Impact of grade and disability on the instructional context of inclusive classrooms. *Education and Training in Developmental Disabilities, 39,* 127–140.

Education for All Handicapped Children Act of 1975, 20 U.S.C. § 1400 *et seq.*

Elliott, J. (2008). Response to intervention: What and why? *School Administrator, 65*(8), 10–18.

Ervin, R. A., Schaughency, E., Matthews, A., Goodman, S. D., & McGlinchey, M. T. (2007). Primary and secondary prevention of behavior difficulties: Developing a data-informed problem-solving model to guide decision making at a school-wide level. *Psychology in Schools, 44*(1), 7–18.

Fairbanks, S., Sugai, G., Guardino, D., & Lathrop, M. (2007). Response to intervention: Examining classroom behavior support in second grade. *Exceptional Children, 73,* 288–310.

Family-teacher partnerships. (n.d.). Retrieved from http://www.pacer.org/mpc/pdf/MPC45.pdf

Fast, J. D. (2003). An in-law comes to stay: Examination of interdisciplinary conflict in a school-based health center. *Social Work, 48*(1), 45–50.

Feifer, S. G. (2008). Integrating response to intervention (RTI) with neuropsychology: A scientific approach to reading. *Psychology in Schools, 45,* 812–825.

Feldman, R., Masalha, S., & Derdikman-Eiron, R. (2010). Conflict resolution in the parent–child, marital and peer contexts and children's aggression in the peer group: A process-oriented cultural perspective. *Developmental Psychology, 46*(2), 310–325.

Fennick, E. (2001). Coteaching. *Teaching Exceptional Children, 33*(6), 60–66.

Fennick, E., & Liddy, D. (2001). Responsibilities and preparation for collaborative teaching: Co-teachers' perspectives. *Teacher Education and Special Education, 24*(3), 229–240.

Fisher, D., & Frey, N. (2001). Access to core curriculum: Critical ingredients for student success. *Remedial and Special Education, 22,* 127–140.

Fisher, R., & Shapiro, D. (2006). *Beyond reason: Using emotions as you negotiate.* New York: Penguin.

Fisher, R., Ury, W., & Patton, B. (1991). *Getting to yes: Negotiating agreement without giving in* (2nd ed.). New York: Penguin.

Fletcher, J. M., Coulter, W. A., Reschley, D. J., & Vaughn, S. (2004). Alternative approaches to the definition and identification of learning disabilities: Some questions and answers. *Annals of Dyslexia, 54,* 304–331.

Friedman Narr, R., Murawski, W. W., & Spencer, S. (2007, Spring). Fostering independence in students with special needs. *The LAUSD Ladder*, pp. 9–10.

Friend, M. (2000). Perspectives: Myths and misunderstandings about collaboration. *Remedial and Special Education, 21*, 130–132, 160.

Friend, M., & Cook, L. (1990). Collaboration as a predictor for school success in school reform. *Journal of Educational and Psychological Consultation, 1*(1), 69–86.

Friend, M., & Cook, L. (2009). *Interactions: Collaboration skills for school professionals* (6th ed.). White Plains, NY: Longman.

Fuchs, D. (2003). On responsiveness-to-intervention as a valid method of LD identification: Some things we need to know. *Perspectives, 29*(2), 28–31.

Fuchs, D., & Fuchs, L. S. (2006). Introduction to response to intervention: What, why and how valid is it? *Reading Research Quarterly, 41*(1), 92–99.

Fuchs, D., Mick, D., Morgan, P. L., & Young, C. L. (2003). Responsiveness to intervention: Definitions, evidence, and implications for the learning disabilities construct. *Learning Disabilities: Research and Practice, 18*, 157–171.

Fuchs, L. S., & Fuchs, D. (2007). A model for implementing responsiveness to intervention. *Teaching Exceptional Children, 39*(5), 14–20.

Fuchs, L. S., Fuchs, D., & Hollenbeck, K. N. (2007). Extending responsiveness to intervention to mathematics at first and third grades. *Learning Disabilities Research and Practice, 22*(1), 13–24.

Fullan, M. (1991). *The new meaning of educational change.* New York: Teachers College Press.

Fullan, M. (2006). Leading professional learning: Think "system" and not "individual school" if the goal is to fundamentally change the culture of schools. *School Administrator, 63*(10), 10–15.

Fullan, M. G. (2007). *The new meaning of educational change* (4th ed.). New York: Teachers College Press.

Furumo, K., & Pearson, J. M. (2007). Gender-based communication styles, trust and satisfaction in virtual teams. *Journal of Information, Information Technology, and Organizations, 2*, 47–60.

Gamble, T. K., & Gamble, M. (2001). *Communication works* (7th ed.). New York: McGraw-Hill.

Gately, S. E., & Gately, F. J. (2001). Understanding co-teaching components. *Teaching Exceptional Children, 33*(4), 40–47.

Gavigan, K., & Kurtts, S. (2009). AT, UD, and thee: Using assistive technology and Universal Design for Learning in 21st century media centers. *Library Media Connection, 27*(4), 54–56.

Gerber, P., & Popp, P. (1999). Consumer perspectives on the collaborative teaching model: Views of students with and without LD and their parents. *Remedial and Special Education, 20*(5), 288–296.

Giangreco, M. F., Baumgart, D. M., & Doyle, M. B. (1995). How inclusion can facilitate teaching and learning. *Intervention in School and Clinic, 30*, 273–278.

Goodman, A. (2008). Student-led, teacher-supported conferences: Improving communication across an urban school district. *Middle School Journal, 39*(3), 48–54.

Grandin, T. (2006). *Thinking in pictures: And other reports from my life with autism* (2nd ed.). London: Vintage Books.

Greenes, C. (2009). Mathematics learning and knowing: A cognitive process. *Journal of Education, 189*(3), 55–64.

Gresham, F. (2007). Response to intervention and emotional and behavioral disorders: Best practices in assessment for intervention. *Assessment for Effective Intervention, 32*, 214–222.

Gronn, P. (2002). Designer leadership: The emerging global adoption of preparation standards. *Journal of School Leadership, 12*(5), 552–578.

Gupta, S. (2008). Mine the potential of multicultural teams. *HR Magazine, 53*(10), 79–84.

Guskey, T. (2003a). Analyzing lists of the characteristics of effective professional development to promote visionary leadership. *NASSP Bulletin, 87*(637), 4–20.

Guskey, T. (2003b). How classroom assessments improve learning. *Educational Leadership, 60*(5), 6–11.

Guskey, T. (2003c). Scooping up meaningful evidence. *Journal of Staff Development, 24*(4), 27–30.

Guskey, T. (2003d). What makes professional development effective? *Phi Delta Kappan, 84*(10), 748–750.

Guskey, T. R., & Jung, L. A. (2009). Grading and reporting in a standards-based environment: Implications for students with special needs. *Theory Into Practice, 48*, 53–62.

Halsey, P. A. (2005). Parent involvement in junior high schools: A failure to communicate. *American Secondary Education, 34*(1), 57–69.

Hargreaves, A. (1992). Time and teachers' work: An analysis of the intensification thesis. *Teachers College Record, 94*(1), 87–108.

Harniss, M. K., Caros, J., & Gersten, R. (2007). Impact of the design of U.S. history textbooks on content acquisition and academic engagement of special education students: An experimental investigation. *Journal of Learning Disabilities, 40*(2), 100–110.

Harris, K. C. (1996). Collaboration within a multicultural society: Issues for consideration. *Remedial and Special Education, 17*(6), 355–362.

Harvey, M. W., Cotton, S. E., & Koch, K. R. (2007). Indiana secondary CTE instructors' perceptions of program expectations, modifications, accommodations, and postsecondary outcomes for students with disabilities. *Journal for Vocational Special Needs Education, 29*(2), 16–32.

Hawkin, L. S., Vincent, C. G., & Schumann, J. (2008). Response to Intervention for social behavior: Challenges and opportunities. *Journal of Emotional and Behavioral Disorders, 16,* 213–225.

Hohenbrink, J., Johnston, M., & Westhoven, L. (1997). Collaborative teaching of a social studies methods course: Intimidation and change. *Journal of Teacher Education, 48*(4), 293–300.

Hopkins, D. (2001). *School improvement for real.* New York: Routledge.

Hopkins, D., Ainscow, M., & West, M. (1994). *School improvement in an era of change.* London/New York: Cassell.

Huber, J. J. (2005). What works for me: Collaborative units for addressing multiple grade levels. *Intervention in School and Clinic, 40*(5), 301–308.

Hughes, C. E., & Murawski, W. W. (2001). Lessons from another field: Applying co-teaching strategies to gifted education. *Gifted Child Quarterly, 45*(3), 195–204.

Hughes-Lynch, C. (2010). *Children with high-functioning autism: A parent's guide.* Naperville, IL: Sourcebooks.

Hunt, P., Alwell, M., Farron-Davis, F., & Goetz, L. (1996). Creating socially supportive environments for fully included students who experience multiple disabilities. *Journal of the Association for Persons with Severe Handicaps, 21*(2), 53–71.

Individuals with Disabilities Education Act Amendments of 1997, 42 U.S.C. § 1400–1487 *et seq.*

Individuals with Disabilities Education Improvement Act of 2004, 20 U.S.C. § 1400 *et seq.*

IRIS Center for Training Enhancements. (n.d.). *Universal Design for Learning: Creating a learning environment that challenges and engages all students.* Retrieved from http://iris.peabody.vanderbilt.edu/udl/chalcycle.htm

Irwin, J. W., & Farr, W. (2004). Collaborative school communities that support teaching and learning. *Reading & Writing Quarterly, 20,* 343–363.

Jackson, C. W., & Turnbull, A. P. (2004). Impact of deafness on family life: A review of the literature. *Journal of Early Childhood Special Education, 24*(1), 15–29.

Jayanthi, M., & Friend, M. (1992). Interpersonal problem-solving: A selective literature review to guide practice. *Journal of Educational and Psychological Consultation, 3*(1), 39–53.

Johnson, E. S. (2000). The effects of accommodations on performance assessments. *Remedial and Special Education, 21*(5), 261–267.

Jones, M., & Carlier, L. (1995). Creating inclusionary opportunities for learners with multiple disabilities: A team-teaching approach. *Teaching Exceptional Children, 27*(3), 23–27.

Joyce, B., & Showers, B. (2002). *Student achievement through staff development* (3rd ed.). Alexandria, VA: Association for Supervision and Curriculum Development.

Kagan, S. (1995). *Cooperative learning.* San Clemente, CA: Kagan.

Kavale, K. A., & Forness, S. R. (2000). History, rhetoric, and reality: Analysis of the inclusion debate. *Remedial and Special Education, 21*(5), 279–296.

Kennedy, J. F. (1961). *Regarding the need for a national plan on mental retardation.* Retrieved from http://www.mnddc.org/parallels2/pdf/60s/62/62-sallinger-pr.pdf

Kim, A., Woodruff, A. L., Klein, C., & Vaughn, S. (2006). Facilitating co-teaching for literacy in general education classrooms through technology: Focus on students with learning disabilities. *Reading and Writing Quarterly, 22*(3), 269–291.

King-Sears, M. (2009). Universal Design for Learning: Technology and pedagogy. *Learning Disability Quarterly, 32*(4), 199–201.

Kluth, P., & Danaher, S. (2010). *From tutor scripts to talking sticks: 100 ways to differentiate instruction in K–12 classrooms.* Baltimore: Brookes.

Kluth, P., & Schwarz, P. (2008). *"Just give him the whale!" 20 ways to use fascinations, areas of expertise, and strengths to support students with autism.* Baltimore: Brookes.

Kortering, L. J., McClannon, T. W., & Braziel, P. M. (2008). Universal Design for Learning: A look at what algebra and biology students with and without high incidence disabilities are saying. *Remedial & Special Education, 29*(6), 352–363.

Kovaleski, J. F. (2007). Response to intervention: Considerations for research and systems change. *School Psychology Review, 36*(4), 638–646.

Kruse, S. D. (2001). Creating communities of reform: Continuous improvement planning teams. *Journal of Educational Administration, 39*(4), 359–383.

Kurtts, S. A., Matthews, C. E., & Smallwood, T. (2009). Solving the differences: A physical science lesson using Universal Design. *Intervention in School and Clinic, 44*(3), 151–159.

Lang, M., & Fox, L. (2003). Breaking with tradition: Providing effective professional development for instructional personnel supporting students with severe disabilities. *Teacher Education and Special Education, 26*(1), 17–26.

Lavié, J. M. (2006). Academic discourses on school-based teacher collaboration: Revisiting the arguments. *Educational Administration Quarterly, 42*(5), 773–805.

Lavoie, R. (2004). *How difficult can this be? The F.A.T. City Workshop: Understanding learning disabilities* [Video]. United States: PBS Videos.

Lavoie, R. (2008). *The motivation breakthrough: Six secrets to turning on the tuned-out child.* New York: Simon & Schuster.

Lee, S., Wehmeyer, M. L, Palmer, S. B., Soukup, J. H., & Little, T. D. (2008). Self-determination and access to the general education curriculum. *Journal of Special Education, 42,* 79–107.

Lee, S., Wehmeyer, M. L., Soukup, J. H., & Palmer, S. B. (2010). Impact of curricular modifications on access to the general education curriculum for students with disabilities. *Exceptional Children, 76*(2), 213–233.

Lengel, T., & Kuczala, M. (2010). *The kinesthetic classroom: Teaching through movement.* Thousand Oaks, CA: Corwin.

Lieber, J., Horn, E., Palmer, S., & Fleming, K. (2008). Access to the general education curriculum for preschoolers with disabilities: Children's school success. *Exceptionality, 16*(1), 18–32.

Linan-Thompson, S., Vaughn, S., Prater, K., & Cirino, P. (2006). The response to intervention of English language learners at risk for reading problems. *Journal of Learning Disabilities, 39*(5), 390–398.

Lovelace, S., & Wheeler, T. R. (2006). Cultural discontinuity between home and school language socialization patterns: Implications for teachers. *Education, 127*(2), 303–309.

Lyman, F. T. (1981). The responsive classroom discussion: The inclusion of all students. In A. Anderson (Ed.), *Mainstreaming digest* (pp. 109–113). College Park: University of Maryland College of Education.

Mackety, D. M., & Linder-VanBerschot, J. A. (2008). *Examining American Indian perspectives in the central region on parent involvement in children's education.* Issues & answers (REL 2008–No. 059). Washington DC: Institute of Educational Sciences.

Madu, C. (2010). Brainstorming. *Psychology Today, 43*(1), 28–28.

Male, M. (1991). Effective team participation. *Preventing School Failure, 91,* 29–36.

Mangin, M. (2007). Facilitating elementary principals' support for instructional teacher leadership. *Educational Administration Quarterly, 43*(3), 319–357.

Margolis, H. (1999). Mediation for special education conflicts: An opportunity to improve family-school relationships. *Journal of Educational and Psychological Consultation, 10*(1), 91–100.

Marino, M. T. (2009). Understanding how adolescents with reading difficulties utilize technology-based tools. *Exceptionality, 17*(2), 88–102.

Marston, D., Muyskens, P., Lau, M., & Canter, A. (2003). Problem-solving model for decision-making with high-incidence disabilities: The Minneapolis experience. *Learning Disabilities Research and Practice, 18*(3), 187–200.

Martin, J. E., Marshall, L. H., & Sale, P. (2004). A 3-year study of middle, junior high and high school IEP meetings. *Exceptional Children, 70,* 285–297.

Marzano, R. J., & Kendall, J. S. (2007). *The new taxonomy of educational objectives* (2nd ed.). Thousand Oaks, CA: Corwin.

Mastropieri, M. A., Scruggs, T. E., Graetz, J., Norland, J., Gardizi, W., & McDuffie, K. (2005). Case studies in co-teaching in the content areas: Successes, failures, and challenges. *Intervention in School and Clinic, 40*(5), 260–270.

Maxfield, D. (2009). Speak up or burn out: Five crucial conversations that drive educational excellence. *Education Digest, 75*(2), 26–30.

McLaughlin, M. J., & Nolet, V. (2004). *What every principal needs to know about special education.* Thousand Oaks, CA: Corwin.

McLaughlin, M. J., Nolet, V., Rhim, L. M., & Henderson, K. (1999). Integrating standards, including all students. *Teaching Exceptional Children, 31*(3), 66–71.

McLeskey, J., & Waldron, N. (2000). *Inclusive education in action: Making differences ordinary.* Alexandria, VA: Association for Supervision and Curriculum Development.

McLeskey, J., & Waldron, N. (2002a). Professional development and inclusive schools: Reflections on effective practice. *Teacher Educator, 37,* 159–172.

McLeskey, J., & Waldron, N. (2002b). School change and inclusive schools: Lessons learned from practice. *Phi Delta Kappan, 84*(1), 65–72.

McLeskey, J., & Waldron, N. (2006). Comprehensive school reform and inclusive schools: Improving schools for all students. *Theory Into Practice, 45,* 269–278.

McPherson, S. (2009). A dance with butterflies: A metamorphosis of teaching and learning through technology. *Early Childhood Education Journal, 37*(3), 229–236.

Meo, G. (2008). Curriculum planning for all learners: Applying Universal Design for Learning (UDL) to a high school reading comprehension program. *Preventing School Failure, 52*(2), 21–30.

Mooney, J. (2008). *The short bus: A journey beyond normal.* New York: Henry Holt.

Moore, M. S. (2010). *What is deaf culture?* Retrieved from http://deafculture.com

Morrissey, K. (2009). The effects of Universal Design for Learning as a secondary support on student behaviors and academic achievement in an urban high school implementing primary level positive behavior support (Doctoral dissertation, Loyola University Chicago, 2008). *Dissertation Abstracts International Section A: Humanities and Social Sciences, 69,* 3902.

Morse, P. S., & Ivey, A. E. (1996). *Face to face: Communication and conflict resolution in the schools.* Thousand Oaks, CA: Corwin.

Mueller, T. G. (2009). IEP facilitation: A promising approach to resolving conflicts between families and schools. *Teaching Exceptional Children, 41*(3), 60–67.

Mueller, T. G., Singer, G. H., & Draper, L. M. (2008). Reducing parental dissatisfaction with special education in two school districts: Implementing conflict prevention and alternative dispute resolution. *Journal of Educational and Psychological Consultation, 18,* 191–233.

Munk, D. D., & Bursuck, W. D. (2004). Personalized grading plans: A systematic approach to making the grades of included students more accurate and meaningful. *Focus on Exceptional Children, 36*(9), 1–11.

Murawski, W. W. (2003). *Co-teaching in the inclusive classroom: Making sure all students find success.* Bellevue, WA: Bureau of Education and Research.

Murawski, W. W. (2006). Student outcomes in co-taught secondary English classes: How can we improve? *Reading & Writing Quarterly, 22*(3), 227–247.

Murawski, W. W. (2008a). *Co-teaching for success: Effective strategies for working together in today's inclusive classrooms.* Bellevue, WA: Bureau of Education and Research.

Murawski, W. W. (2008b, September). Five keys to co-teaching in inclusive classrooms. *The School Administrator, 65*(8), 27.

Murawski, W. W. (2009). *Collaborative teaching in secondary schools: Making the co-teaching marriage work!* Thousand Oaks, CA: Corwin.

Murawski, W. W. (2010). *Collaborative teaching in elementary schools: Making the co-teaching marriage work!* Thousand Oaks, CA: Corwin.

Murawski, W. W., Boyer, L., Melchiorre, B., & Atwill, K. (2009, April). *What is happening in co-taught classes? One state knows!* Paper presented at the meeting of the American Educational Research Association, San Diego, CA.

Murawski, W. W., & Carter, E. (2008). *The role of the administrator in supporting co-teaching: Staff development module.* Winnetka, CA: 2 TEACH.

Murawski, W. W., & Carter, N. (2011). Collaboration and communication with families. In N. Sileo & M. A. Prater (Eds.), *Working with families of children with special needs: Family and professional partnerships and roles.* Upper Saddle River, NJ: Pearson Education.

Murawski, W., & Dieker, L. (2004). Tips and strategies for co-teaching at the secondary level. *Teaching Exceptional Children, 36*(5), 52–58.

Murawski, W. W., & Hughes, C. E. (2009). Response to intervention, collaboration, and co-teaching: A necessary combination for successful systemic change. *Preventing School Failure, 53*(4), 67–77.

Murawski, W. W., & Lochner, W. W. (2009). *Co-Teaching Solutions Systems* [Computer software: http://www.coteachsolutions.com]. Shepherdstown, WV: Wide River Consulting.

Murawski, W. W., & Lochner, W. W. (2011). Observing co-teaching? What to ask for, look for, and listen for. *Intervention in School and Clinic, 46,* 174–183.

Murawski, W. W., & Swanson, H. L. (2001). A meta-analysis of co-teaching research: Where are the data? *Remedial and Special Education, 22*(5), 258–267.

Murawski, W. (in press). 10 tips for using co-planning time more efficiently. *Teaching Exceptional Children.*

Murphy, J. (2001, November). The changing face of leadership preparation. *The School Administrator, 58*(10), 14–17.

Murphy, J. T. (1988). The unheroic side of leadership: Notes from the swamp. *Phi Delta Kappan, 69,* 654–659.

Nevin, A. I., Thousand, J. S., Villa, R. A. (2009). Collaborative teaching for teacher educators—What does the research say? *Teaching and Teacher Education, 25*(4), 569–574.

Nias, J., Southworth, G., & Yeomans, R. (1994). The culture of collaboration. In A. Pollard & J. Bourne (Eds.), *Teaching and learning in the primary school* (pp. 258–272). London: Routledge.

No Child Left Behind Act of 2001, Pub. L. No. 107–110, 115 Stat. 1425 (2002).

O'Connor, R. (2003, December 5). *Tiers of intervention in kindergarten through third grade.* Paper presented at the National Research Center on Learning Disabilities RTI Symposium, Kansas City, MO.

Olivos, E. R., Gallagher, R. J., & Aguilar, J. (2010). Fostering collaboration with culturally and linguistically diverse families of children with moderate to severe disabilities. *Journal of Educational and Psychological Consultation, 20*(1), 28–40.

Oludaja, B. (2000). *Verbal communication styles: Some implications for intercultural listening.* Paper presented at the annual meeting of the International Listening Association, Virginia Beach, VA.

Osgood, R. L. (2008). *The history of special education: A struggle for equality in American public schools.* Westport, CT: Praeger.

Ostensjo, S., Carlberg, E. B., & Vollestad, N. K. (2005). The use and impact of assistive devices and other environmental modifications on everyday activities and care in young children with cerebral palsy. *Disability and Rehabilitation, 27*(14), 849–861.

Park, J., & Turnbull, A. (2001). Cross-cultural competency and special education: Perceptions and experiences of Korean parents of children with special needs. *Education and Training in Mental Retardation and Developmental Disabilities, 36,* 133–147.

Park, J., Turnbull, A. P., & Turnbull, H. R. (2002). Impacts of poverty on quality of life in families of children with disabilities. *Exceptional Children, 68*(2), 151–170.

Poston, D. J., & Turnbull, A. P. (2004). Role of spirituality and religion in family quality of life for families of children with disabilities. *Education and Training in Developmental Disabilities, 39*(2), 95–108.

Prensky, M. (2001). Digital natives, digital immigrants. *On the Horizon, 9*(5), 1–6.

Pugach, M. C., & Johnson, L. J. (2006). *Collaborative practitioners: Collaborative schools* (2nd ed.). Denver, CO: Love Publishing.

Pugach, M. C., & Wesson, C. (1995). Teachers' and students' views of team teaching of general education and learning-disabled students in two fifth-grade classes. *Elementary School Journal, 95*(3), 279–295.

Purcell-Gates, V. (1995). *Other people's words: The cycle of low literacy.* Cambridge, MA: Harvard University Press.

Rea, P. J., McLaughlin, V. L., & Walther-Thomas, C. (2002). Outcomes for students with learning disabilities in inclusive and pull-out programs. *Exceptional Children, 72*(2), 203–222.

Rehabilitation Act of 1973, Pub. L. No. 93–112 (1973).

Renzaglia, A., Karvonen, M., Drasgow, E., & Stoxen, C. C. (2003). Promoting a lifetime of inclusion. *Focus on Autism and Other Developmental Delays, 18*(3), 140–149.

Reynolds, D., & Teddlie, C. (2001). Reflections on the critics, and beyond them. *School Effectiveness and School Improvement, 12*(1), 99–113.

Richardson, V., & Placier, P. (2001). Teacher change. In V. Richardson (Ed.), *Handbook of research on teaching* (4th ed., pp. 905–947). Washington, DC: American Educational Research Association.

Rogelberg, S. G., Barnes-Farell, J. L., & Lowe, C. A. (1992). The stepladder technique: An alternative group structure facilitating effective group decision making. *Journal of Applied Psychology, 77*(5), 730–737.

Rose, D. H., & Meyer, A. (2002). *Teaching every student in the Digital Age: Universal Design for Learning.* Alexandria, VA: Association for Supervision and Curriculum Development.

Rothstein-Fisch, C., & Trumbull, E. (2008). *Managing diverse classrooms: How to build on students' cultural strengths.* Alexandria, VA: Association for Supervision and Curriculum Development.

Rubin, G. (2002, September/October). Schools attuned to learning differences. *Leadership, 32*(1), 12–15.

Salend, S. (2009). Using technology to create and administer accessible tests. *Teaching Exceptional Children, 41*(3), 40–51.

Salend, S. J., & Duhaney, L. M. G. (2002). Grading students in inclusive settings. *Teaching Exceptional Children, 34*(3), 8–15.

Salend, S. J., & Johansen, M. (1997). Cooperative teaching. *Remedial and Special Education, 18*(1), 3–12.

Samovar, L. A., Porter, R. E., & McDaniel, E. R. (2008). *Intercultural communication: A reader.* Florence, KY: Wadsworth.

Samuels, C. (2009). High schools try out RTI. *Education Week, 28*(19), 20–22.

Sanchez-Burks, J., Lee, F., Choi, I., Nisbett, R., Zhao, S., & Koo, J. (2003). Conversing across cultures: East-west communication styles in work and nonwork contexts. *Journal of Personality and Social Psychology, 85*(2), 363–372.

Schmoker, M. (2009). Measuring what matters. *Educational Leadership, 66*(4), 70–74.

Schmuck, R. A., & Runkel, P. J. (1994). *The handbook of organization development in schools and colleges* (4th ed.). Prospect Heights, IL: Waveland Press.

Scribner, J., Sawyer, R., Watson, S., & Myers, V. (2007). Teacher teams and distributed leadership: A study of group discourse and collaboration. *Educational Administration Quarterly, 43*(1), 67–100.

Scruggs, T. E., Mastropieri, M. A., & McDuffie, K. A. (2007). Co-teaching in inclusive classrooms: A meta-synthesis of qualitative research. *Exceptional Children, 73*(4), 392–416.

Sharpe, M. N., & Hawes, M. E. (2003, July). *Collaboration between general and special education: Making it work* [Issue Brief No. (2)1]. Minneapolis, MN: National Center on Secondary Education and Transition.

Shields, C. M. (2000). Learning from difference: Considerations for schools as communities. *Curriculum Inquiry, 30*(3), 275–294.

Shields, C. M. (2001). A dialogue about communities of difference: A rejoinder to Robert Boostrom. *Curriculum Inquiry, 31*(1), 71–76.

Silva, M., Munk, D. D., & Bursuck, W. D. (2005). Grading adaptations for students with disabilities. *Intervention in School and Clinic, 41*, 87–98.

Simpson, C. G., McBride, R., Spencer, V. G., Lowdermilk, J., & Lynch, S. (2009). Assistive technology: Supporting learners in inclusive classrooms. *Kappa Delta Pi Record, 45*(4), 172–175.

Smith, T. E. C. (2001). Section 504, the ADA, and public schools: What educators need to know. *Remedial and Special Education, 23*(3), 335–343.

Smyth, J. (2001). *Critical politics of teachers' work: An Australian perspective.* New York: Peter Lang.

Snell, M., & Janney, R. (2000). Teachers' problem-solving about children with moderate and severe disabilities in elementary classrooms. *Exceptional Children, 66*(4), 472–490.

Snow, K. (2010). *To ensure inclusion, freedom, and respect for all, it's time to embrace people-first language.* Retrieved from http://www.disabilityisnatural.com/images/PDF/pfl09.pdf

Solomon, P. G. (2009). *The curriculum bridge: From standards to actual classroom practice.* Thousand Oaks, CA: Corwin.

Somech, A. (2008). Managing conflict in school teams: The impact of task and goal interdependence on conflict management and team effectiveness. *Educational Administration Quarterly, 44*(3), 359–390.

Song, J., & Murawski, W. W. (2005). Korean-American parents' perspectives on teacher–parent collaboration. *Journal of International Special Needs Education, 8,* 32–38.

Spencer, S. (2005). An interview with Lynne Cook and June Downing: The practicalities of collaboration in special education service delivery. *Intervention in School and Clinic, 40,* 296–300.

Sprick, R. (2009). Doing discipline differently. *Principal Leadership, 9*(5), 18–22.

Stage, S. A., Abbott, R. D., Jenkins, J. R., & Berninger, V. W. (2003). Predicting response to early reading intervention from verbal IQ, reading-related language abilities, attention ratings, and verbal IQ-word reading discrepancy. *Journal of Learning Disabilities, 36,* 24–34.

Sue, D. W., & Sue, D. (2003). *Counseling the culturally different: Theory and practice.* New York: Wiley.

Swanson, H. L., Harris, K. R., & Graham, S. (Eds.). (2003). *Handbook of learning disabilities.* New York: Guilford Press.

Thousand, J. S., Villa, R. A., & Nevin, A. I. (2006). The many faces of collaborative planning and teaching. *Theory Into Practice, 45*(3), 239–248.

Thousand, J. S., Villa, R. A., & Nevin, A. I. (2007). *Differentiating instruction: Collaborative planning and teaching for universally designed learning.* Thousand Oaks, CA: Corwin.

Thurlow, M. L. (2002). Positive educational results for all students: The promise of standards-based reform. *Remedial and Special Education, 23*(4), 195–202.

Tomlinson, C. A. (2004). *Differentiation for gifted and talented students.* Thousand Oaks, CA: Corwin.

Torgesen, J. K. (2003, December). *Operationalizing the response to intervention model to identify children with learning disabilities: Specific issues with older children.* Paper presented at the Responsiveness-to-Intervention Symposium, Kansas City, MO. Retrieved from http://www.rti4success.org/images/stories/ResponsivenessToInterventionSymposium/session4joetorgesen.pdf

Trumbull, E., Rothstein-Fisch, C., Greenfield, P. M., & Quiroz, B. (2001). *Bridging cultures between home and school: A guide for teachers.* Mahwah, NJ: Lawrence Erlbaum.

Tuckman, B. V., & Jensen, M. A. (1977). Stages of small-group development revisited. *Group and Organizational Studies, 2,* 419–427.

Turnbull, H. R., & Turnbull, A. P. (2000). *Free and appropriate public education: The law and children with disabilities* (6th ed.). Denver, CO: Love Publishing.

Understanding IDEA 2004: Frequently asked questions. (2007). Baltimore: Council for Exceptional Children.

Vaughn, S., & Coleman, M. (2004). The role of mentoring in promoting use of research-based practices in reading. *Remedial and Special Education, 25*(1), 25–38.

Vaughn, S., Fletcher, J. M., Francis, D. J., Denton, C. A., Wanzek, J., Wexler, J., et al. (2008). Response to intervention with older students with reading difficulties. *Learning & Individual Differences, 18*(3), 338–345.

Vibert, A., Portelli, J., Shields, C., & LaRocque, L. (2002). Critical practice in elementary schools: Voice, community, and a curriculum of life. *Journal of Educational Change, 3*(2), 93–116.

Villasenor, V. (2005). *Burro genius.* New York: HarperCollins.

Waldron, N. L., & McLeskey, J. (2010). Establishing a collaborative school culture through comprehensive school reform. *Journal of Educational and Psychological Consultation, 20*(1), 58–74.

Wallace, T., Anderson, A. R., & Bartholomay, T. (2002). Collaboration: An element associated with the success of four inclusive high schools. *Journal of Educational and Psychological Consultation, 13,* 349–381.

Walsh, J. M., & Snyder, D. (1993). *Cooperative teaching: An effective model for all students.* Paper presented at the annual convention of the Council for Exceptional Children, San Antonio, TX. (ERIC Document Reproduction Service No. ED361930)

Walther-Thomas, C. S. (1997). Coteaching experiences: The benefits and problems that teachers and principals report over time. *Journal of Learning Disabilities, 30*(4), 395–407.

Walther-Thomas, C., Korinek, L., McLaughlin, V. L., & Williams, B. T. (2000). *Collaboration for inclusive education: Developing successful programs.* Boston: Allyn & Bacon.

Wang, M., Mannan, H., Poston, D., Turnbull, A. P., & Summers, J. A. (2004). Parents' perception of advocacy activities and their impact on family quality of life. *Research & Practice for Persons with Severe Disabilities, 29*(2), 144–155.

Weichel, W. A. (2001). An analysis of student outcomes on co-taught settings in comparison to other special education service delivery options for students with learning disabilities. *Dissertation Abstracts International, 62*(07), 2386. (UMI No. 3021407)

Weiner, I., & Murawski, W. W. (2005). Schools Attuned: A model for collaborative intervention. *Intervention in School and Clinic, 40*(5), 284–290.

Weiss, M. P., & Brigham, F. J. (2000). Co-teaching and the model of shared responsibility: What does the research support? In T. E. Scruggs & M. A. Mastropieri (Eds.), *Advances in learning and behavioral disabilities* (pp. 217–245). Greenwich, CT: JAI.

Weiss, M. P., & Lloyd, J. W. (2002). Congruence between roles and actions of secondary special educators in co-taught and special education settings. *Journal of Special Education, 36,* 58–68.

Welch, A. B. (2000). Responding to student concerns about fairness. *Teaching Exceptional Children, 33*(2), 36–40.

Wepner, S. B., & Bowes, K. A., (2004). Using assistive technology for literacy development. *Reading and Writing Quarterly, 20,* 219–223.

Whittaker, C. R., Salend, S. J., & Duhaney, D. (2001). Creating instructional rubrics for inclusive classrooms. *Teaching Exceptional Children, 34*(2), 8–13.

Wiggins, G., & McTighe, J. (2005). *Understanding by design* (2nd ed.). Alexandria, VA: Pearson.

Wilson, G. L. (2005). This doesn't look familiar! A supervisor's guide for observing co-teachers. *Intervention in School and Clinic, 40*(5), 271–275.

Wolf, M. K., Kao, J. C., Griffin, N., Herman, J. L., Bachman, P. L., Chang, S. M., et al. (2008). *Issues in assessing English language learners: English language proficiency measures and accommodation uses—practice review* (CRESST Report 732). Los Angeles: University of California, National Center for Research on Evaluation, Standards, and Student Testing.

Wood, J., & Turnbull, A. (2004). Impact of deafness on family life: A review of the literature. *Topics in Early Childhood Special Education, 24*(1), 15–29.

Worchel, S. (2005). Culture's role in conflict and conflict management: Some suggestions, many questions. *Journal of Intercultural Relations, 29,* 739–757.

Working Forum on Inclusive Schools. (1995). *Creating schools for all our students: What 12 schools have to say.* Reston, VA: Council for Exceptional Children.

Wormeli, R. (2006). *Fair isn't always equal: Assessing and grading in the differentiated classroom.* Portland, ME: Stenhouse.

York-Barr, J., & Duke, K. (2004). What do we know about teacher leadership? Findings from two decades of scholarship. *Review of Educational Research, 74*(3), 255–316.

Zigmond, N., Magiera, K., & Matta, D. (2003, April). *Co-teaching in secondary schools: Is the instructional experience enhanced for students with disabilities?* Paper presented at the annual conference of the Council for Exceptional Children, Seattle, WA.

Zigmond, N., & Matta, D. (2004). Value added of the special education teacher in secondary school co-taught classes. In T. E. Scruggs & M. A. Mastropieri (Eds.), *Advances in learning and behavioral disabilities* (pp. 55–76). Greenwich, CT: JAI.

Ziviani, J., & Lennox, N. (2004). Meeting in the middle: Improving communication in primary health care consultations with people with an intellectual disability. *Intellectual & Developmental Disability, 29*(3), 211–225.

Index

CORWIN
A SAGE Company

The Corwin logo—a raven striding across an open book—represents the union of courage and learning. Corwin is committed to improving education for all learners by publishing books and other professional development resources for those serving the field of PreK–12 education. By providing practical, hands-on materials, Corwin continues to carry out the promise of its motto: **"Helping Educators Do Their Work Better."**